# THE BONE
# HUNTERS

# THE BONE HUNTERS

*The Heroic Age of
Paleontology in the
American West*

BY

URL LANHAM

DOVER PUBLICATIONS, INC.
*New York*

Published in Canada by General Publishing Company, Ltd., 30 Lesmill Road, Don Mills, Toronto, Ontario.
Published in the United Kingdom by Constable and Company, Ltd., 3 The Lanchesters, 162–164 Fulham Palace Road, London W6 9ER.

This Dover edition, first published in 1991, is an unabridged, slightly corrected republication of the work first published by Columbia University Press, New York, 1973, under the title *The Bone Hunters* (no subtitle).

Manufactured in the United States of America
Dover Publications, Inc., 31 East 2nd Street, Mineola, N.Y. 11501

*Library of Congress Cataloging in Publication Data*

Lanham, Url, 1918–
    The bone hunters : the heroic age of paleontology in the American West / by Url Lanham.
        p.    cm.
    Originally published: New York : Columbia University Press, 1973. Reprinted with corrections.
    Includes bibliographical references and index.
    ISBN 0-486-26917-5 (pbk.)
    1. Fossils—West (U.S.)—Collection and preservation. 2. Cope, E. D. (Edward Drinker), 1840–1897. 3. Marsh, Othniel Charles, 1831–1899. 4. Paleontologists—United States—Biography.
I. Title.
QE718.L36 1991
560.9'73—dc20                                                91-26044
                                                                  CIP

*To my mother and my father*

# CONTENTS

|  | Introduction | ix |
|---|---|---|
| 1 | Scientist in the White House | 1 |
| 2 | Rocks and Fossils | 8 |
| 3 | Joseph Leidy | 18 |
| 4 | The Big Badlands | 23 |
| 5 | The Bone Hunters Come to the Sioux Country | 32 |
| 6 | Othniel Charles Marsh | 47 |
| 7 | Edward Drinker Cope | 60 |
| 8 | The Smoky Hill | 71 |
| 9 | Big Bone Chief | 79 |
| 10 | In Quest of the Great Sea Serpents | 92 |
| 11 | Bridger Basin | 101 |

# CONTENTS

12    West of the Jemez     125

13    Marsh As Partisan     146

14    The Beautiful Judith     154

15    Super-Dinosaurs     166

16    "Dawn Horses" and Birds with Teeth     186

17    Prince Of Collectors: John Bell Hatcher     197

18    The Triumvirate: Hayden, Powell, and King     214

19    Cope As Financier     231

20    Revenge     243

21    After the Battle     262

     Bibliography     273

     Index     281

# INTRODUCTION

A century after the founding of the Republic, the United States was a leader in the scientific exploration of time, with probes extending hundreds of millions of years into the past, explorations that brought to the notice of an astonished world a galaxy of strange and primitive animals that once lived in the vast expanses of the trans-Mississippi West. In the late 1870s, two of the important world centers for research into vertebrate paleontology—the study of the fossils of the backboned animals, the group to which man belongs—were in this country. One was in the laboratories of Yale University, in New Haven. It was the creation of Othniel Charles Marsh, professor without salary at Yale, who financed his research with money from a multimillionaire uncle. The other was a three-story frame house, crammed with fossil bones, at 2102 Pine Street in Philadelphia. It served as the museum annex of the next-door residence of Edward Drinker Cope, erstwhile professor at Haverford College, who lived on an inheritance from his father, a wealthy Quaker farmer.

These two men were of greatly different personalities: Cope a fiery, eccentric genius, devoted to his family and fond of women; Marsh a slow but sure thinker and a lonely and suspicious bachelor. Cope was an adventurous loner, Marsh an accomplished member of the scientific and political power structure. Both were dedicated explorers of the virgin field of western paleontology, and each developed an inordinate jealousy of any success won by the other. They became the most famous haters in the history of science. In a bitter struggle that erupted in the newspapers and the halls of Congress they brought about each other's downfall, and in the course of the battle, each played a role in the economic struggle over the West—whether the arid lands were to be exploited without restraint by wealthy and powerful private interests, or developed in planned, scientific fashion for the general welfare.

A considerable share of this book is devoted to an account of the mistress who ruled the lives of both Cope and Marsh. This was Nature, with an infinite variety of form and mood of which they never tired. There was the western land, with hills and canyons made beautiful by the logic of rock and weathering. There was the dark history of the world, when the countless lives of plants and animals, by their successes and failures, fashioned the wisdom that sustains the lives of all creatures inhabiting the earth today. Cope and Marsh and the small band of fellow explorers who were their satellites prowled insatiably over the dry, rugged landscape of the fossil beds, their sharp eyes searching for traces of a mysterious past that lay out in the bright western sunshine.

Cope and Marsh did not create the science of vertebrate paleontology. They were the inheritors of nearly a hundred years of scientific study of the earth, and of an American tradition in paleontology that began with the founding of the Republic. They were not the only vertebrate paleontologists of their time, since Marsh had as hired assistants men who became noted paleontologists in their own right, and who won their independence from him during his lifetime. Neither did they complete the science, which matured in the hands of two generations of paleontologists who followed them. But they were the central figures in the heroic age of American vertebrate paleontology.

# THE BONE
# HUNTERS

# 1

# SCIENTIST IN
# THE WHITE HOUSE

OF THE FIVE MEN
entrusted with the drafting of the Declaration of Independence
two were, or became, scientists of international renown. One was
the aged Benjamin Franklin, known for his fundamental research
into meteorology and electricity. The other was Thomas Jefferson,
who wrote the draft of the Declaration. In 1797, when Vice-President of the United States and president of the American Philosophical Society, Jefferson read before the society, and published
in its *Transactions,* one of the first technical papers on vertebrate
paleontology in America, "A Memoir on the Discovery of Certain
Bones of a Quadruped of the Clawed Kind in the Western Parts
of Virginia."

Jefferson, then fifty-four years old, had since his youth been fascinated by the Virginia countryside, and by the West, which was then the blue horizon seen beyond the Cumberland Gap. As a young circuit lawyer, he had traveled far through the Virginian wilderness on horseback, visiting backwoods settlements that were sometimes a day's ride apart. He long remembered the beauty of the land, and later was to write in his "Notes on Virginia" with the eye of a naturalist, and even of a geologist years before that science was founded and established in the school curricula:

> The passage of the Patomac through the Blue Ridge is, perhaps, one of the most stupendous scenes in nature. You stand on a very high point of land. On your right comes up the Shenandoah having ranged along the foot of the mountain an hundred miles to seek a vent. On your left approaches the Patomac, in quest of a passage also. In the moment of their junction, they rush together against the mountain, rend it asunder and pass to the sea. The first glance of this scene hurries the senses into the opinion, that this earth has been created in time, that the mountains were formed first, that the rivers began to flow afterwards . . .

A most formative experience of Jefferson's youth was his education at William and Mary's College by Dr. William Small, a young Scotsman who had been influenced by the Enlightenment. The aim of this eighteenth-century European philosophical movement was well expressed by the pronouncement of a University of Glasgow professor that "The intention of Moral Philosophy is to direct men to that course of action which tends most effectually to promote their greatest happiness and perfection; as far as it can be done by observations and conclusions discoverable from the constitution of nature, without any aids of supernatural revelation." Protected by the free-thinking deputy governor of Virginia, Francis Fauquier, Small was able to revolutionize the curriculum at the tiny Virginia college. Of the influence of Dr. Small, Jefferson later said:

2

Dr. William Small of Scotland . . . Professor of Mathematics, a man profound in the most of the useful branches of science, with a happy talent of communication, correct and gentlemanly mannered, and an enlarged and liberal mind . . . most happily for me, soon attached to me, and made me his daily companion when not engaged in the school; and from his conversation I got my first views of the expansion of science, and of the system in which we are placed.

Jefferson's contribution to a science directly concerned with "the system in which we are placed" was based on three enormous claws that were found in the dirt floor of a cave in western Virginia. Of their owner he writes, "I will venture to call him by the name of Great Claw or Megalonyx, to which he seems sufficiently entitled by the distinguished size of that member." Indians had told him legends of great lions that once lived in the forest, and he naturally compared his fossils with that animal, coming to the conclusion that the beast was probably two or three times the size of the African lion. Later he learned that similar claws had been found in South America associated with bones of a gigantic, extinct ground sloth. In spite of his misidentification, Jefferson's name *Megalonyx* is still used for this gigantic sloth, which ranged widely over the United States, until the time of the early Indians.

Jefferson also knew about the bones of other great animals scattered along the banks of the Ohio in Kentucky—the huge vertebrae of mastodons at the Big Bone Lick of Kentucky were used by hunters for campstools—and thought that great animals might still be found roaming the vast continent beyond the Blue Ridge; "In the present interior of our continent there is surely space and range enough for elephants and lions."

After he became President in 1800, Jefferson continued "the tranquil pursuits of science . . . my supreme delight." At the same time, he competently extended the influence of the young

3

Republic to the shores of the Pacific. As early as 1785 Jefferson was concerned about the consequences of exploration in the West by other powers. He wrote that "I find they have subscribed a very large sum of money in England for exploring the country from the Mississippi to California. They pretend it is only to promote knoledge. I am afraid they have thoughts of colonizing in the quarter. Some of us have been talking here in a feeble way of making the attempt to search that country, but I doubt whether we have enough of that kind of spirit to raise the money."

From the presidential office he watched for the chance to get an expedition underway. The opportunity came in 1803 in the shape of a congressional bill concerning Indian trading posts. He included in this a modest appropriation for investigation of a trade route from the Missouri to the mouth of the Columbia. He asked his young private secretary, Captain Meriwether Lewis, to head up the expedition. Lewis chose his friend Lieutenant William Clark to share command, and informally gave him the rank of captain. While Lewis and Clark were on their way West, Jefferson consummated the Louisiana Purchase, which transferred ownership of the land between the Mississippi and the "Stony Mountains" to the United States. Starting out from the Mandan country of the Upper Missouri in April of 1805, with a party of fourteen soldiers, nine Kentucky frontiersmen, an Indian girl named Sacajawea, her new baby, and her French-Canadian husband, the Lewis and Clark expedition reached the Continental Divide in mid-August, and were camped on the cold and rainy Pacific shore by early November.

Jefferson had charged Lewis to find a waterway to the Pacific, to determine the names of the Indian nations and their numbers, and to observe soil, vegetation, animals, minerals, volcanos, and climate. The humane Jefferson also wanted Lewis to distribute "kine-pox" (cowpox) vaccine among the Indians to ward off the smallpox that already was decimating the tribes of the Upper Missouri.

The expedition expended most of its efforts in forcing its way through the wilderness and in gathering enough food to stay alive, but Lewis, an amateur botanist, did an impressive amount of work as a scientist. His lengthy notes on natural history are a priceless record of the red man's West.

Two months out of the Mandan villages, on their way west, Lewis and Clark had gone through what came to be one of the classic fossil-hunting grounds. About a hundred miles below the great Falls of the Missouri, they came upon a beautifully clear stream, flowing from the south through rugged badlands to empty into the Missouri. Clark named it the Judith River after a thirteen-year-old friend Julia (called Judy), whom he later married. In the Judith River badlands pieces of dinosaur bone can be found in abundance, but they lie in the topmost layers of the gigantic bluffs, which rise 800 feet above the river, and Lewis passed by them unaware.

Jefferson did not get a successful bone-hunting expedition underway until the return of the Lewis and Clark expedition, when he asked Clark, now a general, to dig at the Big Bone Lick in Kentucky. Clark collected more than 300 bones, most of them of the elephantlike mastodon, and sent them to Washington by way of New Orleans. Jefferson, who believed that education was the most important aspect of the life of the nation, and dreamed of an entire populace of educated farmers like himself, made one of the rooms of the White House into a museum, where he spread out the fossil bones to show to visitors. In the yard of the presidential mansion he kept a pair of grizzly cubs brought back by the Lewis and Clark expedition.

Like many another scientist and rationalist, Jefferson was an object of abuse from the conservatives of his time as a "French infidel" and "atheist." A famous piece of literature from early America is a satiric poem directed against Jefferson written by the thirteen-year-old prodigy William Cullen Bryant who, no doubt on the advice of his elders, associated science and sin:

> Go, wretch, resign thy presidential chair,
> Disclose thy secret measures, foul or fair,
> Go, search with curious eyes for horned frogs,
> 'Mid the wild wastes of Louisianian bogs;
> Or where the Ohio rolls his turbid stream;
> Dig for huge bones, thy glory and thy theme.
> Go scan, Philosophist, thy ****** charms
> And sink supinely in her sable arms;
> But quit to abler hands the helm of state.

Scholars read the six asterisks as "Sally's," in reference to the contemporary gossip about Jefferson's "black Aspasia."

During the nineteenth century, the Enlightenment's "smile of reason" faded from the high councils of state. Jefferson's friend Tom Paine fell upon evil days, and died abused and neglected. His bones were dug up and taken to England for a traveling show, where the populace could shudder pleasurably at the relics of the notorious atheist. A mastodon also was exported to England, exhibited as the "Leviathan of Holy Writ." But the spirit of Jefferson still lingers about his grave, which bears the epitaph, written by himself, "Here was buried Thomas Jefferson, author of the Declaration of American Independence, of the statute of Virginia for religious freedom, and father of the University of Virginia." His simple farmer's vision of the future of science in America was recorded in a letter to the president of Harvard College:

> What a field we have at our doors to signalize ourselves in. The botany of America is far from being exhausted, its mineralogy is untouched, and its natural history of zoology totally mistaken

or misrepresented. . . . It is for such institutions as that over which you preside so worthily, sir, to do justice to our country, its productions and its genius. It is the work to which the young men you are forming should lay their hands. We have spent the prime of our lives in procuring the precious blessing of liberty. Let them spend theirs in showing that it is the great parent of science and of virtue, and that a nation will be great in both always in proportion as it is free.

# 2

# ROCKS
# AND FOSSILS

Edward Drinker Cope
and Othniel Charles Marsh, as paleontologists, were in the middle of a new science, geology, which was so young that the effective founder of geology was still alive when they began their professional careers. Although observations and theories that would make possible a science of the history of the earth had been accumulating since the reawakening of interest in nature that took place with the Renaissance, these observations were not brought together in a systematic way until the beginning of the nineteenth century. This organization was carried out almost single-handedly by the Englishman Charles Lyell, who created geology as a large-scale and going concern with his three-volume *Princi-*

8

*ples of Geology* which began to appear in 1830 and which he constantly revised for the next forty-two years, keeping pace with and in many ways leading the rapid growth of the new science. His approach to geology is shown by the subtitle to the *Principles:* "An Attempt to Explain the Former Changes of the Earth's Surface by Reference to Causes now in Operation."

Emphasis on what could be seen before one's eyes provided a base for the healthy growth of geology. One of the first results of the science was the realization that the earth must be very old. It could be observed that the landscape was constantly being shaped by the slow forces of erosion. Instead of being permanent structures, the very hills had a history of change that extended over eons of time. Study of the silts and sands carried from the hillsides by streams out into broad valleys and onto deltas showed that hard rocks such as sandstones and shales were obviously ancient sediments of this kind. Analysis of the patchwork of sedimentary rocks scattered over the earth showed that they could be arranged in a vertical sequence, the older at the bottom, that totaled mile upon mile in thickness. The processes of erosion and deposition that can be seen now must have been in operation for millions of years. As a geologic force countering this mass wasting of the highlands, there could be observed the inch-by-inch movements or even catastrophic uplifts of several feet produced by earthquakes.

Civilized societies are so constructed that any new conception produces waves of political disturbance. Lyell wrote that some of his contemporaries believed geology to be a "dangerous, or at least a visionary pursuit." In Lyell's day many of the schools still taught a timetable of earth history that was only an up-to-date version of the following one, published in the sixteenth century and obtained by an analysis of the genealogy since Adam given in the Bible:

9

| EVENT | YEARS BEFORE PRESENT |
|---|---|
| Birth of Christ | 1,561 |
| The Captivity | 2,175 |
| Building of the Temple | 2,589 |
| Departure of Israel from Egypt | 3,070 |
| Abraham | 3,573 |
| The Deluge | 3,865 |
| Creation of the World | 5,521 |

Lyell and his followers also had to combat the influence of speculative scientists. The astronomers had seen nebulae that looked as if they could gradually evolve into solar systems, with planets revolving around a central sun. They concluded that the earth had first appeared as a fiery mass condensed out of a nebular cloud. The French naturalist Buffon in the eighteenth century measured the rate of cooling of a large heated iron sphere to give an estimate of the age of the earth that indicated the biblical estimate to be far too small. Lyell took the position that this kind of approach was too hypothetical to be of any real significance, and that the question of the origin of the earth was not really a scientific one. So far as geological evidence went, it was his opinion that the earth could have existed forever in about its present form.

Paleontology, usually considered a subdivision of geology, is the study of the remains of animals and plants buried in the sedimentary rocks. Whereas Lyell was subversive in giving the earth an age of at least millions of years, his ideas about the meaning of fossils were quite innocuous. His original conception was that the same kinds of animals existed in the past as are now in existence, that there had been no evolutionary change. The absence of the bones of mammals, for example, in the oldest sedimentary rocks was, he thought, merely an illusion: the heat and pressure to which these ancient rocks had been subjected had destroyed the

10

fossils they contained. He was confident that with further geologic exploration, the fossils of the modern groups of animals would be found in sedimentary rocks of all ages.

The only new thing under the sun, Lyell thought, was man himself. He admitted that such objects as the pyramids of Egypt or the stone roads of the Romans would certainly have left traces in the rocks impossible to overlook had they been present in the geologic past. He therefore thought man had been created suddenly in relatively recent times.

Lyell eventually came to the conclusion that he was wrong in thinking that the animal world did not have a history of change. This came about, not from new discoveries in paleontology, but from the influence of his friend Charles Darwin. Darwin published in 1859 his *Origin of Species,* the product of some twenty-five years of observation and thought, a book that convinced most of the scientific world that animals and plants had evolved through time. Darwin came to this conclusion almost entirely from a study of living organisms. What was known about fossils at the time gave little direct evidence to support the theory of evolution.

The modern science of paleontology was systematized a few years ahead of Lyell's organization of geology. The French ex-botanist J. B. Lamarck, at the age of fifty-eight, began publication of what is generally taken as the foundation of invertebrate paleontology: *The Fossils of the Paris Region* (1802–06). Taking into account all animals except the vertebrates, the invertebrate paleontologist deals primarily with shells instead of bones, shells being the limy covering of snails and clams or the jointed armor of arthropods that live in the water.

Modern vertebrate paleontology also began with a study of the rocks of the Paris basin. The Baron Georges Cuvier, who had a thorough knowledge of the anatomy of modern mammals, reptiles, and fishes, could accurately classify the bones found in these

11

Geological history lies in fragments on the broken and eroded surface of the earth. At the base of this hill in northeastern Colorado is a thick sandstone layer that contains fragile shells of oysters that thrive in brackish water and the teeth of small sharks. The sandstone is of the Fox Hills formation, about 100 million years old; the conglomerate blocks near the top are probably of upper Tertiary age, possibly little more than 10 million years old.

sedimentary rocks, where deposits laid down in the sea alternated with the silts and sands washed down from ancient mountains into broad river valleys. A work by Cuvier on these specimens, entitled *Researches on Fossil Bones,* published in 1812, is usually taken as the basis for modern vertebrate paleontology. The educated European of the time was made aware of an ancient Europe that teemed with rhinos, various huge elephantlike creatures, and other mammals somewhat like those that now live only in the tropics. A hundred years later, some of these were brought to life in the paintings and carvings of Stone Age man that were discovered in the caves of France and Spain.

The disappearance of such animals from Europe spoke to Cuvier of unimaginable catastrophes that had taken place in the past, worldwide disasters like that of the biblical flood. The German naturalist Peter Simon Pallas had some years before discovered the fantastic beds of extinct rhinos and mammoths in Siberia, some of them frozen in the ice, with fur and flesh still intact. Cuvier and his followers thought these had been overwhelmed by a sudden deep freeze. However, other scientists pointed out that the shaggy fur of the hairy mammoths and the woolly rhinos could hardly have been an adaptation to life in a tropical climate, and saw these extinct European species as adapted to climates even more rigorous than that of modern Europe, perhaps living amidst tongues of glacier ice.

It was the "catastrophism" of the Cuvier school of paleontologists that was opposed by Lyell. When the theory of an Ice Age in Europe became accepted by geologists, it was seen not as an overwhelming catastrophe, but as a change that took place over thousands or tens of thousands of years, fast enough on the geological scale, to be sure, but hardly a cause for excitement during the life span of an individual.

In America there had as yet been no discoveries of ancient bones as spectacular as that made in the stone and plaster quarries in the suburbs of Paris, so that there was no stimulus to produce an American Cuvier. But by the middle of the nineteenth century the fur traders who had worked their way to the upper Missouri country saw the first of the great boneyards of the West that were to revolutionize vertebrate paleontology. The traders sent scraps of bone as curiosities back to civilization at St. Louis. These finally reached the hands of a man who was to become the "father of American vertebrate paleontology," the Philadelphia naturalist Joseph Leidy.

The tremendous forces involved in mountain-
building are shown by these tilted Carboniferous
rocks which point in the direction of the core of
the Colorado Front Range.

Just as the historian gives names to periods of human history
—the Stone Age, the Renaissance, the Dark Ages, or the Roman-
tic Period—so the geologist divides earth history into time seg-
ments that are given names. It is easy to determine the relative
ages of sedimentary rocks in the same area, since younger sediments are deposited on top of older ones, although in a few parts
of the world, drastic mountain-making movements have over-

turned the original arrangement. However, the sedimentary rocks exist only in scraps and fragments over the surface of the planet, making any kind of historical classification based on the rocks themselves on a worldwide scale quite impossible. What did make a classification of geological time possible was the discovery that sedimentary rocks of different ages have different and characteristic kinds of fossils. Thus three of the major divisions, the eras of geologic time, are named the Paleozoic ("ancient life"), Mesozoic ("middle life"), and Cenozoic ("new life"). It is only within the past few decades that the study of radioactive elements in rocks has made it possible to give absolute time limits to these geologic time intervals. The geologic time chart that we will use as a reference in this book is given on page 16.

In this calendar of events, man—the species *Homo sapiens*— had probably become established on all the continents at the beginning of the Recent epoch of the Quaternary period of the Cenozoic era. The first vertebrates—animals with bone— appeared in the Ordovician period, something like 500 million years ago. The first animals of more than microscopic size, which were simple invertebrates, appeared 600 million years ago at the beginning of the Cambrian period of the Paleozoic Era. Microscopic organisms have been found in rocks 2 or perhaps even 3 billion years old; in this classification this is taken to mark the beginning of the Eozoic era. Evidence from astronomy and geochemistry indicates that the earth was formed some 5 or 6 billion years ago, leaving a long lifeless period of earth history that can be called the Azoic era.

The paleontologist uses the terms of the geologic timetable constantly: Devonian rocks, Permian rocks; the Cretaceous (the time span within which rocks classified as Cretaceous were deposited); Pleistocene sabertooth, Oligocene sabertooth. He uses also the names of what are called "formations." In the West are such formations as the Niobrara, Ogalalla, Dakota, Morrison, or Lance

| Era | Period | Epoch | Time since beginning (millions of years) |
|---|---|---|---|
| | Quaternary | Recent | .025 |
| | | Pleistocene | 2 |
| CENOZOIC | | Pliocene | 5 |
| | | Miocene | 20 |
| | Tertiary | Oligocene | 35 |
| | | Eocene | 45 |
| | | Paleocene | 70 |
| | Cretaceous | | 135 |
| MESOZOIC | Jurassic | | 180 |
| | Triassic | | 230 |
| | Permian | | 280 |
| | Carboniferous | | 345 |
| PALEOZOIC | Devonian | | 405 |
| | Silurian | | 425 |
| | Ordovician | | 500 |
| | Cambrian | | 600 |
| EOZOIC | | | 3,500 |
| AZOIC | | | 5,000 |

Creek, named for geographic localities where the rocks were first discovered or are well displayed, with the locality names themselves often memorializing a person or event or native tribe. A formation is a thick layer of rock, scores or hundreds or even thousands of feet thick, that has considerable geographic extent and differs from rocks above and below it. The differences are related to geologic events. Thus, when a mountain range is newly

16

uplifted, the increased gradient washes sandy and gravelly sediment out onto the surrounding basins. When the range becomes worn down, the fine clays and muds of the kind deposited by the streams before the uplift again appear, sandwiching between them and the older clays the coarse sediments that will become rock of a distinct and recognizable formation. The time span in which a formation is deposited is usually much shorter than that of one of the geological divisions of time. The names of the western geologic formations are uncannily nostalgic; a simple list of the names reads like poetry to the field paleontologist, and stirs up visions of poverty or riches for the oil man. Many of the formation names appear regularly in the business pages of western newspapers, at a high enough usage level that they should appear in dictionaries.

# 3
# JOSEPH LEIDY

W<small>HEN JOSEPH LEIDY</small> in 1870 came to the end of his long reign as the leading vertebrate paleontologist of the United States, he said to a British colleague, "Formerly, every fossil one found in the States came to me, for nobody else cared to study such things, but Professors Marsh and Cope, with long purses, offer money for what used to come to me for nothing, and in that respect I cannot compete with them." Also, when Cope and Marsh entered the science they, by their constant quarreling, turned it into something of a brawl. Leidy thought this disgraceful, and retired from the field to take up the study of microscopic protozoans, which could be scooped up by the millions out of ponds for nothing, and could be studied in scholarly isolation at a desk and microscope.

Leidy was born in Philadelphia in 1823, the son of a comfortably middle-class family. He was a gifted child, early fascinated by natural history. After getting a degree of Doctor of Medicine at the University of Pennsylvania, he abandoned medical practice for teaching and research. Supporting himself for several years in a miscellany of odd jobs, he obtained a position as professor of anatomy at the University of Pennsylvania, which gave him a secure base for a long and uneventful life of scholarship.

Joseph Leidy worked at a time, before the age of the specialist, when a naturalist could write about everything, and in the *Proceedings of the Philadelphia Academy of Natural Science* can be found brief communications from the young Leidy about such diverse subjects as the wings of locusts, the anatomy of the sloth, the red snow of the Arctic (stained by a microscopic plant), and the parasites of fishes. But by the time he was thirty years old he had begun to specialize on fossil bones. In 1853, for example, he contributed a total of fifteen short papers, sometimes only a fraction of a page long, on vertebrate paleontology, with such titles as "On fossil tortoises, from Nebraska," "Remarks on some fossil teeth of a rhinoceros, from Nebraska," and "Reference to a fossil tooth of a tapir." Nowadays the professional scientist scoffs at such "penny postcard" contributions to knowledge, but in Leidy's time they served to keep interest in natural history at a high pitch. The collector gets a good deal of satisfaction in becoming the famous discoverer of a new or rare species. Leidy, by assuring the collector that his discovery would immediately be published and that he would be given full credit for it, soon had a small army of collectors on the lookout for fossil teeth and bones.

The first of the ancient beasts of the American West to wander onto the pages of the literature of science was a titanothere, a large and ponderous relative of the horse. A piece of jawbone with teeth belonging to one of these animals was described by a St. Louis physician, Dr. Hiram A. Prout, in the *American Journal of Science* for the year 1847. The brief paper was entitled "An American species of Palaeotherium," and of the specimen Prout says:

The Palaeotherial bone here described was sent to me some time ago by a friend residing at one of the trading posts of the St. Louis Fur Company, on the Missouri River, From information since obtained from him, I learn that it was discovered in the Mauvais Terre, on the White River, one of the western confluents of the Missouri, about one hundred and fifty miles south of St. [Fort] Pierre, and sixty east of the Black Hills, at a point which would nearly correspond with the intersection of latitude 43° with longitude 26° west of Washington.

The Mauvaises Terres (as the French fur traders called them), or the Badlands, fifteen hundred miles west of Washington, became the main bone-hunting grounds for the next two decades.

By 1851 Leidy had been given this titanothere fossil, and gave it a proper scientific name (which requires both a generic and specific term), calling it *Palaeotherium proutti*. Some hundreds of kinds of fossil vertebrates had already been described from the Old World by Cuvier and his followers, and Leidy naturally had to compare the American fossils with these. The titanothere he thought to be the same as the Old World genus *Palaeotherium*, although more complete fossils discovered in later years showed it to belong to a different group. Even as early as 1851, though, Leidy saw that uniquely American animals had existed in the geologic past. He showed the assembled members of the Philadelphia Academy the fossil skull of a strange sheep-sized grazing mammal that had been sent him from the West, coining the term "oreodon" for it. Oreodon bones turned out to be the most abundant of the larger fossils in some of the western badlands, and are the bones usually found by the beginning collector. These animals must have lived by the millions on the ancient western savannahs. The group appeared and died in North America, isolated by the temporary absence of a Bering land bridge. They were primitive ruminants, or cud-chewing herbivores, whose foot and tooth structure were so primitive that the animals were rendered obsolete when new and more advanced groups of herbivores invaded their domain from the Old World, and they became extinct without leaving any descendents.

During the next twenty years the Badlands were studied intensively, and their wealth of bones described by Leidy. By 1854 there had been some more or less organized collecting expeditions into the Badlands, and enough material had been gathered to write up an account of respectable length. In 1854, Leidy published in the Smithsonian *Contributions to Knowledge* a 126-page account entitled *The Ancient Fauna of Nebraska, a Description of Extinct Mammalia and Chelonia from the Mauvaises Terres of Nebraska.* In succeeding years new specimens from the Badlands and from other fossil beds in the area kept coming in to Leidy. In 1869 he summarized all that was known on the subject in a volume of 472 pages which appeared in the *Journal of the Academy of Natural Sciences of Philadelphia:* "Extinct Mammalian Fauna of Dakota and Nebraska, including an Account of some Allied Forms from Other Localities, together with a Synopsis of the Mammalian Remains of North America."

Leidy says, in the introduction to his book, of the fossil collecting in the Badlands in these early days:

The tertiary deposits of the Mauvaises Terres . . . are remarkable for the great quantity of fossil remains of mammals and turtles they have yielded without further exploration than picking them up from the surface of the country. . . . Most of the loose fossils have been gradually picked up by travellers and others, so that few of a conspicuous character, I am told, now remain. Of those collected, by far the greater part have been submitted to my investigation, and these have amounted to the enormous quantity of between three and four tons in weight.

The fossil beds that Leidy was writing about are of an age that puts them a good 30 million years on the modern side of the Age of Reptiles, so that he was concerned mainly with the mammals. The only large reptiles left in the area were the giant land tortoises, whose shells are abundant in the rocks of the Badlands. When Leidy published his synopsis in 1869, there were 84 species of fossil mammals known from North America, not counting the mammoths and sloths and other mammals that were collected from the later, more superficial deposits of Pleistocene age. Nearly all of these 84 were from the Nebraska and Dakota fossil beds; only 7 were not found there.

# 4

# THE BIG BADLANDS

Driving north from
the valley of the Platte River of Nebraska, toward the Pine Ridge
Indian Reservation of South Dakota, one sees from a great distance the blue-forested hills of the Pine Ridge. Alongside the
road, empty beer cans glitter by the hundreds, the thousands, and
finally the tens of thousands as the border of the reservation is
reached. On the Anglo side of the line is a gasoline station
equipped with a monster refrigerator which is the source of the
cans.

In the normal course of events, the vast and beautiful land of
the reservation would have by now been converted into a half-
dozen luxury ranches, operated as tax evasion devices by absentee
owners. But as it happens, here lives a large percentage of the descendants of the shattered Sioux Indian tribes, regrouping for the
next phase of history.

Beyond the northern edge of the reservation, the terrain opens

Looking north toward the wall of the Big Badlands from the White River which, together with its subsidiary rivulets and the eroding power of wind and frost, has been responsible for carving the badlands out of the soft rock underlying the prairie.

out onto the wide valley of the White River, a tributary of the Missouri that forms part of the northern boundary of the reservation. This rather ordinary prairie stream, shallow and bordered with cottonwood trees, lies at the foot of one of the world's strangest landscapes, a region that bristles with pinnacles and knife-edged ridges of whitish clay 200 feet or more in height. These extend east and west as far as the eye can reach, forming the northern wall of the White River Valley.

This region is now referred to as the Big Badlands, or the

Steep spires about 200 feet high of mid-tertiary sediments in the Big Badlands National Monument.

White River Badlands. Geographers have taken over the term "badlands" for any region where the rocks have been intricately sculptured by erosion, with the White River being what might be thought of as the "type locality" for this kind of landscape. Badlands are always found in elevated, dry regions, where the ground is poorly protected by the vegetation cover. The occasional torrential rains seam the ground with a fine network of gullies, and left standing between the gullies are ridges and spires of naked rock.

One of the "hundred defiles that conduct the
wayfarer through this pathless waste." (John
Evans in his report on the Big Badlands)

The first to write about the Big Badlands was the mountain
man James Clyman, who went by them in 1823 on his way west
from the Missouri. Seeing the milky water of the White River
and the soft white rock of the badlands, he wrote that "the whole
of this region is moveing to the Misourie River as fast as rain and
thawing of Snow can carry it." At the upper rim of the badlands
one can see the beginning of this mass wasting of the land. To the
north is the flat prairie, covered with grass. To the south, at one's
feet, is the impassable jumble of the badlands, and beyond them
the curving line of cottonwoods marking the White River, 200

feet below and a few miles away from the rim. Overhanging the rim is a lip of turf, with its ragged edges crumbling and falling down onto the bare rock. With each rain the surface of this soft, absorbent rock soaks up water and turns to mud which flows into the thousands of torrential streamlets that net the surface of the badlands and carry the mud down to the river valley. The removal of the rock undermines the turf yet farther, which falls off in chunks. In the winter the action of rain is replaced by alternate freezing and thawing that prys off plates of clay and chips of rock. The result is that the strip of badlands slowly moves northward, at the expense of the upper tableland of grass-covered prairie.

In 1939 the most spectacular part of the White River Badlands was converted into the Badlands National Monument. Here a paved road skirts some fifty miles of the rim of the badlands, dipping now and then to the valley floor. The views of wild and uninhabitable country feed the eye of the traveler and soothe the spirit that has been frayed by what he has been told is a high standard of living. The heart of the humanized badlands is the Visitors Center, which feeds the attentive mind. Esthetically pleasing exhibits distill the results of a century of scholarly study of the badlands, telling how they were formed, and reconstructing the life that swarmed in this ancient western river valley. Visitors cluster at the exhibits like butterflies drinking at the nectar of flowers.

In early May the snowbanks from the last blizzard still cling to the shady slopes. The campgrounds are still nearly deserted, and only a few visitors are at the indoor exhibits, but among them is a group of two young women and two long-haired men in costumes appropriate to Jim Clyman's mountain men and their female comrades. What do these modern derelicts see in a collection of old bones?

"We'll put up camp out by Hurley Butte," one is saying.

Although fossils have been mined from the
clays and sandstones of the Big Badlands for
more than a hundred years, more are still
being found as they become exposed by
weathering.

"There's a lot of Pierre shale out there," says another, "but
there's nothing in the Pierre."
"Nothing in the Pierre! Shiyutt! It's full of ammonites!"
So here is the new breed of mountain men.
The outdoor museum is a trail that winds through a small tract
of badlands, leading past bones still embedded in the rock, and

protected by glass from the weather. The ease with which the tourist is led to fossils along this trail should not mislead him as to the real nature of bone hunting. Although the Big Badlands is one of the richest fossil beds in the world, the casual observer meandering through the exposures of bare rock rarely sees a fossil tooth or bone. There are pockets where the fossils are concentrated, but taking the area in its entirety, the chances that a cubic yard of rock chosen at random will contain a fossil are pretty close to zero. The hundreds of fossil skeletons of extinct vertebrates that are mounted in the museums of the world are the result of many millions of hours spent by bone hunters walking with eyes bent to the ground.

The chances of an animal achieving paleontological immortality are exceedingly remote. If its bones are left near the surface, they are usually broken up by weathering within a few years. It is only in those relatively few areas where sediments accumulate rapidly and steadily over tens of thousands and even millions of years that skeletons, or more usually the widely dispersed parts of skeletons, get buried so deeply that they are saved from destruction and impregnated with minerals that toughen and harden them. Then, before the fossils can be found by the paleontologist, the sediments have to be dissected by erosion, bringing the bones again out into the sunlight. Even though a bone has been hardened in the process of fossilization, its life may be short when exposed to the weather, so that the bone hunter has to be on the spot at the instant of geological time when the exposed fossil is on its way to final disintegration. The discovery of a complete fossil skeleton is thus a remarkable intersection of fate lines.

The sedimentary rocks—several hundred feet of clays and sandstones—that form the Big Badlands were deposited in a wide river valley that collected erosional debris from the Black Hills, now visible some eighty miles to the west. These rocks are of Oligocene age, being deposited over a span of a few million years

These huge blocks and crags are remnants of sediment that once filled a wide and green Oligocene river valley.

centered at about 30 million years ago. Some of the highest peaks of the badlands are capped with a layer of younger rock, of Miocene age. The Oligocene rocks are called the White River group, which is divided into two formations, the older Chadron formation, a cool grayish-white layer at the bottom, and the thicker Brule clay, usually tinted with warm buffy tints, lying over it. The Chadron was deposited on a landscape composed of hills of black Pierre shale, a marine rock over a hundred million years older than the Chadron.

.In the sandstones of the Chadron are the bones of the great titanotheres, which give to that formation the name "Titanotherium zone." These bizarre relatives of the horse, some of them with a pair of horns at the front end of the skull, reached the climax of their evolution and became extinct within the confines of the Chadron formation.

Most of the Brule clay was, as the name implies, derived from

30

muds that were deposited in flood stage well away from the main river channels. These wide valleys were the home of vast herds of oreodons, medium-sized grazing animals whose bones give to the lower Brule the name "Oreodon zone." Mixed in with the thick layers of clay are stringers of sandstone deposited in the stream channels. The older, lowermost stream channels are called the *Metamynodon* sandstones, named after the bones of a hippo-sized, amphibious rhino that they contain. Higher up in the badlands are the *Protoceras* sandstones, containing bones of a peculiar horned relative of the deer, with down-turned face and two pairs of horns. In the upper clays the bones of an advanced oreodon, called *Leptauchenia,* are common. Besides these marker fossils, there were camels, tapirs, and giant peccaries with skulls nearly a yard long.

More abundant, even if much less noticeable than the bones of the dominant grazing animals, are the tiny jaws of a host of rabbits and small rodents. Ruling over all were the predators—the hunting dogs and the magnificent sabertooth cats.

Although fossils have been mined from the clays and sandstones of the Big Badlands for more than a hundred years, more are still being found, as they become exposed by weathering. There is much yet to be done by way of reconstructing the life of those distant times, and of building an even more elaborate testimonial than the present museum to man's intelligent concern for nature.

# 5

# THE BONE HUNTERS COME TO THE SIOUX COUNTRY

BY TREATY, THE SIOUX had in 1825 been given title to all the land from the east bank of the Mississippi to the base of the Rockies, and from central Iowa north through the Dakotas. In 1840 the Sioux country was peaceful, and trappers and fur traders had established a track running west for some 300 miles from Fort Pierre, on the Missouri, to what came to be called Fort Laramie, a nonmilitary trading post in southeastern Wyoming. This trail skirted the northern edge of the White River Badlands, and it was travelers on this route who picked up, as souvenirs, the fossil bones that Hiram Prout and Joseph Leidy made known to the scientific world. When these finds began to be noticed in scientific journals, the geologist David Dale Owen was at work on a geological survey of Wisconsin, Iowa, and Minnesota. Upon hearing of the discoveries in the badlands he, in 1849, sent one of his geologists, John Evans, to make a reconnaissance to these fossil beds. With another geologist, five Canadian voyageurs, and an Indian guide and interpreter, Evans set out from an advance base at Fort Pierre and in five days reached the badlands. He writes of the area:

. . . proceeding in the direction of White River, about twelve or fifteen miles, the formation of Mauvaises Terres proper bursts into view, disclosing, as here depicted, one of the most extraordinary and picturesque sights that can be found in the whole Missouri country.

From the uniform, monotonous, open prairie, the traveller suddenly descends, one or two hundred feet, into a valley that looks as if it had sunk away from the surrounding world; leaving standing, all over it, thousands of abrupt, irregular, prismatic, and columnar masses, frequently capped with irregular pyramids, and stretching up to a height of from one to two hundred feet, or more. . . .

The scorching rays of the sun, pouring down in the hundred defiles that conduct the wayfarer through this pathless waste, are reflected back from the white or ash-coloured walls that rise around, unmitigated by a breath of air, or the shelter of a solitary shrub.

The drooping spirits of the scorched geologist are not permitted, however, to flag. The fossil treasures of the way, well repay its sultriness and fatigue. At every step, objects of the highest interest present themselves. Embedded in the debris, lie strewn, in the greatest profusion, organic relics of extinct animals. All speak of a vast freshwater deposit of the early Tertiary period, and disclose the former existence of the most remarkable races, that roamed in bygone ages high up in the Valley of the Missouri, towards the sources of its western tributaries; where now pastures the big-horned *Ovis montana,* the shaggy buffalo or American bison, and the elegant and slenderly-constructed antelope.

In 1850 the Smithsonian Institution sent T. A. Culbertson to the badlands to collect for them. The fossils he obtained, like those gathered by Evans, eventually reached Joseph Leidy for description. In 1853, Evans went to the badlands on another bone-hunting expedition. It was in that year that there came into the field a man who was to become the most famous of the scientific explorers of the American West, the twenty-four-year-old Ferdinand Vandiveer Hayden.

Hayden had been a farm boy, working on an uncle's farm as a refugee from a broken home. When old enough to support himself, he walked away to Oberlin College and managed to work his way through to a college degree. From there he went on to train as a physician.

While a student at Albany Medical College, Hayden became acquainted with James Hall, State Geologist for New York, with the result that when he got his medical degree in 1853 (which he did not use until he enlisted in the Union Army in 1862 as a surgeon) he set off on a fossil-hunting expedition to the Big Badlands, with expenses paid by Hall. Joseph Leidy wrote to Hall in April, 1853, "I am glad to hear you are going to send Mr. Hayden to the Mauvaises Terres which, with its remains, I view as a darling child." A pair of German collectors were also on their way to the badlands, and Leidy wrote, "The information of two German collectors going there this summer has annoyed me exceedingly and I am delighted to hear you possess the same patriotic feelings as myself." In some way the Germans were deflected from their goal, turning south to Texas and Oklahoma to collect fishes. As it happened, the paleontological exploration of the West remained almost entirely an American venture.

This taste of western exploration brought Hayden back to the Sioux country in 1854 as a free-lance. For two years he roamed the Upper Missouri country, as far west as Fort Benton and the junction of the Yellowstone with the Bighorn, eking out a living by occasional work for the traders. Sometimes he traveled under the protection of the American Fur Company, sometimes alone. The Sioux war began in 1854 with a clash at Fort Laramie, and began to spread east through the Dakotas. Now Hayden's fossil collecting ground became dangerous, but legend has it that the Indians, who called him "the man who picks up stones while running," thought Hayden insane, and thus a holy man, a person not to be harmed. Hearing of Hayden's return to the West, Leidy wrote to him in 1854, from Philadelphia, "For whom are you now collecting? How are you especially engaged?. . . . If I can be of any service to you, or can in any way promote your objects let me know it. If you wish to make a sale of any of your specimens, for further explorations, I will see what may be done by subscription in our Academy."

To avenge the defeat handed the U.S. Army at Fort Laramie, in which a detachment consisting of a lieutenant and twenty-nine infantrymen was killed to the last man, the Army ordered an expedition to strike a chastising blow at the Sioux gathered north of the Platte River in Nebraska. This expedition was led by General William S. Harney, a cavalry officer. Attached to Harney's staff was a young lieutenant, Gouverneur Kemble Warren, of the Corps of Topographical Engineers who, like Hayden, was to win fame as a scientific explorer of the West. Warren's job was to write up general accounts of the geography of the field of action, as well as the combat operations themselves.

The campaign was to be launched from Fort Kearny, on the Platte, late in the summer of 1855. In July, Warren was far to the north, at Fort Pierre, making a survey of that military post. In order to be certain to get to Harney's headquarters in time for the operation he, instead of going downstream by boat and then west up the Platte, struck out directly south from Fort Pierre, crossing the White River some distance east of the badlands, and traversing the difficult sandhill country of northern Nebraska. Traveling swiftly with a small party of mountain men, without fires or tents, he managed to avoid the numerous Sioux war parties, and reached headquarters with two days to spare.

With Harney's force, he marched westward up the wide valley of the Platte. Early in September the expedition came upon a band of Sioux camped along Blue Water Creek, a northern tributary of the Platte. According to Warren, the general called the Indian leaders out to parley under a white flag, in the meantime bringing his own forces into attack position. When the trap was set, Harney told the Indians they had better start fighting. The position of the Sioux was hopeless, and 86 were killed, at the cost of only five U.S. soldiers. Warren writes of the aftermath of the Battle of Blue Water Creek:

I aided in bringing in the wounded women and children who were found near the place to which the Indians first fled. These had secreted themselves in holes in the rocks, in which armed savages also took shelter, and by firing on our men compelled them, in self-defence, to fire back, which caused the destruction of the women and children, whom the soldiers were unable to distinguish in the confusion and smoke. Near one of these holes two soldiers, five Indian men, seven women, and three children were killed and several wounded. . . .

The Indians were killed in places far apart, and in situations where the dead bodies could not easily be seen, so that it was almost impossible to make a correct estimate of the slain after the fight. I passed very close to one body several times without discovery and till the fourth day after, when my attention was only attracted to it by a group of ravens.

After dealing this blow to the Sioux, Harney's force, accompanied by Warren, marched on to Fort Laramie, which had been converted into a military post in 1849. Then, during October and November, they marched north and east through the Sioux country, into the Big Badlands, and thence to Fort Pierre.

Warren wrote up the battle of Blue Water Creek, the military geography of the Sioux country, and its natural history as a report to "Brevet Brigadier Gen. W. S. Harney, commanding, 'Sioux Expedition.'" This report was "read" to the Senate, where the motion to print it was referred to the Senate Committee on Printing. Perhaps influenced by Warren's candid report on the Blue Water episode which was at variance with the official report released by Harney and by the unmilitary descriptions of birds and flowers that were included in the geographic section, this committee sent back their decision, "resolved that it be not printed."

The senator who was chairman of the Committee on Military Affairs retaliated by moving that the report of the Committee on Printing be amended by striking out the word "not." After a postponement, the Senate finally voted to have Warren's report printed.*

In his introduction, Warren says that "In the Appendix to my report will be found an interesting memoir, from Dr. F. V. Hayden, of examinations lately made by him in Nebraska." Warren realized that Hayden knew more about this vast region in the corner between the Platte and the Missouri than anyone, and the Appendix, which was Hayden's first scientific publication, marked the beginning of two more years of collaboration between Warren and Hayden in the exploration of the Sioux country.

Hayden had been making his own exploration of the badlands in the spring of 1855, and this furnished part of the information, along with that gathered in 1853 and 1854, that he put in the report published by Warren. Hayden writes:

* It appeared as Senate Executive Document No. 76, 34th Congress, 1st Session, with the title "Explorations in the Dacota country in the year 1855."

To present an idea of the country on the White river, and the modes of travelling on the prairie, I will give a brief digest of my journal, made on a tour to the Bad Lands, in the spring of 1855. I started from Fort Pierre May 7, with an Indian as guide, one voyageur and a boy, with several horses and two carts, for the purpose of making a collection of mammalian and chelonian fossils in that remarkable cemetary. The weather was warm, and the sun shining brightly. Most of the usual spring birds had come, and the ravines and water courses were green with grass and the foliage of trees. . . . Myriads of flowers enamelled the prairies and honey bees were industriously at work by thousands among the Leguminous blossoms. I was not aware that this little inhabitant of civilization had wandered so far into the western wilds, until he appeared here.

Of the fossil hunting he says,

After partaking of a delicious dinner of antelope meat, I started out, accompanied by my voyageur, and ascending an elevation which was above the bad ground, looked down upon one of the grandest views I ever beheld. The denuded area was nearly square in form, and the immense flat concretions that projected out from the sides of the perpendicular walls in regular seams, and at about equal distances above each other, resembled some vast theatre; indeed it reminded me of what I imagined of the amphitheatre of Rome, only nature works on a far grander scale than man. We climbed with great difficulty down the steep sides, following the main channel of the little stream and after much winding through this labyrinthian sepulchre, we came to an open plateau covered with fine grass, and in the centre a beautiful grove of cedars, and through the whole a stream of milky water wound its way to the White river, about five miles distant. All

38

around us were bare, naked whitened walls, with now and then a conical pyramid standing alone. We felt very much as though we were in a sepulchre, and, indeed, we were in a cemetary of a pre-Adamite age, for all around us at the base of these walls and pyramids were heads and tails, and fragments of the same, of species of which are not known to exist at the present day. We spent that day and the following exploring the cemetary, which the denuding power of water had laid open for our inspection, and many fine specimens rewarded our labors. . . .

Contrasted with most of the country on the upper Missouri, the White river valley is a paradise, and the Indians consider it one of the choice spots of the earth. Indeed, when supplied with an abundance of meat, they always resort here and spend their time in amusements or in cultivating their numerous gardens which are scattered throughout the valley. The Brulés and Yanktons raise a considerable amount of corn and other vegetables, and with very little attention they get a tolerable crop.

Hayden merely takes it for granted that the White River "paradise" is to change hands. He writes that "The greatest deficiency that will be felt here will be a scarcity of wood for fuel, and, like other portions of the upper Missouri country, no coal need be sought after" (that is, he thought there were no coal-bearing formations in the region). He then makes the suggestion that pine logs be rafted from the forests of the Black Hills down the "Sheyenne" River.

In his 1855 report, Warren asked Congress for $50,000 for additional exploration of the Sioux country, before the still quiescent Indians of the more remote areas "became maddened by the encroachments of the white man." This turned out to be a good stratagem, for the money became available for Warren and Hayden to make additional explorations during 1856 and 1857.

In 1856 Warren and Hayden explored the Missouri from Fort
Pierre to Fort Union at the mouth of the Yellowstone, and that
river itself somewhat beyond the mouth of the Powder River.
They collected extensively while carrying out their normal mapping duties, making a rich haul of both fossils and animal skins.

Hayden was struggling desperately to become firmly established
in the field of western scientific exploration, and before the year
was out, Lieutenant Warren learned something of the ways of the
politician-scientist. In the fall of 1856 some newspaper articles
written by Hayden came to the notice of the War Department
that mentioned an exploration in the Upper Missouri, led by a
certain naturalist-geologist [Hayden] and sponsored by an organization called the "Topographical Bureau." Warren was mentioned, but only in such a way, as Warren said, to be "damned by
faint praise." The War Department complained to Warren, and
Warren to Hayden, writing that:

> You know that I labored nearly as hard in making the actual
> collection of natural history objects as you did; most of the
> large animals were killed or skinned and brought in by me;
> many of the birds I prepared entirely; my men did a great
> deal; many of the articles necessary to their preservation I
> purchased at my own expense, my accounts having been
> stopped. . . . I only employed you on my right to engage
> *three* assistants, one of whom was to have been the astrono-
> mer which position I filled myself on purpose to leave the
> place open to you. All the transportation, etc., of your
> branch I provided for. I gave up half our boat and all our
> comfort to the collection, and all of us rowed like laborers to
> bring it a portion of the way down the Missouri River. You
> may be sure it was no agreeable thing to me to see in a paper
> like the *National Intelligencer* that you had "conducted" the
> exploration, when all this labor had been actually performed
> by me and at my own risk and responsibility.

". . . a valley that looks as if it had sunk away from the surrounding world; leaving standing, all over it, thousands of abrupt irregular, prismatic, and columnar masses, frequently capped with irregular pyramids . . ." (John Evans, in a geological report on the Big Badlands)

But Warren was not one to hold a grudge, and apparently satisfied that the tongue-lashing had good effect, he appointed Hayden as an assistant the following year. Perhaps he thought better of Hayden as a geologist than as a physician, since he pointed out to Hayden that the War Department had already given him a physician who was supposed to act also as a geologist, but since this man was a good physician and a poor geologist, he split the

41

appointment so as to make Hayden the geologist, observing that "you need not therefore prepare any medicines or instruments of surgery, any further than you wish to practise on yourself."

The expedition of 1857 was ordered by the War Department to look for new routes for wagon roads north of the Platte and to explore the Black Hills. Warren and Hayden, packing by mule train with a force of twenty men, penetrated to the north part of the Hills, where "we were met by a very large force of the Dakotas, who made such earnest remonstrances and threats against our proceeding into their country that I did not think it prudent for us, as a scientific expedition, to venture further in this direction. Some of them were for attacking us immediately, as their numbers would have insured success; but the lesson taught them by General Harney, in 1855, made them fear they would meet with retribution, and this I endeavored to impress upon them."

Warren's ability to see the native's point of view is shown by the following analysis of the situation, which is worth repeating as showing the internal contradictions of this and many another exploring expedition of his time that were both acquiring scientific knowledge and representing a power implacably dedicated to "storm the citadels of barbarism" and destroy the Indian's way of life. Warren's narrative appeared in a Report of the Secretary of War to the Congress.

The grounds of their objections to our traversing this region were very sensible, and of sufficient weight, I think, to have justified them in their own minds in resisting; and as these are still in force for the prevention of the passage of any other party of whites not large enough to resist successfully, they are of sufficient importance to be repeated here. In the first place, they were encamped near large herds of buffalo, whose hair not being sufficiently grown to make robes, the Indians were, it may be said, actually herding the animals. No one was permitted to kill any in the large bands for fear

of stampeding the others, and only such were killed as strag-
gled away from the main herds. Thus the whole range of the
buffalo was stopped so that they could not proceed south,
which was the point to which they were travelling. The intention of the Indians was to retain the buffalo in their
neighborhood till their skins would answer for robes, then to
kill the animals by surrounding one band at a time and completely destroying each member of it. In this way no alarm is
communicated to the neighboring bands, which often remain
quiet almost in sight of the scene of slaughter.

For us to have continued on then would have been an act
for which certain death would have been inflicted on a like
number of their own tribe had they done it; for we might
have deflected the whole range of the buffalo fifty or one
hundred miles to the west, and prevented the Indians from
laying in their winter stock of provisions and skins, on which
their comfort if not even their lives depended. Their feelings
towards us, under the circumstances, were not unlike what
we should feel towards a person who should insist upon setting fire to our barns. The most violent of them were for immediate resistance, when I told them of my intentions; and
those who were most friendly, and in greatest fear of the
power of the United States, begged that I would "take pity"
on them and not proceed. I felt that, aside from its being an
unnecessary risk to subject my party and the interests of the
expedition to, it was almost cruelty to the Indians to drive
them to commit any desperate act which would call for chas-
tisement from the government.

But this was not the only reason they urged against our
proceeding. They said that the treaty made with General
Harney gave to the whites the privilege of travelling on the
Platte and along the White river, between Fort Pierre and
Laramie, and to make roads there, and to travel up and
down the Missouri in boats; but that it guaranteed to them

that no white people should travel elsewhere in the country, and thus frighten away the buffalo by their careless manner of hunting them. And finally, that my party was there examining the country to ascertain if it was of value to the whites, and to discover roads through it, and places for military posts; and that having already given up all the country to the whites that they could spare, these Black Hills must be left wholly to themselves. Moreover, if none of these things should occur, our passing through their country would give us a knowledge of its character and the proper way to traverse it in the event of another war between themselves and the troops. I was necessarily compelled to admit to myself the truth and force of these objections.

Perhaps this report by Warren, coupled with his previous record for objectivity, was the last straw for the authorities in Washington. At any rate, he was abruptly pulled out of the field of western exploration and given a post as an instructor at West Point. He next appears on the field of combat at the Battle of Gettysburg, where with his keen sense of topography he detected an undefended strategic hill, which he occupied with a small force brought together on his own initiative; this was the turning point of the battle. Today a bronze statue of Gouverneur Kemble Warren looks out over the peaceful meadows and woodlands of the battleground.

Hayden now got a new master. A newcomer to the West, Captain William Raynolds, replaced Warren, and led the exploratory work during 1859 and 1860. Raynolds was not enthusiastic about western exploration. Although he wrote that the Indians were both "indolent and ignorant" (ignorant of the geography of the area Raynolds was supposed to study?), he was on their side to the extent that he thought the whole Sioux country, including the Black Hills, was worthless, fit only for savages.

Going west to the Yellowstone country, the expedition worked its way south to the Oregon Trail in south-central Wyoming, which by this time was already well marked and heavily traveled. Here, where there was a good supply of liquor at a trading post, the military escort got drunk, the nondrinking Raynolds lost control of them, and the escort, together with their lieutenant, deserted. Hayden was left there for the winter, cooped up with Raynolds. The captain turned out to be a religious fanatic, and Hayden spent much of the winter arguing theology with him.

In the spring, Raynolds and Hayden went into the Lewis and Clark country of the Montana mountains, trying to get to the geyser and hot springs region of the Upper Yellowstone, but were turned back by deep snow.

The badlands for a time disappeared from the stage of history. Warren, as a result of his reconnaissance of 1855, played down the military value of the Fort Pierre–Fort Laramie road through the badlands region: "when we consider that the train for transportation from Fort Pierre to Fort Laramie must be procured from the States at a distance of 500 to 600 miles, it is doubtful if at any time economy would select this route as a channel through which to supply Fort Laramie." The track was abandoned, and the badlands were left as a wilderness until the end of the Sioux war.

The Sioux war lasted for thirty-five years. In December of 1890, Chief Big Foot led the last armed band of Sioux south through a defile in the Big Badlands. At Wounded Knee Creek, fifty miles to the south, they were intercepted and captured. An attempt to disarm them met with resistance, and two hundred Indians, men, women, and children, were slaughtered, with the loss of twenty-nine soldiers.

Hayden did not become a vertebrate paleontologist, and the fossil bones and teeth he collected went to Joseph Leidy for study. In collaboration with his friend Fielding Bradford Meek, who was his companion on the first expedition to the badlands in

1853, Hayden described many of the fossil shells found in rocks laid down on the floor of the Cretaceous sea that once covered the center of the American continent. This, and some stratigraphic geology, were his main contributions as a scientist. After the Civil War, when he enlisted in the Union Army as acting assistant surgeon and became successively post surgeon and surgeon-in-chief of a cavalry division, he turned more and more to administration and writing. It was as a man close to the sources of power in Washington that he affected the lives of the bone hunters who came to the West after the Civil War.

# 6

# OTHNIEL CHARLES
# MARSH

$A T$ ABOUT THE TIME
that Ferdinand Hayden was making his escape from a career as a
medical doctor to the freedom of the new western lands, another
farm boy, Othniel Charles Marsh, was taking the first steps to free
himself from the hated drudgery of farm life. The star of freedom
was a remote and fabulously rich uncle, George Peabody.

Peabody owned one of the world's largest mercantile companies, and lived much of the time in England to take care of
banking and brokerage interests. Happily for a large assortment
of siblings, nieces, nephews, and in-laws, he was a bachelor, and
happily for the world at large, he was a philanthropist with belief
in the worth of education. During his lifetime he spent $2 million
for such enterprises as a library at Peabody, Massachusetts, a museum of natural history at Yale, a museum of archeology and eth-

nology at Harvard, and an art gallery, music academy, and library at Baltimore. He gave $3.5 million for elementary schools and teacher's colleges in the South; and in England, $2.5 million for low-cost housing for the poor.

Othniel's mother was the beautiful Mary, sister of George Peabody. She died when Othniel was three, and as the boy grew up, he found himself the eldest child of a family of several stepbrothers and stepsisters on a farm that was on the edge of failure, in spite of some help from Uncle George. Othniel's lot was one of almost unremitting labor, but the dull existence of life on a poverty-stricken farm was leavened by his father's interest in fossils, which were abundant in the rocks exposed by the diggings for the nearby Erie Canal. This area, near the town of Lockport, New York, became widely known for its rich fossil beds, and attracted the attention of a retired Army officer, Colonel Ezekiel Jewett, who was famous in academic circles as a highly competent collector. Jewett moved to Lockwood, became acquainted with the Marsh family, and the young Othniel became his fast friend. The colonel despised the pretenses of the academicians, and besides being a better field man than any of them, was an expert in hunting and advanced profanity.

Perhaps because of the amateur standing of his scientific mentor, Colonel Jewett, it did not at this time occur to Marsh to try to get an education that would qualify him for a profession. Instead, he thought of getting away from the farm by becoming a surveyor or a carpenter. These vague plans came to nothing, and when at twenty-one he got a small cash settlement from property which had been held by his mother, he decided to go to school at Phillips Academy at Andover, although with no particular program of study in mind.

The first year at the academy was, after life on the farm, pure pleasure, mainly spent in shooting ducks and playing at games of dice. The important woman in his life at this time seems to have

48

been Aunt Judith Russell, another sister of the rich Uncle George. Probably it was her influence that gave him second thoughts about the potentialities of a good education, for in the summer before his second school year he reformed.

Marsh went to work arranging the mineral collection at the Essex Institute of Salem, a museum and library which had been established four years earlier. He then spent the rest of the summer assiduously collecting minerals in New York and Massachusetts. In the fall he went to work in, or on, the academy.

Although still much the country bumpkin, he was several years older than his classmates, and, as one of his classmates put it, "made a clean sweep of all the honors of Phillips Academy." He was invariably at the top of his classes, graduated valedictorian, was an accomplished newspaper writer and editor, and became the most powerful of the school politicians. When it turned out that he was not a good rhetorician in debate, he became manager of the debating team. His identity as a man with a passion for minerals and natural history became settled. He now became the grasping collector. An entry in a copybook of maxims reads, "Never part with a good mineral until you have a better, and never let a fine one go in the expectation of getting (at a future time) something for it." During the summers he went farther afield on expeditions, collecting minerals and fossils in Nova Scotia, acquiring experience that was later to help him on his way as a professional scientist.

With Aunt Judith as a go-between, Othniel received regular financial help from George Peabody. There would seem to be no doubt but that a good deal of the motivation for his astonishing performance at Phillips Academy was to prove his worth to his uncle. Upon his graduation in 1856, at the age of twenty-four, Marsh wrote to his uncle, with the introductory apology that he would have written him sooner in thanks for his generosity, but thought that his benefactor would be more impressed by action than words. In the same letter he says that "if it is in accordance with your wishes" he wanted to enter Yale College, and concludes with the promise that "so far as it may be in my power to prevent it, you shall never have the occasion to regret the kindness which you have shown me for my dear mother's sake."

That fall, Marsh began classes at Yale, with George Peabody promising expenses and a hundred dollars a year pocket money. When Marsh came to Yale, the renowned geologist and zoologist James Dwight Dana was professor of natural history and geology. Dana fought for more science at Yale, with some success, for in the mid-50s the balance of power began to tip, with the professors of science outnumbering professors of theology eight to five.

As a Yale undergraduate, Marsh may well have obtained one of the best all-round educations that could be had in a university. Noah Porter, who taught "Mental and Moral Philosophy," was ranged on the side of orthodox religion as the main ordering force in civilized affairs. At the other extreme was Dana, pleading for science, asking "why not have here, The American University —where nature's laws shall be taught in all their fullness, and intellectual culture reach its highest limit!" At this time, the senior faculty taught the students themselves, instead of turning them over to the tutors, as had been done in previous years, bringing the undergraduates in contact with some of the world's leading scholars.

The philologist James Hadley taught a course in Greek that was said to be the best course in science in Yale College. Hadley was an authority on several ancient languages, including Sanskrit, whose study was one of the harbingers of evolutionary thought, some decades before the publication of Darwin's *Origin of Species*. Sanskrit, about thirty years previously, had been shown by European scholars to be an extraordinarily significant fossil language, being the ancestor of the great family of languages to which English belongs. Progressive students, abandoning the theory of the Tower of Babel, were busy tracing out lineages of European tongues, and the laws of their change, much as Marsh and Cope were, in the 1870s, to be tracing out the family trees of vertebrate animals.

Hadley was highly proficient in studying language with this dynamic evolutionary approach, and several of his technical papers were highly regarded throughout the world. He wrote a "Brief History of the English Language" for an introduction to *Webster's Dictionary*, and this still appears, revised by a modern author, in the 1959 edition of the *New International*. His discussion of languages "kindred" to English, and of their evolutionary history, has the same outlook as any discussion of a group of animals and their relatives written by a good paleontologist. It probably is not too far-fetched to think that Hadley's influence on Marsh's intellectual development was considerable, although the influence was doubtless not at the conscious level, since Marsh never showed much interest in ideas for their own sake. Marsh had the most solid comprehension of Darwinian thought of any of his important American contemporaries in geology, and avoided pitfalls that many a distinguished paleontologist has fallen into.

Marsh developed a style of writing that was forceful and eminently clear, a trait that served him well in later life. At times the influence, exerted at an impressionable age, of the crudely powerful Colonel Jewett is combined with the Yale polish in strange ways, as in a collection of rather trite stories of his adventures in the West, intended as part of an autobiography which, however, he did not publish.

While at Yale, Marsh, as at Andover, managed to be the well-rounded student—a member of the rowing team, the "most celebrated sportsman," the envied escort of what a colleague cryptically called "the blue dress," eighth in scholastic ranking in a graduating class of 109, and a member of Phi Beta Kappa. He had no intention of living at Yale in threadbare fashion as a poor relation. The average Yale expenses were estimated officially at $200 to $300 a year. Marsh pushed expenditures as close to $1,000 a year as he dared, in the face of warnings by Aunt Judith, who doled out the money, and who thought this profligacy would bring him to disaster. Occasionally Marsh asked for more money from his father, saying that he could get it from his uncle, but that in doing so he ran the risk of losing "ten times" the amount in the future.

The home life of Othniel Marsh while at Yale was on the other hand quite atypical. He occupied four rooms on the third floor of a private home. These and the attic he filled to overflowing with a huge collection of minerals and fossils, so that the owner of the house had to prop up the floors. The landlady described him as "very odd," and that for most people it was "like running against a pitchfork to get acquainted with him." However, he delighted the landlady's tiny daughter by carrying her on his shoulder up the stairs to show her "real gold" and "fool's gold," while telling her that he trusted no one else to see these valuable specimens.

Marsh, several years older than most of his classmates, was called "Daddy," or "Captain." The *Yale Literary Magazine* for his senior year (1859–60) has this account of him, written by a classmate:

Captain's portly form looks odd enough in his well-worn shooting jacket; which tell, however, many a tale of swift destruction to innocent snipe and plover, in its ooze-drabbled edges, and the evident traces of Charm's [Marsh's dog, famous on the campus] muddy paws. His moustache, too, takes a still fiercer curl as he carefully sifts the powder into his flask. One cannot look at him without thinking of Kingsley's ideal naturalist. "He must be strong in body, able to haul a dredge, climb a rock, turn a boulder, walk all day uncertain where he shall eat or rest; ready to face sun and rain, wind and frost, and to eat or drink thankfully anything, however coarse or meagre; he should know how to swim for his life, to pull an oar, to sail a boat, and ride the first horse which comes to hand; and, finally, he should be a thoroughly good shot and a skillful fisherman; and, if he go far abroad, be able on occasion to fight for his life."

It was during the time that Marsh was at Yale that his life style became fixed. He settled firmly on the goal of a professorship in geology. He amassed collections on an impressive scale. He laid much store on the value of material things, and lived in as elegant a fashion as possible. He drifted away from the society of women; those of his own age laughingly referred to him as "Oh See" Marsh, in allusion to his dislike of his given name and the use of the initials O.C. Acting upon impulse became utterly foreign to him. He rarely made a mistake, except when it came to judging the extent to which he could impose upon his inferiors.

Early in the summer of 1860 Marsh wrote to George Peabody, announcing his desire to prepare himself for a professorship of natural science at Yale or some other college. Peabody replied that it was obvious that his nephew's "character and exertions" entitled him to continuing financial support, so that Marsh embarked on two years of graduate study in Yale's new Sheffield School of Science. That winter the Civil War broke out, and Marsh was offered a commission as major in a Connecticut regiment, which he declined on account of defective eyesight, although a year and a half later he wrote his father that he was still trying to make up his mind whether or not to go into the Army.

During the summer of 1861 Marsh explored the gold fields of Nova Scotia, and published a report on this new discovery. This, his first scientific paper, attracted attention even in England, and was an early example of Marsh's well-developed ability to identify and capitalize on the dramatic.

Othniel Charles Marsh, "a slow but sure thinker" who played his cards close to his chest. He founded the great collection of vertebrate fossils at Yale's Peabody Museum. (From *Science*, 1889)

As was said earlier, Marsh had done field work in Nova Scotia while a "high school" student at Andover. On one of these trips he had collected a pair of fossil vertebrae. While a graduate student at Yale, he showed these fossils to the famed Louis Agassiz, of Harvard, the authority on fossil fishes. Agassiz jumped to the conclusion that the bones were of the highest scientific importance, representing an unheard of combination of fish and reptilian characteristics, and sent a letter to Marsh's professor, the younger Benjamin Silliman, which Silliman published in the Yale-dominated journal, *The American Journal of Science*.

Agassiz, after saying that the specimens had been shown him by Mr. Marsh, a student at Yale, made a few general remarks on the remarkable features of the bones ("I do not believe there is a vertebra known thus far, in which are combined features of so many vertebra"), and then, from the eminence of his new Harvard Museum of Comparative Zoology, went on to say that "Whatever be the fate of these remains, be sure that they are preserved where they will be duly appreciated."

Marsh, with the slow and tenacious anger that characterized all his professional life, set about to "duly appreciate" the remains and to pin back the ears of the great Harvard scientist. He first published a short note giving a name to the fossil, *"Eosaurus Acadianus,"* thus establishing himself as the scientific author of the name. Then during much of the next year he worked up an exhaustive 16-page report on the two bones, which included even a chemical analysis, as well as elegant illustrations of the specimens. A notch on the rim of one of the vertebrae, which had led Agassiz to think it so remarkable, was shown by Marsh, who completed the job of clearing the matrix away from the bone, to be merely an artifact caused by accidents of preservation.

Then, acknowledging the help of the well-known anatomist Jeffries Wyman, he plodded through a long demonstration that proved the animal was not at all related to the fishes, and in fact belonged to an already known group of extinct reptiles. The fossils, however, were still remarkable because they represented the oldest known true air-breathing reptiles, so old that they "add another to the arguments that have been brought against the so-called 'Development Theory' [that is, the theory of evolution] and they show with how great caution we should receive the assertions so frequently and confidently made . . . . of the exact date of the creation or destruction of any form of animal or vegetable life." Marsh, on the basis of these two vertebrae, gives a confident reconstruction of a 15-foot-long reptile, adapted for life in the sea, but having to come to the surface to breathe.

This paper, like his account of the gold fields of Nova Scotia, made a wide and favorable impression on the scientific fraternity. But in the long run, Marsh and Agassiz both turned out to be wrong. More complete fossils showed *Eosaurus* to be an amphibian, not a reptile, of a geologic age that placed it comfortably within what is known as the "Age of Amphibians."

After getting a Master's degree at Yale in 1862, Marsh determined to go to Germany, at the time the world leader in university science, to complete his formal training. Here he attended classes in geology and biology by the hundreds, absorbing information from the lecture-loving Germans. (The story is told of a nineteenth-century German professor who, when confronted by two doors, one reading "Entrance to lectures on the Kingdom of God," and the other reading "Entrance to the Kingdom of God," without hesitation chose the former.)

At the time Marsh was in Germany, the country was seething with political agitation coincident with the rise of Prussia to power in the German Confederation, and with the attempt to restrict liberal thought. In the thick of the fight were the university professors, with the German apostle of Darwin, Ernst Haeckel, a leader on the side of democracy. Marsh must have here obtained good insight into the nature of Darwinism which, coupled with his earlier training at Yale made him, as had been said, a sound evolutionary biologist. However, his letters to his professors at Yale say little about the politics of evolution, perhaps since he knew well the mind of Noah Porter, then president of Yale College and hostile to the new theory. His notes taken from the lectures of the paleontologist Ferdinand Roemer credit the latter with opening a lecture with "Three cheers for Lincoln!" who had just been reelected President.

It has been said that Marsh was offered a professorship at Yale in 1862 when he obtained his M.S. degree, an offer he declined in order to study abroad. The only documentation for this is in one of Marsh's unpublished autobiographies. That the question was a delicate matter is shown in a letter to his father at Lockport, written in the summer of 1862, complaining about an article that appeared in the local newspaper: "The published statement that I am *expecting* a Professorship at Yale would do not a little towards preventing my getting it."

On his way to Germany, Marsh visited his Uncle George, now nearly seventy years old, who, he learned, intended to give a large sum of money to Harvard. Marsh brought up in a general way the possibility of support for Yale also, and set in motion the machinery that he hoped would get him the coveted professorship.

Marsh wrote to the geologist and mineralogist, Benjamin Silliman, Jr., a powerful figure in Yale politics, giving him the details of the proposed gift to Harvard, and asked his opinion as to how Yale could best use a donation to support the sciences. He cautioned Silliman against writing Peabody directly, gave the reasons for Peabody's devotion to Harvard (most of the Peabody family had gone there), and went on to say that "I have at present no interest in any institution except Yale. I shall use all my influence with Mr. P. in her favor and I think there is a fair prospect of success."

Silliman, and Dana, in whom Silliman confided, let the matter stand, putting their trust in Marsh. They also gave Marsh a précis of a plan for establishing a "Peabody Museum" at Yale. In May of the following year Peabody came to Germany for his health, and summoned Marsh to a conference at Homburg, a famous health resort, also noted for its gambling casinos.

Silliman received from Marsh two letters in the same envelope, one dated 10 May 1863, which inquired as to which branch of geology Marsh should specialize in while studying in Germany. "Supposing, for example, that during my stay in Europe, I should study Chemical Geology . . . . would there be an opportunity available of making such attainments useful on my return?" The other letter, written toward the end of May, gave Silliman the news that Peabody, whom Marsh had talked to a few days before, would give Yale College a legacy of $100,000 to promote natural science, and that there was every possibility that the legacy might be replaced by an imminent gift.

Silliman's response was joyful. What to do? Become a paleontologist. Make a large collection of European fossils (apparently at his own, that is, Peabody's, expense). You have only to demonstrate your fitness in order to be appointed to a chair at Yale. However, the amount of your uncle's bequest is not great enough to pay your salary; ask for more. Professor Dana's response is more authoritative; he says briefly that the only position available would be in paleontology, and that there should be no difficulty in getting him an appointment (no mention of salary).

Marsh's reply included the comments that he was agreeably surprised that they could offer him a professorship, although it was not entirely out of line with the encouragement he had been given before and, brilliantly, "I am sure my proposed connection with Yale will please Mr. P. as he has of late manifested no little interest in my future scientific prospects, and several times expressed a wish that I might obtain a position at Yale or Harvard." Some time later, he writes to another correspondent, "So much for mineralogy, which with me is a reminiscence of the past, and yet I think it not unlikely that a tender feeling for my 'first love' will always remain."

The impasse with Yale remained—they did not want to pay for Marsh's professorship (since they saw that there would be no need to do so)—and when it finally became apparent to Peabody that the money would not be forthcoming, he offered to pay it himself. Marsh, however, refused, making no doubt a correct estimate of the ultimate effect of such an action. The Yale professors had judged their man correctly: the outcome was that Marsh accepted an unpaid professorship, which left him without teaching obligations and gave him a free hand for research. Allowances and a bequest from his uncle, as it turned out, gave him enough money to live comfortably and to amass the rich collection of fossils that he eventually donated to Yale.

# 7

# EDWARD DRINKER
# COPE

Edward drinker cope,
born in 1840, was nine years younger than Othniel Marsh, but
as a result of the accident of being a child prodigy, was almost
an exact scientific contemporary of his great antagonist, publishing his first scientific paper in 1859, while Marsh entered the
scientific arena with his paper on the Nova Scotia gold fields in
1861, at the age of thirty.

The slowly developing Marsh, at twenty-one gives us this ponderous introduction to his first journal: "Believing that a diary,
with regular additions, will be highly advantageous in improving
my style of writing, and penmanship, and also a valuable assistant
to my memory, I shall now commence to note down the most important events of each day, in as plain and concise a manner as
possible."

Five years earlier, the six-year-old Cope had begun his journal, a long account of the events of a voyage by sea to Boston, with childish but penetrating sketches of ships and scenery and wildlife, and such writing as, "We saw some Bonetas swimming alongside of the vessel; they're long slim fish & they twist about like eels. We saw a Man-of-war, which looked like a large Jellyfish only he was dead." And after docking at Boston: "The next day we went home and now my journal is done."

At eight he described the specimens in the Philadelphia Academy of Natural Sciences, in a more mature fashion. He saw "Several small skulls of birds of different sizes and forms; some of them had red, black and large bills. Among them were about five skulls of Toucans that had very large bills, which were of brownish yellow around the mouth shading off into brown." He also was already observing fossils, noting "Some saurians which were fossil skeletons that were found in the rocks of England, but it was very curious that they are monstrous sea lizards (See Figure *Ichthyosaurus*). In the centre of the room, there were two rows of fossils, such as ammonites, starfish, &c."

His father, one of a clan of wealthy Quakers, was a retired farmer who owned a large stone house on a picturesque eight-acre estate. Edward's mother died when he was three; his father remarried three years later. The father himself gave his family of four children (Edward was the eldest) a carefully supervised education, about equally divided between Quaker religious discipline on the one hand and the study of an excellent library and the natural history of the beautiful surrounding countryside on the other. The happy results of Edward's heredity and early training are evident enough in his childish journals and letters, which give an impression reinforced by a playmate's recollections of him as being so active both physically and mentally as to make people laugh, and their "attention was instantly caught by his quick and ingenuous thought, expressed in a bright and merry way."

Edward's formal schooling began with a Quaker day school at the age of nine, and continued, at twelve, with a Quaker boarding school at Westtown, near Philadelphia. While away at school, a lively correspondence went on between him and his father and sisters, with elegant pink-edged parchment for his sisters, plain paper for his father. Soon after he got to the boarding school, the twelve-year-old boy wrote his father, "I like Westtown very much, & most of the boys; I am very busy at one thing or another, but this last week seems almost a month, & the thought of staying here 23 of them seems rather dreary. If I *would* I *could* be *very* homesick, but I wont if I can help it. One boy this morning cried at a great rate, & seemed unwell; he was sent to the nursery."

Away from home, and probably growing, although much undersized for his age, he became much preoccupied with the problem of nutrition. In the same letter, he told his father, "I guess father when thee gave me $\frac{1}{4}$\$, thee forgot the cost of Stamps (U.S. and Westtown), Ice cream &c. . . . I leave it to thee about furnishing me more 'goodies.' Though thee may be surprised at it, yet I tell thee, that what thee would think too much is not atall so, as boys get very hungry between meals."

Ten days later, he heard from his father about the matter, and in another letter returned to the problem with the same kind of careful analysis that he had shown a few years before in describing the specimens in the Philadelphia Academy.

Thee talks about "miserable goodies"; by goodies I don't mean candy, cakes pies, &c (though I confess they don't appear to do *any* harm) but crackers, figs, walnuts, shelbarks, & the like. If I, who have just eaten 3 big pieces of pie, & drunk a porringer full of milk, cant bear these, I must be a rather strange boy. On "pie night," at supper, I never stop under 2 pieces of pie; & a Westtown piece is about 6 inches long by 4 wide at the top by $\frac{3}{4}$ inch thick, & yet with all that I am as well as could be.

By the time he was fourteen, Cope was writing his younger sister Mary Anna in happy teenage chatter:

I think what thee says about Mary B. Evans' going out of meeting beats the bugs entirely. I think AB ought to be mobbed most certainly. If I had been in M.E.'s place I think I should not have paid the least attention, but just gone on. . . . I might have come over but for my foolishness or rather, thoughtlessness, once, when Josephs Scattergood and Snowden were here. The former asked me rather abruptly whether I had seen you lately. I know from his manner that he would have taken me over that very afternoon; but I not thinking, replied, "No, but I expect to go before long.'

On the summer when he was fourteen, the young Cope was put to farm work by his father in hopes of improving the health of the rather frail, undersized boy, and this was continued for the next four years. His father also had in mind preparing him for the life of a practical farmer, which provided the basis for a quiet but fierce struggle between the two which lasted into Cope's early manhood.

After finishing his schooling at the age of fifteen, Cope set about learning, at the insistence of his father, the profession of farming. This he continued until 1860, when he was twenty, although his interest in science was growing day by day. A letter written in 1859 to his father shows the conflict. He had discovered for himself the difference between the superficially similar bank and rough-winged swallows: "I obtained the other day a specimen of a rare *swallow,* that burrows into sand banks,—but not the 'sand-martin,' which is common. The species in question has the 'fibrillae' of the first quill converted into sharp, recurved, horny hooks, to assist it in its entrance to its deep hole."

In the same letter he said, about farming, "Tho' the cultivation of corn is a very necessary thing yet the time spent in cultivating it in the present manner seems almost wasted to me. The amount of it is there must be more machinery about it, and less poking." And going on to a more general consideration, "Tho' I do not think I would become much interested in a business of making money for its own sake, as many men are, yet the latter is a very useful asset in the furtherance of those things in which one is interested & in getting along generally—all which is sufficiently obvious."

Cope began his campaign to get out of farming and into science in earnest with a strategic move detailed in a letter to his father written in 1860. Joseph Leidy, the famed zoologist and paleontologist, was lecturing in anatomy at the University of Pennsylvania in Philadelphia. Cope gave good reasons why the coming winter would be a favorable time to hear these lectures, which "I have been wanting for some time to attend." As to the value of the course, "the knowledge of human and comparative anatomy would be of immense service to one desiring a knowledge of the proper manner of treating stock," and honesty forces him to add, "of comparative zoology." He enrolled in the course that winter.

Little is known about the details of the influence of Leidy on Cope, but in 1861 Cope became a member of the Philadelphia Academy of Natural Sciences, in which Leidy was most influential. Four years later he accepted the post of curator there (apparently without pay), a position he held for ten years.

At twenty-one, Cope was given a farm, called McShag's Pinnacle, by his father, but instead of working it himself, the young Cope soon put it out to rent. With the income he plunged into the scientific life, quickly becoming acquainted with most of the leading naturalists of the country, in part through his activities at the Philadelphia Academy, in part through visits to the Smithsonian Institution at Washington.

Cope's stage of development at the age of twenty-one, as a member of the Cope Quaker aristocracy and as shown in his letters to

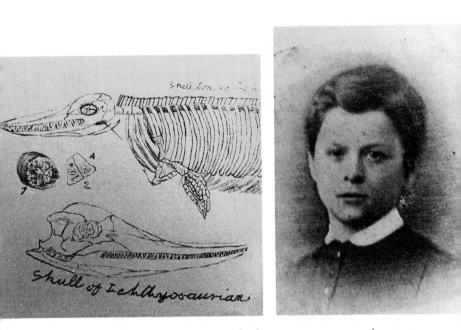

Sketch (left) made from a museum specimen at
age eight by Edward Drinker Cope (right; here
aged ten). (From *American Geologist*, 1900)

his father from Washington, is in striking contrast to that of
Marsh, who at this age had been an earnest and unsophisticated
beginning high-school student. In January of 1861, Cope wrote of
the political situation: "Senator Seward seem to be gaining the
confidence of people here. . . . If Seward is left to manage things
I am sure all will be right. Get the country safely under the control of the next administration, with a territorial compromise if
necessary, and then the Republican victory will be complete. . . .
I attended the last levee of the President."

After his life at Philadelphia, the scientific attainments of the
academicians at the Capital did not much impress him. In the
same letter he wrote: "I have now been here 11 days. I have come
to the conclusion that Washington is decidedly a second-rate

place. Though there are two professors and a doctor in the boarding-house, they are all unsatisfactory, trifling people. The habitues of the Smithsonian, though undoubtedly very superior as regards scientific attainments, are not unexceptionable. Two fairer men than Profs. Henry and Baird are hard to find."

In writing his sister, Cope gave a glimpse of the pleasant student life in his self-organized university of the world: "I have three rooms to myself, which are most conveniently arranged. One I have luggage in, the other, books & specimens. It is indeed the paradise of the student. I have called on several old friends, among them Prof. Henry's daughters." (Henry was the famous physicist and head of the Smithsonian.)

He was again in Washington in the winter of 1863, when news of the war appeared in letters to his sisters:

> I hear sundry stories of the war, from various men. . . . Soldiers are occasionally knocked down and robbed in the streets of Washington now. Last night, one was brought into the Smithsonian, and found to have a rib broken, and be otherwise injured. . . . Tell Jammy I had a present of a Boa Constrictor the other day. I am having the blood vessels injected for study. . . . I am afraid Dick Chase was killed at the battle of Murfreesboro.

Early in 1863 Cope's father sent him on a European trip, no doubt prompted by a Quaker desire to keep him from enlisting or being drafted into the Union Army. The young Cope's health also was poor, and apparently he was entangled in a love affair not approved of by his father. Although the flow of sparkling letters to his family continues, he is in psychological difficulty. In a letter to his father written on shipboard while crossing to Europe he said: "It is perhaps of great advantage that I have had the outside of my sensibilities scorched into a crust. . . . My affection for those like myself who have had to arm themselves against a pain-

66

ful destiny, increases, naturally; and I can perhaps now sympa-
thize with and understand what in thee seemed to me once to be
stoicism, and most opposed to happiness." This seems a bit strong
to be taken as an expression of grief over a broken love affair, although desolate lovers have before this thought themselves facing
a "painful destiny." Against the meager context available in biographical material that has been published, one could venture a
guess that Cope feared progressive insanity, although this seems
pure hypochondria in the face of the letters filled with intelligence and gaiety that abound in his published correspondence
with the Cope clan.

While in London in 1864, finishing up scientific work before
his return home, Cope discussed his own mental characteristics in
a letter to his father. His father had been writing about the mental problems of a woman (her name deleted in published correspondence), close to them both, and Cope was discussing his own
situation in an effort to help his father do something for her. He
said: "I need every possible aid to distract myself from myself,
and if I do not have it my health suffers; what it would result in
if my various outlets for my activities were not to my hand, I cannot tell—but I do not much doubt, in insanity." If he concentrated on one subject too long, "Existence becomes a burden; little occurrences are magnified into great griefs." During this
troubled, introspective phase, Cope began to destroy the scientific
drawings and notes he had made in Europe; only the intervention
of friends prevented this partial suicide.

More than twenty years later, when Cope and Marsh were engaged in open warfare, Marsh took advantage of this period in
Cope's life to slander him in the newspapers, with this account:

> My acquaintance with Professor Cope dates back twenty-five
> years, when I was a student in Germany at the University of
> Berlin. Professor Cope called upon me and with great frank-
> ness confided to me some of the many troubles that even

then beset him. My sympathy was aroused, and although I had some doubts of his sanity, I gave him good advice and was willing to be his friend. During the next five years I saw him often and retained friendly relations with him, although at times his eccentricities of conduct, to use no stronger term, were hard to bear.

While the close supervision of Cope's education by his father helped produce a *Wunderkind,* the dark side of the relationship showed up in the exaggerated difficulties of this storm and stress period of his life. The evils of the abnormally close and prolonged child-parent relationship were compounded by the fact that the training was saturated with religion. Even for several years after his return to the United States Cope, while on the surface an active and brilliant professional scientist, was in private life a religious fanatic, embarrassing even his devout Quaker compatriots by his outpourings of religious fervor.

Perhaps a case could be made that Cope's preoccupation with religion (which subsided after the death of his father) marred his evolutionary studies, but this is doubtful, and at any rate profitless to pursue. Cope was in America the leader of the Lamarckian (as opposed to the Darwinian) theory of evolution, which holds that the activities and desires of the animals themselves were a directing force in evolution. However, although the Lamarckian view has since been shown to be inconsistent with known facts, it was in Cope's time the dominant view among paleontologists. It was only his opinion that Lamarckian evolution was an indication of the operation in evolution of a supernatural guiding intelligence that put Cope's speculations beyond the pale of science.

While in Europe, Cope had taken in the usual tourist sights, visited the large museums and studied their collections, made the acquaintance of many of the leading scientists and picked the brains of some, and bought specimens and books. This, together

Edward Drinker Cope, "a fiery, eccentric genius," reckless in politics and combat. His large collection of fossil vertebrates is now at the American Museum of Natural History. (From *Science,* 1897)

with his work at the Philadelphia Academy of Natural Sciences and the Smithsonian Institution, took the place of a university education. It was a kind of experience that lay at the opposite pole from the methodical scholarship of Marsh. Soon after his return from Europe Cope, in the fall of 1864, got a job as professor of zoology at Haverford College. The following year he married a distant cousin, Annie Pim, who had a Quaker background like his own. A year later his only child was born, the always beloved

Julia who, with Annie, was an audience for a remarkable series of letters he wrote from the scenes of his bone-hunting forays in the West.

Cope's teaching experience at Haverford was, in fact, a continuing education in natural history. He had his students collect insects, for example, and although he for the most part ignored the insects in his varied publications, his letters from the field showed, even late in his life, that he had a good grasp of this group of animals. He also began to take classes in chemistry. As for the job itself, after a hopeful year or two he became disenchanted, and resigned before the third year of teaching was out. He now turned all of his attention to managing the farm and his scientific research, but the farm even then was in the way of his research. In 1869, when he was twenty-nine years old, he wrote to his father:

> My way of health does not adapt me for a routine position. I have occupation enough before me to last for years, but my opportunities of doing it well are much diminished by my capital being locked up in another business. I have enough capital to get a house and have a going income beside—but the present arrangement produces the smallest income and puts me to the most expense.

His "occupation enough" was his independent scientific activity. He would have enough capital to finance this if he could sell the farm and invest the money. This he soon did, and launched himself into a full-time scientific career.

In 1870, Cope published his first scientific paper on fossil vertebrates; for some years previously—ever since 1859—he had been publishing voluminously on living vertebrates. He roamed the eastern states, observing and collecting. At least one trip to some dinosaur beds along the East Coast was made with his friend Marsh. In 1871, he made his first trip to the western fossil fields.

# 8

# THE SMOKY HILL

Western Kansas is covered with a flat veneer of sediments that were washed down from the Rocky Mountains by long-vanished rivers. This sheet of soft rock, belonging to the Ogalalla formation, of Miocene age, produces the surface of the High Plains. In the latter half of the nineteenth century, the tenacious sod of these Plains was being broken by homesteaders and, along the Smoky Hill River, a wagon road made its way to the mines of Colorado. This prairie stream has cut through the smooth surface of the Plains, down through the Tertiary sediments, and into the chalky rocks of an ancient sea floor, shattering them by erosion to create a miniature wilderness of badlands which lies below the level of the surrounding country.

These marine sediments belong to the Niobrara formation. The Cretaceous sea in which they were deposited covered the heart of North America, from the Arctic coast to the Gulf of Mexico, and from Utah nearly across Kansas. This shallow sea, which has been called the American Mediterranean, washed a shoreline inhabited by dinosaurs. In its mild skies flew great leather-winged reptiles and dainty sea birds. Fishes several yards in length thronged the waters, in company with an astonishing assortment of gigantic swimming reptiles, some imitating the fishes in shape and habits, others paddling heavy turtle-like bodies that bore a long sinuous neck and toothy skull.

Fossils were discovered in the Smoky Hill Badlands in the 1860s by a professor at Kansas State College, Benjamin Mudge. Mudge was educated for the law, and had, while a practicing lawyer in Massachusetts, become acquainted with Othniel Marsh, then a student at Phillips Academy and a fellow mineral collector. His interest in science led him to abandon law, and he went to work as a chemist in oil refineries in Kentucky. The abolitionist sentiments of this New Englander drove him out of the South just before the Civil War broke out. Coming to rest temporarily in Kansas, he got an appointment as professor of natural history at the college in Manhattan, Kansas. His path again crossed that of Marsh when he wrote to the Yale professor in 1866 about his discovery of fossil bones in the chalk beds of western Kansas. Some years later he was fired over a disagreement with the college administration, and became a hired hand for Marsh, collecting bones in the West.

To the descendants of the pioneer farmers who had lived along Hackberry Creek and the Smoky Hill, in Gove, Trego, and Lane counties, there was known a pair of bone hunters whose name was legendary among them as men of a free-roving life—Sternberg, father and son. As a boy I visited relatives there, and climbed among the chalk bluffs. Here I heard tales from the poverty-stricken farmers, hard pressed by drought and the Great Depression, of the wealth that was to be had if one could find a fossil, and sell it to the professors, as did the Sternbergs.

A few years later, as a freshman college student at Boulder, Colorado, I heard again of Sternberg. An advertisement in the local newspaper announced for sale a fossil from Kansas. I went along with the director of the University Museum to the address given, in a small foothills town. Here in a barren frame house, almost completely without furniture, with curtainless windows open to the dusty roadside, was a woman with several children, she with the familiar Depression look of the times, frightened and dazed. She told us that she thought the time had come to sell something that had long been kept in the family, a fossil given them by their friend Sternberg. She took us into another room where, on the floor, propped up against the wall, was a slab bearing some dozen specimens of the beautiful free-swimming crinoid *Uintacrinus,* a relative of the starfish, and an inhabitant of the Cretaceous sea of Kansas. She folded her arms to say, "I'm asking five hundred dollars for it." With shocked disbelief she learned that $50 was all the fabulous university could pay for the fossil. Gently breaking the news to her, the professor left her with some hope by promising to send the address of Ward's Natural Science Establishment, a buyer and seller of fossils.

Charles H. Sternberg (the father; later, another son, George, also collected in the Smoky Hill) was a gentle, energetically self-sacrificing man who in some future century that praises those who love nature might well be established in the sainthood. He grew up in New York state, in Mohican country, and writes in his autobiography, *The Life of a Fossil Hunter:*

Fifteen years of my life were spent in Otsego County, New York, at dear old Hartwick Seminary, where my father, the Rev. Dr. Levi Sternberg was principal for fourteen years, and my grandfather, Dr. George B. Miller, a much-loved, devout man, professor of theology for thirty-five. The lovely valley of the Susquehanna, in which it stands, lies five miles below Cooperstown, the birthplace of the Walter Scott of America, James Fenimore Cooper, and my boyhood was spent among scenes which he has made famous. Often my companions and I have gone picnicking on Otsego Lake, shouting to call up the echo, and spreading our tablecloth on shore beneath the very tree from which the catamount was about to spring upon terrified Elizabeth Temple.

When a boy, Sternberg, in a fall out of a barn loft, injured his leg in such a way as to make him a permanent cripple; yet he was able to walk many thousands of miles through the badlands, prospecting for bone. In 1867, when he was seventeen, he and his brothers emigrated to a ranch on the lower Smoky Hill River, some one hundred miles east of the Niobrara chalk badlands. There was still Indian fighting; a U.S. Army guard was posted to defend the Sternberg ranch, and when one morning in July a band of Indians approached, Sternberg was prevented from joining in the shooting by the black sergeant in command, who called, "Let the citizens keep in the rear." Quantities of lead were sent through the air toward the Indians, who, although at distant range, beat a retreat. The Sternbergs were very much a part of the scene in pioneer Kansas; Sternberg's oldest brother, who eventually became Surgeon-General of the Army, was an Army doctor in the area.

In this region, near the towns of Ellsworth and Kanopolis, the Smoky Hill River has exposed layers of Cretaceous rock of the Dakota formation. These rocks are stream and shoreline deposits of an age just before the land sank under the Cretaceous sea that produced the Niobrara chalk exposed farther west. In the Dakota, the young Charles found fossil leaves of semitropical trees. This

Charles H. Sternberg, internationally known as a free-lance fossil hunter. (From his autobiography, *The Life of a Fossil Hunter*, 1906)

awakened his imagination, and the boy became absorbed in collecting and studying these fossils. He writes:

At the age of seventeen, therefore, I made up my mind what part I should play in life, and determined that whatever it might cost me in privation, danger, and solitude, I would make it my business to collect facts from the crust of the earth; that thus men might learn more of "the introduction and succession of life on our earth."

Sternberg combed the hills looking for fossil leaves. He describes the discovery of one of the best localities, where he found leaves a foot in diameter:

One night I dreamed that I was on the river, where the Smoky Hill cuts into its northern bank, three miles southeast of Fort Harker. A perpendicular face in the colored clay impinges on the stream, and just below this cliff is the mouth of a shallow ravine that heads in the prairie half a mile above.

In my dream, I walked up this ravine and was at once attracted by a large cone-shaped hill, separated from a knoll to the south by a lateral ravine. On either slope were many chunks of rock, which the frost had loosened from the ledges above. The spaces left vacant in these rocks by the decayed leaves had accumulated moisture, and this moisture, when it froze had had enough expansive power to split the rock apart and display the impressions of the leaves.

Other masses of rock had broken in such a way that the spaces once filled by the midribs and stems of the leaves admitted grass roots; and their rootlets, seeking the tiny channels left by the ribs and veins of the leaves, had, with the power of growing plants, opened the doors of these prisoners, shut up in the heart of the rock for millions of years.

I went to the place and found everything just as it had been in my dream.

Although devout, Sternberg was no mystic, and goes on to say:

Probably my eyes saw the specimens while I was chasing an antelope or stray cow and too much occupied with the work

76

in hand to take note of them consciously, until they were revealed to me by the dream, the only one in my experience that ever came true.

Over the years Sternberg made remarkable collections of fossil leaves from the Dakota formation near Ellsworth, totaling many thousands of specimens and hundreds of species. Of the first specimens collected, he sent some to the Smithsonian, where they were used in scientific work published many years later. In 1872 he met the leading paleobotanist of the time, Leo Lesquereux, who was out West to inspect these famed fossil beds. Lesquereux was a Swiss emigrant, deaf in his old age, who is remembered for his ability to lip-read in three languages as well as the fact that he became a world authority on the living mosses and on fossil plants. Lesquereux made a strong impression on Sternberg:

> I do not remember how long we talked. I only know that the golden moments sped by all too rapidly; and from that hour until his death in 1889 we were in constant correspondence.
>
> After this all my collections were sent to him for description. Over four hundred species of plants like those of our existing forests along the Mexican Gulf, some beautiful vines, a few ferns, and even the fruit of a fig, and a magnolia flower petal so far found in the coarse sandstone of the Dakota Group, have rewarded my earnest efforts.

Sternberg became internationally known as a free-lance fossil hunter. The life was a hard one, with the few hundred dollars from a hard-won collection being spent to finance yet another expedition into the badlands. But it was an improvement over the life of a farmer:

> My father was unable to see the practical side of the work. He told me that if I had been a rich man's son, it would doubtless be an enjoyable way of passing my time, but as I

should have to earn a living, I ought to turn to some other business. I say here, however, lest I forget it, that although my struggle for a livelihood has been hard, often indeed, bitter, I have always been financially better off as a collector than when I have wasted, speaking from the point of view of science, some of the most precious days of my life attempting to make money by farming or in some other business, so that I might live at home and avoid the hardships and exposures of camp life.

# 9

# BIG BONE CHIEF

M ARSH'S FIELD WORK
in the West began in 1868, nearly twenty years after the pioneer
exploration by John Evans in the Big Badlands of South Dakota
had opened up the western fields. That year the annual meeting
of the American Association for the Advancement of Science was
held in Chicago. On the program was a rail excursion to the western end of the Union Pacific line, which then was at a point
about midway across Wyoming. Marsh had seen a newspaper report of fossil bones of human beings, tigers, and elephants that
were dug up from a well near the railroad at the station of Antelope Springs, in western Nebraska, so particularly wanted to make
the trip. He also wanted to bring back living specimens of the
tiger salamander, whose larval or "mud puppy" stage had been
found in Lake Como, in Wyoming.

Field work at Antelope Springs consisted of a few minutes
spent looking over a rockpile thrown up beside the well. Marsh at

once picked up bones and teeth of an extinct miniature horse, and of camel, turtle, and peccary. The conductor was anxious about getting the train underway, so Marsh instructed the station master to get more. Marsh wrote that "a hatfull of bones was my reward when I passed Antelope returning East, for the station master had kept his promise. As we shook hands, I left in his palm glittering coin of the realm."

Farther west, in the wilderness between Laramie and Rawlins, he found the salamander he was after. In getting to Lake Como, he passed by, or even perhaps through, one of the world's greatest dinosaur boneyards. It is hard to understand how he remained oblivious of this locality, where at that time giant leg bones were scattered about like logs in a lumbering operation. It is even said that one of the workers on the railroad, which ran just south of the boneyards, told him about the fossils. Whatever the reason, he showed no awareness of their existence until nearly ten years later.

On his return to New Haven, Marsh began laying plans for a large-scale bone-hunting expedition to the West. However, a flare-up of Indian hostilities made an expedition the following year out of the question. He made good use of the time to perfect his plans for an expedition in 1870. As was always characteristic of Marsh, he worked with an eye for the public relations side of the venture as well as the scientific side.

Marsh arranged military protection for his party by going to the top—Generals Sherman, Sheridan, and Ord were all brought into his schemes. Sherman was commanding general of the Army, and Marsh had from him a letter that opened the way for help from every Army post. Two members of the party wrote up excellent accounts of the expedition that appeared in the New York *Weekly Herald* and *Harper's New Monthly Magazine*. Marsh wrote bulletins from the field to a leading scientific journal, the

*American Journal of Science,* lending an air of drama to the expedition.

Marsh recruited his personnel from the Yale student-body. Few of the eleven students that he selected were particularly interested in science, but they were healthy, enthusiastic, and daring, and they were able to pay their own expenses. Nearly all later in life became distinguished public figures. Henry Sargent, a sophomore and the one given credit for finding the most specimens, became a member of the Yale Corporation and head of a great hardware company. Charles Reeve, who apparently found nothing worth recording, became the first American chief of police in Manila. Only one, George Grinnell, became a professional scientist.

The plan of the expedition was to work north and south from the line of the Union Pacific Railroad. Their first stop was North Platte, Nebraska, near Fort McPherson, where they picked up a military escort. They then worked their way north and west to explore the Oligocene and Miocene rocks exposed in vast areas of western Nebraska. Sixty miles due north, by horseback and wagon, brought them to the valley of the Loup Fork River, where the country is even today relatively wild and uninhabited. The party had an escort of 43 troops, with the famous Indian scout, Major Frank North, as guide (Buffalo Bill also was with them for a short time). One of the students, Charles Betts (who was to become a patent lawyer), says in the account published in *Harper's* of this part of the trip:

> The guides rode about a mile in advance of the column. The major pointed out the least difficult paths; while the Indians, with movements characteristic of their wary race, crept up each high bluff, and from behind a bunch of grass peered over the top for signs of hostile savages. Next in line of march came the company of cavalry. . . . and with them rode

Tertiary bluffs along the Colorado-Wyoming
boundary, explored by Marsh and Cope.

the Yale party, mounted on Indian ponies, and armed with
rifle, revolver, geological hammer, and bowie-knife. Six army
wagons, loaded with provisions, forage, tents, and ammunition, and accompanied by a small guard of soldiers, formed
the rear.

As night closed over our geologists, cut off from civilization, in a country infested by hostile Indians, and they saw
around them the tents, the bivouac fires, the soldiers standing in picturesque groups, the horses cropping in the twi-
light, the corral of wagons and packing sentinels beyond,
they felt "in for" something more than science. This fact was
more forcibly impressed by day, as hour after hour they
marched over burning sand hills, without rocks, or trees, or
sign of water, while the thermometer stood at 110° in the
shade of the wagons. After fourteen hours in the saddle, one
of the soldiers, exhausted with heat and thirst, finally exclaimed, "What *did* God Almighty make such a country as

this for?" "Why," replied another more devout trooper, "God Almighty made the country good enough, but it's this deuced geology the professor talks about that spoiled it all!" . . .

After five days of such trials we hailed with joy the fresh running water of the Loup Fork. . . . Our geological labors now commenced. The sides of the river were indented with canyons, in which were exposed the strata of the ancient lake, weathered into the formation known as *mauvaises terres,* and full of fossil remains. A strong guard was each day detailed to accompany our party, while the main body marched up the river. The soldiers not only relieved us from all fear of surprise, but soon became interested and successful assistants; but the superstition of the Pawnees deterred them for a time from scientific pursuits; for Indians believe that the petrified bones of their country are the remains of an extinct race of giants. They refused to collect until the professor, picking up the fossil jaw of a horse, showed how it corresponded with their own horses' mouths. From that time they rarely returned to camp without bringing fossils for the "Bone Medicine-man"!

The expedition then moved on to Fort Russell, near Cheyenne, and again under military escort went south to work for seven days in the Miocene and Oligocene bluffs of northeastern Colorado. They then made their way north and east to Antelope Springs and into the maze of badlands near Scottsbluff, and finally back toward Cheyenne along the valley of Horse Creek. Near Horse Creek are towering cliffs of Miocene rock at Bear Mountain where, on the summit, scraps of bone still can be found lying about on the surface. The explorers found the fossil beds of northeastern Colorado to be rich in fossils of rhinos, oreodons, rabbits, and small rodents. Then, as now, the country surrounding the string of bluffs which forms the north wall of the valley of the Platte swarmed with rattlesnakes.

The party then took train westward past Como Bluff, with its still untouched hoard of multi-ton dinosaur bones, to a point where they could leave the railway line for the Uinta basin, which lay south of the Uinta range. They made an epic journey over the eastern end of the Uintas, riding muleback and pulling wagons over the trackless wilderness. When the wagons fell apart, they transferred the supplies to saddle packs. Attaining the south slopes of the Uinta range, they saw lying at their feet a vast expanse of virgin Eocene rock, the Uinta Badlands. After descending to the fossil beds, they worked their way back north over the crest of the Uintas, cutting their way through down timber, that bane of travel through high-altitude coniferous forests.

Upon their return to the Union Pacific line and after sightseeing tours to Salt Lake City and San Francisco, the party collected in the cliffs of Green River shale near Kemmerer, in southwest Wyoming. In these rocks, deposited in a huge Eocene fresh-water lake, they collected the elegant, coal-black skeletons of fossil fish that abound there. They now headed for the Smoky Hill, though the season was late, and they did not get into the Niobrara chalk beds until late November.

In the Smoky Hill chalk, on his first major expedition, Marsh made the most remarkable discovery of his life. Riding to camp late one evening, after a hard day's work collecting fossils, he found himself following a deeply cut buffalo trail, so deep and narrow that his stirrups brushed against the rock on either side. In the gathering dusk he saw, about a dozen feet from the trail, an interesting looking bone. Upon dismounting and picking it up, he could see that it was remarkably thin and hollow and had an end joint like nothing he had seen before. There was no time to look for the rest of the animal, so he put the bone in a soft pocket, cut a deep cross in the rock, and went on his way.

After the party reached New Haven in mid-December, Marsh sat down to serious work on this small hollow bone. The articular surface showed it to be the end of a finger joint, and since it was thin-walled and hollow, he concluded that it could be nothing other than the finger of a pterodactyl, a group of extinct flying reptiles which had wings constructed of skin stretched on the enormously elongated outermost of the three fingers of the hand. Judging from the size of the specimen, the wing span of the animal must have been 20 feet or more. No pterodactyl of this size was previously known from North America. On this meager evidence he published a description that placed in the skies above the Kansas sea great flimsy dragons, fantastic contraptions of skin and drinking-straw bones.

Next spring Marsh was again in the Smoky Hill, and rode the buffalo trail down to the cross he had cut in the rock. In a few minutes he had found more of the wing bone. Following it through the rock to its end, he proved on the spot that his estimate of the size of the animal was correct. Over the years Marsh accumulated a hoard of bones representing hundreds of these Smoky Hill pterodactyls, including 10 fairly complete specimens. However, he never made an intensive study of these fossils.

After the first expedition of 1870, Marsh took student parties to the West for three successive years—in 1871, ten students; in 1872, four; and in 1873, thirteen. Besides visiting the old localities, they explored new fields, such as the Eocene rocks of the Bridger basin north of the Uinta Mountains, the Oligocene and Miocene badlands in the John Day River basin of Oregon, Tertiary rocks in Idaho, and the valley of the Niobrara River north of the Loup Fork country.

Marsh went on only one more fossil-hunting expedition, this in 1874, when he assembled a party of guides and soldiers at the Red Cloud Indian Agency in Nebraska for a brief sortie (which yielded two tons of fossils) into the Big Badlands. This was accomplished in the face of dangerous pressure from the Sioux, who were trying to turn back an invasion of gold hunters into the Black Hills.

These five summers in the West laid the basis for the Yale

collection of fossil vertebrates, which was soon to become the finest in the world. They also made Marsh widely known among the Army men and frontiersmen of the West, and among the Indians, who called him the "Bone Medicine Man," and later, as his fame grew, "The Big Bone Chief." (There also was another sobriquet coined by the Indians. Evidently Marsh had sometimes the mannerism of an Englishman who sputters a stream of comments, such as "What? What's that?" and, from addressing his horse in a similar fashion, gained the title "Heap Whoa Man.") The image of himself as an intrepid frontier outdoorsman lay very near his heart, for Marsh sedulously promoted this aspect of his life for the public.

Marsh built for himself an elegant eighteen-room mansion in New Haven, and to this bachelor home invited a constant round of visitors. Here they saw a kind of museum, crammed with art objects, curios, and memorabilia, built around his western adventures. The central attraction was the octagonal reception hall, called the Wigwam, which was dominated by a buffalo head mounted on the wall, and furnished with a large round table, covered with mementos of his life in the West. One visitor recalls, "After a luncheon planned to satisfy even the appetites of Yale undergraduates we were taken to the 'Wigwam,' a sort of trophy room filled with mementos and treasures from all over the world. Here a scalp or pair of buckskin leggings, or a frontiersman's pistol would recall some incident of the west and Yale seniors became small boys again, listening to tales of Indian savagery, or of hair-breadth escapes from stampeding buffalo."

Marsh was a good entertainer, as testified by acquaintances and by the western adventure stories that have come from his own hand. Those who, when the occasion permits, have their own stock of adventure stories to tell, will recognize in Marsh a master of the art. Marsh wrote five chapters of a projected autobiography. This was never completed, nor was any part of it published

View from the summit of Bear Mountain. The Miocene rocks of which it is composed have been stripped by erosion from the plains seen in the distance.

during his lifetime, but some of the western material was included in the biography *O. C. Marsh: Pioneer in Paleontology* by Charles Schuchert and Clara Mae LeVene. Of one of these stories, depicting an episode of the first expedition to the Smoky Hill in 1870, these authors say, "it was on this expedition that Professor Marsh staged the spectacular buffalo hunt that established his reputation, once and for all, as a hunter endowed not only with plenty of courage, but with an almost uncanny ability to send a bullet from a rifle exactly where he wanted it to go."

The party had found themselves in the midst of a huge buffalo herd, and the captain of the military escort decided to make this the occasion of a hunt. The bone hunters were cast in the role of spectators, Marsh being placed in the ambulance, which was drawn by four mules, to watch from a safe vantage point. "This was tame sport for me," says Marsh, "who had had considerable experience with other large game, and after watching the hunt for awhile, I rebelled, and made friends with the ambulance driver by means of some good cigars." Marsh said, "Driver, do you want a Five Dollar Bill?" "Mighty bad," was the reply. "Then put me alongside those three buffalo, where I can get a fair shot, and here is your money."

At the crack of the whip the four mules carried the swaying ambulance at top speed over the uneven prairie. Pulling alongside the first victim, Marsh drew up his Winchester and "aiming low, just behind the fore-leg, where his heart should be, I fired, and down he came. I saw nothing more, for the frightened mules were in the air, each plunging for himself, and the driver could not hold them. The ambulance rocked fearfully, and I thought every moment it would go over, but I was willing to take the chance, and only lost my hat."

Marsh now asked, "Do you want another V?" and off they went after more buffalo. Another animal was brought to a halt by a shot from the Winchester, but Marsh pressed on with, "I have one more V for you; help me get that fine fellow, and we'll turn back." A mad dash of a hundred yards, another shot, and the leader of the group of buffalo was brought to his knees. Marsh leaped from the ambulance to finish him off. "The driver suddenly exclaimed, 'Look out, he's going for you!' The bull sprang to his feet, and with head down and eyes and nostrils flaming, made a dash for me. I just had time to jump aside, and before he could turn, gave him another shot, which pinned him to the ground, and victory was mine."

Marsh concludes the story with, "Around camp fires in various parts of the West, I have since heard the story of that ambulance hunt with many variations, but what I give here is the official account."

After 1874, the smoke of the campfire was replaced by the cigar smoke of exclusive men's clubs, which Marsh came to haunt as he

South face of Bear Mountain, a sheer cliff of Miocene rock in southeastern Wyoming. The 1870 Yale student expedition led by Marsh made pioneer scientific explorations in this area.

grew older. After his virtual retirement from active field work at the age of forty-four, he relied on a band of professional bone hunters, both temporary hired hands and those who became more or less permanent members of his staff, to collect for him.

Stories of a quite different sort from those told by Marsh himself, related by members of Marsh's field and laboratory staff in the days when he had retired from the field, no doubt diffused out into the Yale student population. Some of his assistants became deeply disenchanted and volubly critical, becoming a trial to him in his later years. One of these was Samuel Williston, of Kansas, who in 1875 joined one of Marsh's hired field parties, as a result of one of the members being frightened off by the danger from Indians. Williston eventually got a doctorate at Yale (with a thesis on a group of living insects, since Marsh forbade him to work on fossils), and became a world authority on fossil reptiles. Writing in 1897, in a report of the Kansas Geological Survey, he says of Marsh's role in Kansas paleontology and the Indian wars:

The Niobrara deposits have been famous for the past twenty-five years for the abundance, variety and perfection of its vertebrate remains. Many tons of fossils have been collected for various institutions and individuals, among which may be mentioned Yale and Harvard Universities, and University of Munich, and of Kansas, the National Museum, Professor Cope, etc. In his publications Professor Marsh has stated, or left it to be inferred, that his personal explorations in this as in other fields were extensive and that the larger part of the fossils described by him were the results of these explorations. The actual fact is that since 1875, when my personal relations with Professor Marsh began, he himself did no field work, his knowledge of the formations being derived from a few transient and hasty visits to the different fields where his collectors were at work. . . . His reference to the personal dangers encountered by hostile Indians is amusing in the extreme to all those who know the facts. I think I can say without fear of dispute by those who know the facts that Professor Marsh never ran any greater danger from Indians than when he entertained Red Cloud at his home in New Haven. This statement I think is called for in justice to his collectors who did expose themselves to real and often imminent dangers from hostile Indians, but who were rarely or never mentioned by him in his publications.

Williston says further, in another report of the Kansas Geological Survey:

The few months of collecting by Marsh and Cope was under ample protection of soldiers. While yet the danger was fully as great or greater, the various other parties spent over thirty months in the same regions with no other protection than what their own rifles and revolvers afforded. Immigrants were massacred almost within rifle shot of the parties at different times, but fortunately no encounter was had by the explorers, though at times the danger was escaped almost marvelously.

Yet, in spite of the scoffers, it is clear that Marsh and his student collectors, on their memorable expeditions into the western fossil fields, launched American vertebrate paleontology into its heroic period.

# 10

# IN QUEST
# OF THE GREAT SEA
# SERPENTS

IN MODERN TIMES
there is only one group of reptiles that can live its entire life cycle
in the high seas. These are some of the sea-snakes, extremely ven-
omous animals, up to six feet in length, and with the tail flattened from side to side in such a way as to make them efficient
swimmers. They never have to come out on the land, and they
give birth to living young at sea. Next in sea-going ability are the
sea turtles, which are almost perfectly adapted for life in the
ocean, where some of them spend their lives, except for the intervals when the female comes ashore to lay her eggs in beach sand.
The estuarine crocodile of south and southeast Asia occasionally
crosses hundreds of miles of ocean, so that it has become widely
dispersed throughout the islands of the Malay Archipelago. On

the Galapagos Islands are some husky lizards, up to 4 feet long, that live on rocks at the edge of the sea. They have a tail shaped so as to make a good paddle, but spend most of their lives basking on the shore, entering the water only to feed on seaweed.

The situation was far different in the geologic past, when the sea was dominated by several groups of reptiles, some of large size, in the way that the whales and porpoises, and the tribes of such semi-aquatics as the walruses and seals, dominate the modern oceans. These marine reptiles, except for the sea turtles, became, for reasons unknown, extinct by the end of the Mesozoic, along with their gigantic brothers on the land, the dinosaurs. In North America the most famous graveyard for their bones is the Niobrara chalk of the Smoky Hill Badlands.

By late Cretaceous times, when the waves of the American Mediterranean rippled over the future wheat fields of Kansas, the reptiles already were veterans of the sea, with several types having become adapted to life in this environment. Those best fitted for marine life went about it in one of two ways; either becoming shaped like fishes, so that they swam by powerful movements of a flattened tail, or by changing the legs into huge paddles.

In the black Jurassic shale of south Germany are found remarkably preserved fossils of one of the most successful groups of marine reptiles, the ichthyosaurs, in which the most advanced types almost exactly imitated the body form of their fellow inhabitants of the sea, the great sharks. The legs were modified into fins used only for steering. In one of the German fossils, a number of young ichthyosaurs are in the body and outside near the birth canal, indicating that these reptiles had evolved the ability to produce living young, a useful adaptation for life in the open seas.

It is strange that the well-adapted ichthyosaurs should have become extinct just before the beginning of the Cretaceous, so that none are found in the Kansas chalk. What it shows is that the misfortunes of the great reptiles did not come as a single blow, but that there was rather a succession of hard times during the Mesozoic, the last one wiping out the few remaining dinosaurs and great "sea serpents."

The other ancient and successful group of marine reptiles, dating back to Triassic times, were the plesiosaurs, which perfected the paddle method of swimming. Some were short-necked types, but most had very long, flexible necks, so that they were described as looking like a snake strung through the body of a turtle. These managed to survive until the time of the Kansas sea, and their skeletons are found in the chalk beds of the Smoky Hill. Some of the long-necked plesiosaurs attained a maximum length of 50 feet. (When Cope found his first plesiosaurs in the Smoky Hill, after seeing a skeleton going into one side of a hill and apparently emerging on the other, he wrote that this "sea serpent" was 75 feet long.)

After the extinction of the ichthyosaurs that had lived in the seas for 50 million years, another group of reptiles moved in from the land or coastal waters to fill the ecological vacuum. These were the mosasaurs, near relatives of the large terrestrial monitor lizards, up to 12 feet long, that still live in the Old World tropics. The mosasaurs never became as highly adapted for life in the sea as did their predecessors, and with their long, slender tail looked more like a bull-necked serpent than a fish. Indeed, they had little time to achieve a high degree of adaptation, for in a geologically short time after their appearance in the Upper Cretaceous, they became extinct, along with the plesiosaurs and the last of the dinosaurs. The mosasaurs, some of them 30 feet long, fairly swarmed in the ancient Kansas sea. When Marsh was in the Smoky Hill in 1870, he once had seven of their skeletons in view at one time.

Cope, after his resignation from Haverford College, had settled at Haddonfield, across the Delaware from Philadelphia. This was handy to the marl beds of New Jersey, which were marine and coastal deposits of approximately the same age as the Niobrara chalk of Kansas, and like them contained the skeletons of both plesiosaurs and mosasaurs. Cope often went bone hunting in the marl beds, and had by 1870 written several papers on his discoveries. Joseph Leidy had in 1865 brought together all that was known about the reptiles of these New Jersey fossil beds in his *Cretaceous Reptiles of the United States,* so that it would seem that Cope had only to provide information supplementary to the work of his former teacher. However, Cope had privately expressed dissatisfaction with Leidy's work, which is written in a curiously dry and noncommittal style. When the well-known British zoologist and paleontologist T. H. Huxley reviewed Leidy's book in 1868, he said of Leidy and Cope:

> Altogether we must, while expressing our thankfulness for the memoir [by Leidy], such as it is, say that it is the least able contribution to paleontology that we can remember. Its best praise is that it contains no quackery; its worst condemnation is that it contains no science. It will always be valuable for its plates. We look forward with hope, that remains so precious will some day be elucidated, and doubt not that the accomplished author [Cope] of the *Arctifera* and discoverer of *Laelaps* [a large carnivorous dinosaur from the New Jersey marls], will make available to scientific students the descriptions of his Philadelphian brother Professor.

The fossils in the Jersey marls were mainly isolated bones. When Cope heard of the results of Marsh's first expedition to the Smoky Hill fossil beds, where complete skeletons were not uncommon, he decided to waste no more time on the second-rate eastern fields. In the fall of 1871 he was on the train for Kansas. By the time he reached the fossil beds, Marsh had been through them twice, with large parties, but Cope wrote to his wife,

"Marsh has been doing a great deal, I find, but has left more for me, and one of his guides is at Fort Wallace, *left behind,* and in want of a job. Prof. Mudge wanted to accompany Marsh and Marsh wouldn't let him go! I'll let him go!" Anyway, there were plenty of fossils: "It appears that the fossil reptiles and fishes are legion, out there, that the whole country is filled with them. That one has only to go after them to obtain them."

Cope was furnished with a small military escort. The soldiers worked as bone hunters; "The officers and men are by this time much interested in our studies and give us every aid." In late September: "The weather is lovely. The Indians are peaceable and nowhere in this region at present. Prairie dogs and antelope are in thousands and the wolves howled at us as we worked on the bluff." He is far from being a bloody-minded sportsman: "I carry a canteen or haversack and they tried to lend me a military hat and revolvers, but I left them behind as I hate the sight of them"

Cope's adventure stories are reserved for his five-year-old daughter Julia: "When we were hunting one day, I rode up a little place and came on two old bull buffalos and ran at them with my mule. The old fellows ran away and I went after them for a while and then went another way." Danger and threat of violence are depicted, with the appropriate happy endings: "I must tell thee about the wolves. They go together in large packs and sometimes in pairs. . . . I rode away on my mule and ran onto twenty live wolves only a short way off. . . . Wolves eat men when they are hungry but they have enough buffalo meat now to keep them quiet. . . . Then I must tell thee about the rattlesnakes. They are almost the only kind of snakes that bite people and kill them, but there are more here than any other kind of snake." When he collected a rattlesnake "it was not quite dead and tried to bite me but was too much hurt. So I put him in a bag, and will show him to thee in alcohol when I get home."

Cope published in 1875 a survey of the vertebrate fossils discovered by himself and others in the Niobrara chalk of Kansas, as part of a *Report of the U.S. Geological Survey of the Territories. Volume II: Cretaceous Vertebrata.* In it he gives this account of the fossil hunting grounds:

> In portions of Kansas, tracts of this kind [mauvaises terres] are scattered over the country along the margins of the river and creek valleys and ravines. The upper stratum of the rock is a yellow chalk, the lower bluish, and the brilliancy of the color increases the picturesque effect. From elevated points, the plains appear to be dotted with ruined villages and towns whose avenues are lined with painted walls of fortifications, churches, and towers, while side-alleys pass beneath natural bridges or expand into small pockets and caverns, smoothed by the action of the wind carrying hard mineral particles. But this is the least interesting of the peculiarities presented by these rocks. On the level surfaces, denuded of soil, lie huge oyster-like shells, some opened and others with both valves together, like remnants of a half-finished meal of some titanic race, who had been frightened from the board never to return. These shells are not as thickened as many fossil oysters, but contained an animal which would have served as a meal for a large party of men. One of them measured twenty-six inches across.
>
> If the explorer searches the bottoms of the rainwashes and ravines, he will doubtless come upon the fragment of a tooth or jaw, and will generally find a line of such pieces leading to an elevated position on the bank or bluff where lies the skeleton of some monster of the ancient sea. He may find the vertebral column running far into the limestone that locks him in his last prison; or a paddle extended on the slope, as though entreating aid; or a pair of jaws lined with horrid teeth, which grin despair on enemies they are helpless to resist.

When Cope's account was published, scarcely more than five years after work on the Kansas Niobrara beds had begun on a large scale, a wealth of vertebrate fossils from the Kansas beds had been brought to light. A total of 84 species, nearly all of them new, and most of them named and described by Cope, were found. Of these, 4 were birds. There were 4 species of pterodactyls, all of the gigantic, toothless kind originally discovered by Marsh. Cope compares his contribution to that of Marsh in his account of these Kansas dragons:

> The flying saurians are pretty well known from the descriptions of European authors. Our Mesozoic periods had been thought to have lacked these singular forms until Professor Marsh and the writer discovered remains of species in the Kansas chalk. Though these are not numerous, their size was formidable. One of them (*Pterodactylus occidentalis,* Marsh) spread eighteen feet between the tips of its wings, while the *P. umbrosus,* Cope, covered nearly twenty-five feet with his expanse. These strange creatures flapped their leathery wings over the waves, and, often plunging, seized many an unsuspecting fish; or, soaring at a safe distance, viewed the sports and combats of the more powerful saurians of the sea. At night-fall, we may imagine them trooping to the shore, and suspending themselves to the cliffs by the claw-bearing fingers of their wing-limbs.

In the Cretaceous sea of Kansas, as in the modern oceans, there swam gigantic turtles. *Protostega,* which was collected by Cope, reached a length of 12 feet, not much bigger than the modern leatherback sea turtle, which grows to 10 feet or more.

The great paddle-swimming reptiles, the plesiosaurs, were represented by only 3 species. They had reached their climax many tens of millions of years before the Kansas sea existed.

The dominant sea serpents in the Niobrara chalk were the mosasaurs, which Cope called the *Pythonomorpha,* named for their resemblance to the giant serpent of Greek mythology. Cope distinguished 26 species of these in the chalk beds. With their long tails and relatively short paddles they were exceedingly snakelike, and indeed belong to the modern group of reptiles to which the living snakes and lizards belong. Here, as on other occasions, he had some trouble in estimating size, displaying the well-known fisherman's bias. He found mosasaurs that he claimed were 75 feet long, which, a hundred years later, the textbooks have shrunk to a length of 30 feet. One of Cope's giants, as described by him in the following passage, clearly belongs to the category of fish that got away (or at least part of it got away):

The giants of the *Pythonomorpha* of Kansas have been called *Liodon proriger,* Cope, and *Liodon dyspelor,* Cope. The first must have been abundant, and its length could not have been far from seventy-five feet; certainly not less. . . . The *Liodon dyspelor* was probably the longest of known reptiles, and probably equal to the great finner whales of modern oceans. The circumstances attending the discovery of one of these will always be a pleasant recollection to the writer. A part of the face, with teeth, was observed projecting from the side of a bluff by a companion in exploration, Lieut. James H. Whitten, United States Army, and we at once proceeded to follow up the indication with knives and picks. Soon the lower jaws were uncovered, with their glistening teeth, and then the vertebrae and ribs. Our delight was at its height when the bones of the pelvis and part of the hind limb were laid bare, for they had never been seen before in the species, and scarcely in the order. While lying on the bottom of the Cretaceous sea, the carcass had been dragged hither and thither by the sharks and other rapacious animals, and the parts of the skeleton were displaced and gathered into a small area. The massive tail stretched away into the bluff, and, after much laborious excavation, we left a portion of it to more persevering explorers.

Of fishes, there were 48 species, 12 of them sharks. Among the fossils of the Smoky Hill most often exhibited in museums, the best known is the giant fish *Portheus*, related to the herrings and tarpon; its skeleton measures 13 or 14 feet. The fishes of this Cretaceous sea had a more primitive cast than those of the modern ocean, on account of the preponderance of types related to the herrings. Nowadays the dominant bony fishes of the sea are the tunas and such relatives as the groupers, perch, and bass, with perfected swim bladders and fin structure that fits them perfectly for life in the limitless depths of the sea.

By the middle of the 1870s, both Cope and Marsh had almost abandoned the rich fauna of the ancient Cretaceous sea of Kansas, but its study continues to the present day, and the picturesque badlands still stand as a small wilderness in the sea of wheatfields.

# 11

# BRIDGER BASIN

IN THE YEARS AFTER Lewis and Clark had opened a way across the tumbled ranges of Montana and Idaho, the mountain men, in search of beaver pelts, found these northern mountains too rugged, and the Blackfeet Indians too hostile, to ply their trade, so that they turned to the country farther south. In southern Wyoming they found the dreamed-of easy crossing of the Continental Divide. West of the present town of Rawlins lie the barren low hills of the Red Desert; in crossing this, the traveler finds that he has imperceptibly crossed the Divide. In the first half of the nineteenth century the explorations of the mountain men opened up this route, which was to become the track of the first transcontinental railway, and then a main automobile highway to the Pacific.

The man who knew this country best was Jim Bridger, who in 1825 had been the first to explore the Great Salt Lake. In 1834 Bridger set up a trading post a hundred miles west of the Divide, in the wide basin that lay at the foot of the Uinta Mountains. When the Union Pacific Railroad was completed more than twenty years later, it passed near Fort Bridger. The town became a base of operations for the pioneer bone hunters who wanted to explore the sedimentary rocks that flank the Uintas and the badlands that extended for hundreds of miles to the north between the great mountain ranges of western Wyoming.

After the Civil War, Ferdinand Hayden, out of the Union Army, took to the western fields again. He began pushing his explorations farther west, and by the late 1860s was sending to Joseph Leidy, still the reigning monarch of American vertebrate paleontology, fossil bones he had collected in the Bridger basin. The bones were blackened; they were old; they were of the Eocene epoch, from a time near the beginning of the Age of Mammals.

Western Wyoming, northeastern Utah, western Colorado, and western New Mexico are the domain of the Eocene badlands. Along most of the eastern front of the Rocky Mountains, sediments of Eocene age did not accumulate, or if they did, they were later carried away by new cycles of erosion. But between the mountain ranges west of the Divide, the erosional debris of the mountains, from the time of their origin at the end of the Cretaceous, settled in the intermontane basins and accumulated for some 60 million years, until Pliocene times, piling to a depth of thousands of feet, with Eocene and in some places Paleocene sediments lying well-protected at the bottom.

In this Eocene country is a peculiarity of landscape that was remarked on by the first geological explorers, and that is related to the persistence of the Eocene badlands. The rivers here have a habit of slicing through mountain ranges, instead of going around them. South of Thermopolis, the Wind River cuts a gorge through the Bridger Mountains. The Green River flows south into the eastern end of the Uinta Mountains, meanders casually through them in a spectacular canyon, and emerges to continue on its way to the Colorado. A tributary of the Green, the Yampa, runs through the heart of a huge rock dome to produce what is called Split Mountain.

The pioneer geologists explained the remarkable canyons of this part of the West by assuming that the mountain ranges, when they originated in Paleocene times, were slowly uplifted beneath the river systems. The cutting powers of the streams were great enough to match the uplift, producing the trans-mountain canyons. However, it is now believed that these "thruway" canyons are very much younger than the mountain ranges themselves, perhaps not being cut until Pliocene times, some 60 million years after the mountain uplift. It is postulated that the young mountain ranges had only the ordinary type of canyon, with streams originating at the summits, and cutting the usual canyons in the mountain flanks. During the Eocene, these streams carried vast quantities of sediments into the intermontane basins. Throughout the Oligocene and Miocene, deposition continued, burying the Eocene rocks beneath thousands of feet of new sediments, and eventually smothering the mountain ranges themselves in their own debris. This, together with minor uplift and depression, produced a nearly flat landscape on which developed the ancestor of the present Green River system. With a general uplift of the whole region in Pliocene times, the rivers gained new eroding power. They began to carry away the soft Tertiary sediments, gradually uncovering the preexisting mountain ranges. These ranges, as they now exist, are therefore called "exhumed" mountains. As the mountains were exposed and adjacent sediments carried away, the rivers were gradually let down onto the hard rocks of the mountains, sawing into them to produce the trans-mountain canyons. In the basins between the mountains, nearly all of the Oligocene and Miocene sediments were stripped away. Patches of some of these younger sedimentary rocks can still be

Wind River formation, northwest of
Riverton, Wyoming.

found high on the flanks of the Uintas. Left in the basins were
the Eocene sediments, which have been carved into some of the
most extensive badlands in the world.

When Othniel Charles Marsh in 1870 began his systematic exploration of the western fossil hunting grounds, he wisely by-
passed, except for one brief foray, the classic White River Badlands of South Dakota, which during the previous twenty years
had been skimmed of their scientific riches by collectors who sent
their specimens to Joseph Leidy. Instead, he concentrated on
three areas that had been only lightly touched—the Miocene and
Oligocene badlands along the South Platte, some few hundred
miles south of the Big Badlands; the Cretaceous chalk bluffs
along the Smoky Hill River of western Kansas; and the Eocene
badlands at the foot of the Uinta Mountains. Casual observation

of those who had gone before him had showed the unmistakable gleam of paleontological gold in the Eocene badlands.

Three basins lined with Eocene badlands lie at the base of the Uinta Mountains, a range rising to a height of about 13,500 feet and extending east-west for over a hundred miles, just south of the Wyoming border, in the state of Utah. On the north side is Bridger basin. Around the east end of the mountains is the Washakie basin, containing somewhat younger Eocene rocks, as well as more recent Tertiary formations. South of the Uintas is the large and paleontologically rich Uinta basin, site of the Utah and Ouray Indian Reservation, and with badlands of upper Eocene age. The Uinta basin was almost completely unknown geologically in 1870, and Marsh was the effective scientific discoverer of it and its Eocene animals.

Upon their arrival at Fort Bridger late in August, 1870, the Yale party spent a couple of weeks collecting near the town, especially in the badlands a few miles to the southeast that were called Grizzly Buttes (so named, according to one account, because a fur trapper had found there a skull he thought to be that of a grizzly bear—actually that of an Eocene mammal), a locality that was to become famous in the annals of Eocene bone hunting. Then, with military escort, they made preparations to set out for the goal that had brought them to Fort Bridger—the virgin country south of the Uinta Mountains. The student Charles Betts, who wrote an account of the expedition in an article for *Harper's* magazine called "The Yale College Expedition of 1870," said of this jaunt: "No exploration of this region had ever been made; but hunters and Indians had brought back fabulous stories of valleys strewn with gigantic petrified bones."

Marsh had hoped to be able to cross directly over the summit of the Uintas, but a guide who knew the way could not be found. They then set out by wagon down the valley of the Green River, to make a flanking movement around the eastern end of the range. The wagons soon had to be abandoned, on account of the rough terrain. Beyond Brown's Hole, an old-time summer rendezvous for the trappers, high canyon walls forced them to leave the river, and they climbed up onto the high table lands that mark the eastern end of the Uintas, and worked their way southward. Betts wrote of the view when they came into sight of the Uinta basin:

A grand scene burst upon us. Fifteen hundred feet below us lay the beds of another great Tertiary lake. We stood upon the brink of a vast basin so desolate, wild, and broken, so lifeless and silent, that it seemed like the ruins of a world. . . . The intermediate space was ragged, with ridges and bluffs of every conceivable form, and rivulets that flowed from yawning canyons in the mountainsides stretched threads of green across the waste, between their falling battlements. Yet through the confusion could be seen an order that was eternal. For as, age after age, the ancient lake was filled and choked with layers of mud and sand, so on each crumbling bluff recurred strata of chocolate and greenish clays in unvaried succession, and a bright red ridge that stretched across the foreground could be traced far off, with beds of gray and yellow heaped above it.

In a technical paper published the following year, Marsh christened the region the Uinta basin. The giant bones were not seen, but turtles and mammals of a prosaic size abounded, so that they made "collections in this region to the satisfaction of even our enthusiastic professor," wrote Betts. At Fort Uintah Marsh found a guide who knew the direct route back to Fort Bridger across the range. On the way they encountered strata of rock deposited in the same Cretaceous sea that rippled over the Smoky Hill of Kansas, and found on this distant mountain range the first fossils of

Eocene badlands of the Bridger basin,
with the High Uintas in the background.

the elegant crinoid *Uintacrinus,* which later was also found on
the Smoky Hill.

In August of 1871 Marsh had another field party of Yale men
working in the Bridger basin. Among the ten participants, several
were mentioned in Marsh's technical papers as having discovered
new species of fossils: G. G. Lobdell, Jr. (later, a manufacturer),
Theodore Peck (brick manufacturer), Oscar Harger (Marsh's
hired scientific assistant), and Harry Ziegler, a repeater from the
1870 expedition (a new fossil mammal from the 1871 expedition
was named by Marsh *Platygonus ziegleri*). Although some species

107

of mammals had by the Eocene evolved to rather large size, the majority were small, and some of the most desirable specimens to be found in the Bridger Badlands were inconspicuous and hard to find, in contrast to the gigantic reptiles the party had been hunting in Kansas some weeks before. One of the party wrote:

A large part of the collection in this region was of the remains of small animals. The fossils were generally found in the buttes, and on account of their minuteness their discovery was attended with much difficulty. Instead of riding along on the sure-footed mule and looking for a gigantic telltale vertebra or ribs, it was necessary to literally crawl over the country on hands and knees. . . . Often a quarter of a mile of the most inviting country would be carefully gone over with no result, and then again some one would chance upon a butte which seemed almost made of fossils. When two or three found such a prize at nearly the same time, lines would be drawn around each claim with as much care as when valuable mineral land is located; for it must be remembered that each man had full credit for all his discoveries, and the thought of having one's name attached to some rare specimen in the Yale Museum led to sharp competition.

Although the whistle of the locomotive had for two years past signaled the arrival of mass civilization in the Bridger country, the Yale students found themselves in a land relatively unspoiled. A dispatch from the expedition, posted from Great Salt Lake City, and published in the New York *Times* of October 17, 1871, said:

. . . the fishing is superb. During the two weeks we spent on Henry's Fork, twenty-eight miles east of the fort, over one thousand trout were caught, and still the supply seemed inexhaustible. In one day three men landed 379, the united weight of which was over three hundred pounds. Besides this superfluity of fish, our larder was supplied with sage-hen, rabbit, beaver, antelope and deer. Wolves, coyotes, and puma we shot at in vain, and upon the grizzly bear [encountered only well up into the Uintas] we gazed at a safe distance with great respect.

As soon as the snow melted from the forests of the Uinta range, the Indians set fire to the forests, in the belief, according to the correspondent, that it would be converted to fresh grassland that would bring back the vanished herds of buffalo. "Day after day we saw the heavy clouds of smoke rising, and night after night the mountain-sides were masses of flame." The party's military guard of ten men came from the remnants of two demoralized companies that had manned the post. Of 160 men, 100 had deserted in two months, because of a reduction in pay ordered by Congress.

As Marsh became acquainted with the fossils of the Bridger basin he remarked on the abundance of crocodilians and of large aquatic turtles. These, and the fossils of large snakes that he discovered, indicated that the cold and windy desert hills of western Wyoming once were the scene of lush forests, bathed in mild tropical airs. More detailed knowledge of the structure of the primitive mammals found there, especially of the structure of their feet, showed that they were forest animals, in contrast to the prairie and savannah mammals, adapted for running over hard ground, that had been found in the Oligocene and Miocene badlands east of the Divide.

It had now become clear that the Bridger basin, with its store of primitive mammals of kinds previously not known from North America, was of considerable scientific importance, and the two final Yale student parties, those of 1872 and 1873, again collected in the area.

In 1872 Joseph Leidy, still the dean of American vertebrate paleontology, came to the Bridger basin on his first (and last) expedition to the western badlands, on invitation from his friend Dr. James Van A. Carter, resident physician at Fort Bridger. Carter, and another medical man, Dr. Joseph K. Carson, United States Army, and surgeon of the post, had between 1868 (when Carter made the original discovery of bone in the Bridger basin) and 1871 collected large quantities of fossils in the region and sent them to Leidy for description. Leidy, an habitue of the lecture hall and laboratory, apparently was overwhelmed by the Bridger country. He writes, "No scene ever impressed the writer more strongly than the view of these Bad Lands" (hardly any scene could contrast more strongly with Leidy's green eastern forests), and described his feelings while walking through the maze of canyons, "it requires but little stretch of the imagination to think oneself in the streets of some vast ruined and deserted city," a quite reasonable simile in this forsaken wilderness. His friends took him into one of their collecting spots forty miles southeast of the fort, where he could pick up teeth and bone scraps to his heart's content.

Although Leidy had been publishing on the fossils of the Bridger basin for several years, Marsh had by 1872 come to regard the whole of southwestern Wyoming and adjacent parts of Utah as his private domain, and at that time, and for some years after put obstacles in the way of other bone hunters who wanted to collect there. The advent of the shy and retiring Joseph Leidy in 1872 was of little concern to him, but Marsh's Eocene idyll was truly shattered when that same summer Edward Drinker Cope arrived in the basin, with intent to collect fossils.

Cope had the year before joined forces with Hayden, becoming a member of the United States Geological Survey of the Territories. He got no salary, but had the privilege of publishing his longer technical papers at government expense and could, in theory, get supplies from military posts.

Marsh claimed to have extracted a promise from Hayden that his Survey would stay out of the Bridger basin country, but Cope decided to intrude into Marsh's territory in southwestern Wyoming regardless of any agreement. He arrived in Fort Bridger in mid-July, and set about suborning some of Marsh's hired men who had been trained by Marsh in previous years. Soon, however, Cope found the situation too difficult in Marsh's territory at the center of the basin (perhaps Marsh's Yale party had arrived), and spent the rest of the season in the younger Eocene of the Washakie basin, a good many miles to the east of Marsh's digs, and in another locality, the Ham's Fork country, well to the north of Fort Bridger.

One of Marsh's men who was hired by Cope, Sam Smith, an enthusiastic gossip, wrote to Marsh that Cope had to sleep "in the Government hay yard" and "took his meals at Manleys—hitoned for a bone sharp." In late August Smith wrote Marsh that "whe got one tusk and part of the jaw nearly one foot long I think the same kind that Prof Lidy got part of the tusk of hear that he is blowing about." A local resident and friend of Marsh told him that Smith had "hired himself to Cope and was going out with him and that he had showed him some of the fossils gathered for you." W. B. Scott, of the next generation of paleontologists, and friend of Cope's, wrote that Sam Smith vanished in the late 1880s, and that his bones, when found, indicated he had been murdered.

When Cope wrote to the commanding general of the region, Brigadier E. O. C. Ord, to explain his presence in Fort Bridger, he claimed to be "in charge of the department of Paleontology for the Survey of 1872." Then, with logic not quite clear, he proposed to stay in the Bridger area to write up the paleontology of the district, since the main Hayden party was going to Yellowstone, where there were no fossils. He informed the general that no Army horses or saddles were to be had at Fort Bridger because Hayden's party had taken them all; could the general order that more be provided from neighboring military posts? As it turned out, he had to pay for wagons, horses, and mules from his own pocket.

Cope's entry into the Bridger basin was much less auspicious than that of the Marsh groups, with their well-disciplined students and large military escorts. Cope could get no escort from the impoverished Fort Bridger post, but "I . . . don't need one in this country, of which I am heartily glad." He had brought with him from Chicago a professor of biology and two younger would-be scientists who were to help him and learn the business of western exploration, but disagreements arose from the beginning, and Cope parted company with them before starting field work. He finally assembled a party of four hired men, including a guide who had previous bone-hunting experience in the region, but had trouble with the men as the work progressed. One of the teamsters followed some strayed mules thirty-five miles, providentially found a saloon where he stayed drunk three days, the mules starving in the meantime, then stole $20 worth of provisions to set by as a reserve in anticipation of being fired.

In spite of such difficulties Cope, with valiant efforts carried off rich plunder from Marsh's territory. A sharp-eyed, hard-working field man, he found many fossils. With a quick mind and good memory, he wrote up his discoveries on the spot, and sent off manuscripts to his editors and printers in Philadelphia by mail or telegraph for quick publication.

Marsh had during the previous winter written up some of the results of his 1870 and 1871 expeditions to the Bridger basin, and these were now appearing at intervals in the *American Journal of Science,* a prestigious, Yale-edited journal that was at the disposal of Marsh for publication of his work. Cope's publications from the field in the late summer of 1872 began to fall like bombshells into Marsh's literary garden, since both were describing and naming fossils collected in the same general area.

The rules governing the christening of animals with scientific names—scientific nomenclature—hold that the name first proposed, by being published in "the literature," is the one that is to be accepted by the scientific world at large. This is the rule of priority. The question then became, for each of the long-extinct Eocene beasts of southwestern Wyoming, would Cope or Marsh be the author of its name. And one should add, or would Leidy, since he also, without coordination with the other two, was in 1872 busily naming these animals. To anticipate, the result was a world-famous debacle in the science of nomenclature.

The law of priority is nearly infallible, at least in theory, since the chances of two scientists naming the same animal on the same day are vanishingly small, but Cope and Marsh accomplished this miracle in the Bridger basin episode. Of the fossil animal *Limnotherium rostratum* Cope (in technical literature, the two-word scientific name is followed by the name of the person who christened the animal), Cope writes: "Professor Marsh states that this species is the one he named *Limnotherium affine* in a paper in the *American Journal of Science and Arts,* the advance copies of which bear date August 7, 1872. This is also the day of publication of the paper in which the name *Tomitherium rostratum* [Cope had in the meantime changed the generic term *Limnotherium* to *Tomitherium*] was proposed." Since the publications did not state the hour of their appearance, Cope used the quantitative superiority to claim credit for the new species. "Professor Marsh's description is extremely brief consisting of five lines and six measurements. . . . My original description was fuller, consisting of seventeen lines and seven measurements." This small lemur, with a skull two or three inches long, belonged to a genus which was given a total of seven generic names by Marsh, Cope, and Leidy: *Notharctus, Hipposyus, Limnotherium, Telmalestes, Telmatolestes, Thinolestes,* and *Tomitherium.* No doubt some of the duplication was the result of descriptions based on fragmentary remains, which could not be properly associated until more complete jaws and skeletons were found. Leidy's *Notharctus* is the oldest name, and is the one used today.

The fossils that most appealed to Cope and Marsh were the ponderous, herbivorous uintatheres, the largest and most spectacular animals of the Wyoming Eocene, and at the time utterly new, quite unlike anything known in the Eocene of Europe. Their multihorned skulls, the size of that of a modern rhino, but with a tiny brain, were the prizes of the race for Eocene fossils. The uintatheres suffered much from the frantic efforts in the early 1870s of Marsh, Cope, and Leidy to get credit for names. A few comments on the history of some of the names will illustrate the point.

Joseph Leidy named the first uintathere in a paper that was published on August 1, 1872, describing the new genus *Uintatherium.* On August 17, Cope sent off to the secretary of the American Philosophical Society, as a telegram, what paleontologists rather proudly refer to as one of the most bizarre papers in the history of science:

> I have discovered in Southern Wyoming the following species: *Lefalophodon* Cope. Incisor one tusk canine none; premolars four, with one crescent and inner tubercle; molars two; size gigantic.—*Dicornutus;* horns tripedral cylindric; nasals with short convex lobes.—*Bifurcatus,* nasals with long spatulate lobes.—*Expressicornis,* horns compressed and acuminate.

This was published for Cope in Philadelphia on August 19. The nonsense name *Lefalophodon* was a misspelling committed by the telegraph operator. Cope corrected it to read *Loxolopho-don* (which means "crested tooth") in a paper published August 22. However, Cope had already published the name *Loxolopho-don* for another fossil mammal which was not a uintathere. Fortunately, he was flinging about new names recklessly enough that there was one available for the new uintathere; this was *Eobasileus,* published August 18. At about the same time, Marsh published the new names *Dinoceras* and *Tinoceras.* He mistakenly thought that Cope's *Eobasileus* was the same, not realizing that the fossil beds just east of the Bridger basin, where Cope collected, were younger than the Bridger beds, and that Cope's animal was a different and more recent uintathere, farther along in evolution. Anyway, *Dinoceras* and *Tinoceras* turned out to be the same as Leidy's *Uintatherium,* published about three weeks earlier.

Marsh alone of the three men assembled enough specimens to make a really solid contribution to our knowledge of the uintatheres. Fifteen years after the hectic season of 1872, Marsh published a 237-page volume entitled *Dinocerata: a monograph of an extinct order of gigantic mammals,* in which complete restorations of the skeletons were made. In deference to this massive contribution, his name *Dinocerata* is used in some modern classifications as a group name for the uintatheres, although Marsh's genus *Dinoceras,* on which it is based, is a synonym of Leidy's *Uintatherium,* so that legalists probably would regard the use of *Dinocerata* as unlawful. Although Marsh eventually won recognition as being the real authority on uintatheres, he did not win the superficial struggle for priority in scientific names, losing out to Leidy, who had begun publishing on the Bridger basin first, and to Cope.

Leidy foresaw the difficulties that lay in wait for future students of the uintatheres, and when he came (in 1873) to summarize the results of the 1872 collecting, and of his earlier writing on the fossils from the Bridger areas, he said, in characteristic understatement:

> The interest excited by the numerous discoveries of vertebrate fossils in the Western States and Territories has led to the recent explorations of Professors Marsh and Cope, both of whom have obtained rich collections. The investigations and descriptions, by these gentlemen, of some of the fossils from the same localities, have been so nearly contemporary with my own, that, from want of opportunity of comparison of specimens, we have no doubt in some cases described the same things under different names, and thus produced some confusion, which can only be corrected in the future.

The matter of assigning names to plants and animals, living and fossil, seems to many a trivial one, yet it is one of the necessary features of natural science. Human thought processes are such that every object or entity has to be denoted by a name, and the despairing naturalist, bedeviled by the near impossibility of assigning fixed names to the kaleidoscopic, shifting world of living nature, answers his critics, "Well, I've got to call it *something!*"

The problem is solved, more or less satisfactorily, by selecting a type specimen, which is preserved as a reference in museums, and which serves as a fixed point, or anchor, for the name which the systematist invents for the species, or population of animals from which the type specimen has been more or less arbitrarily selected. The many hundreds of type specimens named by Leidy, Cope, and Marsh, preserved in the great museums of the United States, act as survey markers in the limitless map of the life of the vanished past that is still being sketched by paleontologists.

Until the 1872 season in the Bridger basin, Marsh and Cope

116

had maintained a somewhat wary friendship, made uneasy chiefly by the fact that Cope had already beaten Marsh to the description of several fossils that Marsh had thought were rightfully his. In 1868, Cope was writing to Marsh in this vein:

> I have in the meantime found what is perhaps a branched sponge which I desire for the Academy, but lend it to thee if it be of any interest to thee. . . . We are all well here, and still hoping for *good weather*. With kind regards I am thy friend
>
> Edw. D. Cope

By 1870 Cope had begun to advise his elder colleague on scientific matters. Marsh had just written up some important discoveries of fossil birds, and Cope wrote to him:

> Please have my thanks for the proof of the bird MS. l am much interested in them and think thee remarkably fortunate in getting the specimens.
>
> As we sometimes take the liberty of alluding to each others "great mistakes," I would make one criticism on the diagnoses of the birds, i.e., that thee does not "come up" to the generic relationships nor show any reason why the genera names are different from those existing. This is the Leidyan method, and one that rendered one *written science* a riddle, and leads foreigners to underrate our abilities (?). Characters or nothing! . . .
>
> With kind regards
> E. D. Cope

Cope to Marsh, 1 January 1873:

> I send you some small specimens I recently received from Kansas as having been abstracted from one of your boxes! Of course they are yours.

Marsh to Cope, 27 January:

The Kansas fossils you sent came all right. Where the rest? and how about those from Wyoming?

The information I received on this subject made me very angry, and had it come at the time I was so mad with you for getting away Smith [a collector who worked for Marsh in the Bridger basin] I should have "gone for you," not with pistols or fists, but in print. I came very near publishing this with some other transgressions including a certificate from Mr. Kinne but my better judgement prevailed. I was never so angry in my life.

Now dont get angry with me for this but pitch into me with equal frankness if I have done anything you don't like. In haste yours very truly

O C Marsh

Cope to Marsh, 30 January 1873:

I never knew of any losses sustained by you, or specimens taken by anyone, till those were sent me that you now have. . . .

On the other hand some appropriative person has stolen *Chlorastrolites* Hyposaurus jaw etc. from me.

All the specimens you obtained during August 1872 you owe to me. Had I chosen they would have been all mine. I allowed your men Chew and Smith to accompany me and at last when they turned back discouraged, I discovered a new basin of fossils, showed it to them and allowed them to camp and collect with me for a considerable time. By this I lost several fine things, although Smith owed me several days work.

Early in 1873 Cope, at a party given in New York for the distinguished English scientist John Tyndall, met Marsh face to face, and in a letter to his father said, "I met many friends from all parts of the East and as far as Washington S; among others Marsh! who stuck to me like a leech and I hope became fully satisfied that I was not a thief. It seems persons had been writing to him and had wronged me very greatly. As to the dates I said nothing."

The scientific public learned of the growing quarrel between Cope and Marsh in the pages of the *American Journal of Science* and the *American Naturalist,* where the dispute turned mainly on two questions: the matter of dates of publication and the accuracy of interpretation of the fossil remains. Both scientists had issued preprints of their papers on the Eocene fossils, and took the dates on which these were mailed out as the date of publication. Date of publication of course determined who of the two was to be given credit for discovery. The barrage of papers that Cope fired from the Bridger country caused most of the difficulty, since Cope was not at hand to supervise their publication. The result was a mass of self-contradictory errors which probably convinced Marsh that Cope was deliberately falsifying dates of his publications in order to gain priority. But even if he thought Cope was lying, Marsh did not say so in print. An example showing the tone of the dispute is the following communication that appeared in the *American Journal of Science,* 1873, entitled "Note on the Dates of Some of Prof. Cope's recent Papers, by O. C. Marsh."

The Proceedings of the American Philosophical Society, vol. xii, No. 89, just published (Feb. 6th, 1873), contain several communications from Prof. Cope on vertebrate fossils from Wyoming. There are some errors with regard to the dates, bearing the same way with those pointed out on pp. 118 and 122, which should be corrected. In the table of contents of this number, under the stated meeting, August 15th, 1872, eight papers by Prof. Cope are enumerated; and it might be

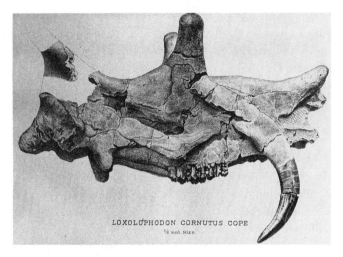

LOXOLOPHODON CORNUTUS COPE
⅛ nat. size.

One of Cope's uintathere discoveries
in the Bridger area. This skull was 29
inches long. (From 6th Annual Report of
the Hayden Survey, 1873)

inferred that they were read on that day. In fact, however, there was no meeting of the Society on the 15th, the regular August meeting having been held Friday, August 16th, at which three only of these papers were read by title, or entered on the records. At the next regular meeting, September 20th, 1872 five papers by Prof. Cope were announced or read by title. But as now published in the Proceedings, four of these purport to have been read September 19th, 1872, when no meeting was held on that date. The actual publication of these papers, by distribution is of course a distinct matter, and the evidence is conclusive that none of these were so published before Oct. 29th, 1872, and some of them not until long after.

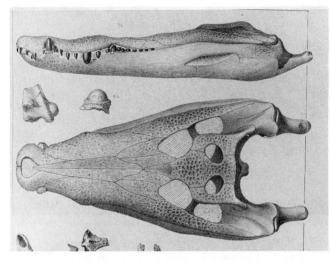

Bone fragments and skull of *Crocodilus affinis* Marsh, collected by Cope on Smith's Fork of the Green River, in southwestern Wyoming. (From "Cope's Bible," 1884)

Marsh commented on various others of Cope's papers in such detail that Cope privately referred to him as "the Professor of Copeology at Yale."

Both Cope and the officials in charge of publication at the offices of the American Philosophical Society handled his scientific papers from the Bridger basin in such chaotic fashion that it would be hard to pin a charge of deliberate deception on Cope. Cope wrote to his father, in 1873, "I have another lesson of the weakness and depravity of human nature on hand, which confirms previous ones. The acting Secretary of the Philos. Soc. not being a paid officer has been careless and indifferent." The Secretary had changed dates, mutilated, lost, and delayed publication of his papers of the previous season, Cope wrote. Furthermore,

Marsh was able to get the Society to pass a motion of censure against Cope for printing papers before they were read; Cope was "disgusted at the meanness of the proceedings."

Cope and Marsh, when they began studying the fossils from the Eocene badlands at the foot of the Uinta Mountains, only gradually realized that they were seeing a mammalian fauna much different from anything known before. As a result, both made many errors, and frequently changed their minds as the work progressed. Marsh described his first uintathere as a titanothere, comparing it to the gigantic beasts described by Leidy from the Dakota Badlands. Before finally putting it in the group where it now rests, he decided it was a proboscidean, and called it *Mastodon,* an entirely different sort of creature that did not come into existence until tens of millions of years after the close of the Eocene. Cope at one point also thought the uintatheres were related to the elephants, and published illustrations in a popular magazine showing them equipped with long trunks, but more complete skeletons later revealed a neck long enough for the animal to reach the ground without such an appendage.

Early in 1873 Marsh was beginning to get perspective on the uintatheres, and in the *American Journal of Science* referring to Cope's work (but his remarks are equally applicable to his own): "It is important, therefore, that accurate information on them [the uintatheres] be promptly made public, especially as serious errors on the subject have already appeared in various scientific publications, and are being widely disseminated." He said of Cope's uintathere: "This mythical *Eobasileus,* under the Professor's domestication, has changed its character more rapidly than Darwin himself ever imagined for the most protean of species. . . . Surely, such an animal belongs in the Arabian Nights, and not in the records of modern science."

By the summer of 1873 both Cope and Marsh were tiring of the game, and Cope wrote in the *American Naturalist:*

To sum up the matter, it is plain that most of Prof. Marsh's criticisms are misrepresentations, his systematic innovations are untenable, and his statements as to the dates of my papers are either criminally ambiguous or untrue. I might now proceed to characterize the effrontery of such proceedings in fitting terms, but forbear, believing that with a little change of scene the author of them will be as glad to bury them in oblivion as the writer of this notice.

For nearly twenty years after, the animosity between Cope and Marsh flowed underground, but all the while gaining in strength, so that when it surfaced again in 1890, each was out to destroy the scientific and moral reputation as well as the livelihood of the other.

Besides his scientific papers, Cope maintained a flow of letters to his father. He sent the seeds of various plants, and some cacti, for the farm garden, and kept him up to date on the various discoveries of fossils. He camped much of the time in the Ham's Fork country, well to the north of Fort Bridger. There was plenty of deer and antelope for meat. Sage hens and grouse were abundant, but could be eaten only when young, on account of their eating the leaves of the "sage" or wormwood (*Artemisia*) that covers vast areas of the West. He had to hide the meat from the magpie, a striking bird unknown to the easterner, but which Cope noted was to be seen in Europe.

By early October Cope had collapsed in the field from overwork and some sort of infection. "During my fever I had terrible visions and dreams, and saw multitudes of persons, all speaking ill of something and frustrating my attempts to sleep." He dosed himself with what seems to have been a favorite remedy—a powerful mixture of opium, quinine, and belladonna. "I am favored with a good appetite and my nights are positively happy under the influence of an opiate." One could imagine that were this concoction still available at the corner drug store, there would be little use for the members of the A.M.A., except perhaps for occasional surgery.

After a few weeks's convalescence at Fort Bridger, cared for by his wife, Annie, he recovered enough to return east by train. He again took to the field the following summer.

# 12

# WEST
# OF THE JEMEZ

F$_{LANKED ON THE NORTH}$
by the San Juan Mountains of Colorado, and on the east
by the Jemez range of New Mexico, lies the vast San Juan basin,
pulsing with the strange mechanical life of clanking steel arte-
ries that carry natural gas. Scattered through the naked badlands
and the forests of piñon are clusters of uninhabited metal buildings at the well sites, humming away as they carry out their designated work. Most of the human life is concentrated in a few over-
sized modern towns that supervise the extraction of the coal, gas,
and oil that impregnate the immense volume of sedimentary rock
cradled in the basin. Along the walls of such sheltered valleys as
the Canyon Largo or Canyon Gobernador, and on desolate hill-
tops, far from existing water, are the dusty ruins of vanished
Indian civilizations.

In early Tertiary times, streams from the ancestral Jemez and San Juan ranges carried mud and sand out into the San Juan basin, depositing them on the late Cretaceous rocks that contain rich coal beds. These Tertiary sediments became the rocks of the Nacimiento and San Jose formations, which are of Paleocene and lower Eocene age, older than the sediments of the Bridger basin. These formations were virgin territory for the bone hunters in the early 1870s, and for once Cope was ahead of Marsh when he arrived in the basin in 1874.

The circumstance that led to Cope's entry into the bone-hunting grounds of New Mexico was his temporary desertion from the Hayden Survey. In 1873 Cope, as a member of the Survey (he wrote that "Hayden only gave me $250, as he was very short of funds this year") went back briefly to the Bridger basin, visited the Cretaceous dinosaur beds of eastern Wyoming, and collected many fossils from the bluffs of Miocene and Oligocene rocks that form the northern wall of the Platte River in northeastern Colorado. Dissatisfied both with Hayden's parsimony and with the fact that the Hayden Survey was operating in regions already well known to the vertebrate paleontologists, Cope decided for the next year to join a competing survey that was conducted by the Army Corps of Engineers. This party was commanded by Lieutenant George Wheeler, and was charged with making a geologic and topographic survey of New Mexico.

When Cope joined the Wheeler Survey in 1874, he apparently did not have the San Juan basin in mind, but he did know that there were Tertiary badlands of much more recent (Miocene) age farther east, in the vicinity of Santa Fe. Also, one of Wheeler's men, F. Klett, had the year before found fragmentary remains of mammals in these badlands. In mid-August of 1874, the party to which Cope was attached had reached the badlands, which are spectacularly developed at San Ildefonso, and found in them rhinos, camels, horned deer, horses, and mastodons. Wheeler had put the zoologist H. C. Yarrow in charge of the party, to administer a schedule designed to carry out its primary function, that of mapping the geology and terrain of designated parts of New Mexico and southern Colorado.

Cope, after digging up some of the splendid fossils at San Ildefonso, wanted to stay. Yarrow wanted the group to move on, as ordered. Cope wrote his father, from Taos, "It is absurd to order stops where there are no fossils, and marches where fossils abound." And, "All this comes from the system of orders and regulations which it is customary to issue for the government of parties of engineers, but which are useless for explorers, for unknown objects in new fields."

Cope therefore set about to dismantle Wheeler's plans for the campaign. He argued his case with Yarrow with such effect that Yarrow, in despair, offered to hand over the command to Cope and go home, but Cope preferred a different tactic. He went, in company with Yarrow, to the regional military headquarters at Santa Fe to confer with General Gregg, the regional commanding officer. After Yarrow presented his case, Cope explained how it was that the official instructions made it impossible to collect fossils. "To my delight," Cope wrote his father, "the Gen. at once took my view of the case and set the Dr. [Yarrow] at liberty to violate and disregard the points which I had found so objectionable. . . . Everything will, I hope, go on swimmingly and the results will, I suspect, be equal to or better than any season I have yet had. For which I am thankful to the good Father of us all."

No doubt the whole procedure was illegal, for Lieutenant Wheeler was presumably under orders from headquarters at Washington, but Cope got away with it and before he left New Mexico, abundantly fulfilled his prediction that it would be his best season, for in August and September of 1874 he made the most important scientific discoveries of his life. Wheeler may have been impressed by these discoveries, but there is no record that

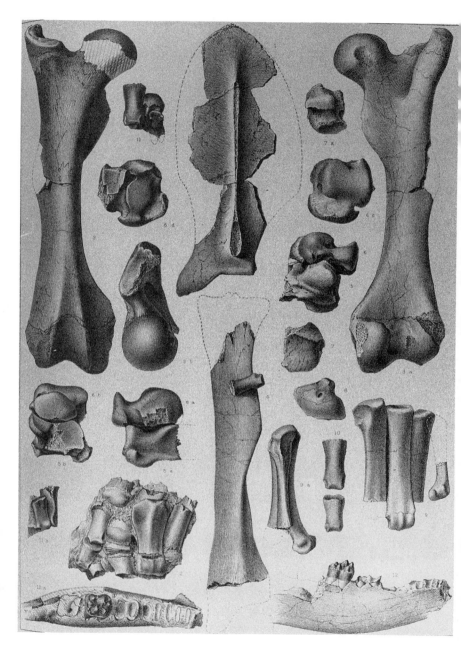

128

Cope was asked to work again with the Wheeler Survey in subsequent years.

Unlike Marsh, who seems to have directed his energies while on field trips to fossil bones, making useful friends, and acquiring valuable primitive art, Cope was interested in the whole sweep of natural history, collecting all sorts of live reptiles and amphibians for his scientific work, and maintaining more or less of an amateur interest in flowers, birds, and insects. He often sent seeds or living plants home. On the Wheeler expedition he wrote his father of a jointed globe cactus, with flat spines, and a long-spined Opuntia, which he boxed up for shipment for planting at Fairfield: "I took them to the express agent who refused to take them without prepayment of freight which I had not the cash to do, but some of my friends here will probably induce him to send it."

In making the trip, mainly on horseback, from Pueblo to Santa Fe, over a pass into the San Luis Valley, past the soaring peaks of the Sierra Blanca massif and across the sage brush plains bordering the gorge of the Rio Grande, he recorded in his letters home over 30 species of plants, which he apparently recognized from memory. "The pass is beautiful and a perfect flower garden," he wrote. He made the climb several hundred feet down the basalt cliff of the canyon and "found in the bottom in piles of fallen rock, some large flocks of sheep and on the water's edge 15 or 20 men butchering and washing them. I borrowed a hook and line from a boy and fished with mutton and caught a number of nice fishes."

Cope was never happier than when out in the field, and his zest for the passing scene extended to the life of the people, whom he often enthusiastically criticized from the condescending and prej-

(On facing page) Fragments of the skeletons of species of Periptychus, the largest of the known mammals at or very near the beginning of the Cenozoic, the Age of Mammals. The femur in the upper right of the photo is 5½ inches long. (From "Cope's Bible," 1884)

udiced standpoint of a white male Protestant (in particular, a Quaker) of his time:

> I rather like these Spanish Americans. They are of medium, some above medium, size and all well and stoutly built. They are often very dark and of straight black hair. They are lively and pleasant. The chief fault in their expression is the absence of intelligence. I am agreeably disappointed in them. The signoras and signoritas are often handsome, and only need intelligence to bring out real beauty.

Cope was quite free with pronouncements on politics, religion, or morals, and published many controversial articles and essays, even in scientific periodicals. (It should be pointed out that these have not survived as significant contributions to thought although some are amusing and incisive.) When he went to Europe, for example, his reactions to old traditions were not unlike those of Mark Twain as the Innocent Abroad. As with Twain, the Catholic Church was one of his favorite targets. In his correspondence to his intimates we encounter such opinions as "No doubt the Catholic religion is adapted to a low state of spiritual development" or "I am now in peaceful Leiden. . . . No more priests and nonsense; all is clear and quiet and sensible; as though their water had washed them clean of catholicism and water had made them think."

In New Mexico, with a culture quite old by American standards, Cope again came in contact with a Catholic tradition, this time as the repository of information Cope found worth knowing. In mid-August of 1874 he writes "We found here [at El Rito] a very intelligent priest Antonio Lamy and from various quarters gained most valuable information as to localities of fossils." (Did Cope have the first name right? Willa Cather's Archbishop was Juan Lamy, Archbishop of Santa Fe in 1875.)

Apparently it was one of Lamy's acquaintances who showed

Cope some fossil teeth from the yet unexplored badlands beyond the blue range of the Jemez Mountains, which loom in the sky west of Santa Fe. Cope recognized these teeth as those of *Bathmodon,* a good-sized animal he had described from collections made from near the western edge of the Bridger basin of Wyoming. This was from the Wasatch formation, of Eocene age and somewhat older than the Bridger formation. The Wasatch, even of Wyoming, was still little known, and Cope knew that if there also were fossil-bearing Wasatch Badlands in western New Mexico, he had within his grasp an almost completely new fauna, one still untouched by his competitor, Othniel Charles Marsh.

Cope dispatched his assistant, W. G. Shedd, on a reconnaissance over the Jemez to examine the badlands, while he himself, working until the end of August, completed his investigation of the Pliocene Santa Fe beds. The Survey party then headed west over the Jemez range, en route to Pagosa Springs, Colorado, as their orders directed. To get to Pagosa Springs, they were to swing north before reaching the Eocene badlands of the San Juan basin, but Cope kept going on a beeline to the fossil beds, continuing to make a shambles of Wheeler's plans. "We got as far as this point far up the Rio Chama," he wrote his father, "when I had to divert the route laid down in the official instructions from Wheeler in order to make the discovery I expected." Dr. Yarrow and some of the rest of the party objected, but on September 5, "knowing that to obey orders was to kill the expedition I resolved to risk a violation of them and took the guides, Mr. Shedd and a pack animal and left the concern with rations for 4 men for 7 days."

As soon as he reached the edge of the badlands (he was "delighted to find them Eocene . . . of the character of those at Evanston, Wyoming"), he picketed his horses and on the eroded hillsides of dark clay began to find bone, first of a turtle, and then teeth of *Bathmodon.* Everything was "rare and strange," older than the Fort Bridger formations, "the most important find in geology I ever made, and the paleontology promises grandly."

In mid-September, Wheeler sent a message to Cope, who was still working in the Eocene badlands, to come immediately to base camp at Tierra Amarilla, some forty miles to the northeast, to confer regarding an emergency brought about by the death by accidental shooting of the topographer, P. R. Ainsworth, and Yarrow's recall to Washington. Cope cached the fossils he had collected and set out for Wheeler's camp, where he found that he was now the ranking member of the party, next to Wheeler. Evidently Wheeler was impressed with Cope's discoveries, for Cope was allowed to return to the badlands with men and supplies for extended exploration. But Cope wrote his father that when he tried to get his salary from Wheeler, he could only collect half, and "I can not therefore send the $125 thee kindly lent me until the end of the season."

The Eocene badlands of the eastern edge of the San Juan basin, where Cope worked in the late summer and early fall of 1874, were not very rich in fossils. He wrote that the work was much harder than in the Oligocene beds of northeastern Colorado, that he might prospect for a mile or more without seeing a fossil, and even when found, the fossils usually were badly broken. However, they were of great antiquity, of an age little-studied in North America, and they existed in great variety. By mid-October he thought that he had collected 90 species of vertebrates. He classified the soft rocks of these badlands as belonging to the Wasatch formation, which covered a vast territory in western Wyoming, several hundred miles to the north. In modern classifications the San Juan basin Eocene rocks are considered to be different from those farther north, and are called the San José formation. The San José Badlands cover the eastern two-thirds of the basin, at their eastern edge lapping over the low Continental Divide, and edging close to the forested fringe of the Jemez Mountains.

132

Cope worked the San José Badlands until near the end of October, then moved farther south, to Nacimiento (now called Cuba), where he discovered older rocks, lying underneath the San José, which he named the Puerco formation. Realizing that fossils from these ancient Tertiary beds would be of great scientific interest, he looked eagerly for bone, but found nothing but pieces of petrified wood. But time was running out, with cold weather setting in, and on October 28 he headed north for Pueblo, Colorado.

The Puerco formation (now called the Nacimiento) eventually brought Cope even more renown than the San José. Fourteen years later, in 1888, Cope wrote to his now-grown daughter Julia, ". . . at the A. Phil. Soc. [American Philosophical Society] I read a paper on the Fauna of the Puerco formation. This is a very 'Copish' formation, for I discovered it, and named all the 107 Vertebrata which it contained. It is the oldest Mammalian fauna of any extent—there are 93 mammalia, and its types are ancestors of those of later ages. It has enabled me to explain how and what the origin and changes in Mammalian anatomy (Osteology) have been."

Although the Puerco was a "Copish" formation, Cope saw it only briefly, in the fall of 1874 (as just related), and in an area where it was poor in fossils. Unknown to Cope, the Puerco forms an immense area of badlands in the western part of the San Juan basin. Today a highway skirts the edge of some spectacular Nacimiento Badlands, southeast of the town of Bloomfield, which lie along the edge of the Canyon Blanco. Here there is a rich layer of fossil-bearing rock, discovered after the time of Cope and his collectors. Capping the Puerco (Nacimiento) beds is a remnant of the San José formation that produces the strangely overhanging walls and summits of Angel Peak. The Puerco fossils were discovered by David Baldwin, who began work in the San Juan basin in 1876, collecting for Marsh, but in 1880 he transferred his allegiance to Cope. Fortunately for Cope, Marsh had

failed to recognize the importance of the Puerco fossils and had packed them away unstudied. Cope began to describe them in 1881, thus opening up a new chapter in American vertebrate paleontology.

When Cope described the first of the discoveries made in the New Mexico Puerco, he for some reason departed from his usual practice of giving credit to the collector, and did not mention Baldwin. In 1884, however, in making a summary of what was by then known of these Paleocene beds, he wrote that "In 1881 I employed Mr. D. Baldwin to collect fossils in the Puerco formation of New Mexico, which I discovered in 1874. Mr. Baldwin's success has had a very important bearing on the science of paleontology. He has obtained more than sixty species from that formation, nearly all of which were new to science." In a more comprehen-

Scenes from near Gallina, New Mexico, in the Eocene badlands where Cope made his greatest paleontological discoveries. Cope assigned these rocks to the Wasatch formation; in modern terminology they are called the San José.

sive work on the Puerco, published in 1888 (the paper referred to in the already-quoted letter to his daughter) he says that

> While the formation [the Puerco] possesses lithological peculiarities, no clue to its importance in geologic chronology was known until the discovery of vertebrate remains was made in 1880, by Mr. David Baldwin. With the evidence derived from this material, the writer has been able to interject into the series of epochs of geological time a period which must have possessed many peculiarities, and which differed in such important essentials from those which preceded and from those that followed it, that an immense interval between them is proven to have existed, such as had not been previously suspected.

Mammals presumably first came into existence about 200 million years ago, toward the end of the Triassic. For the next 130 million years, throughout the rest of the Mesozoic, little is known of their history, since their fossils are rare, except in a few restricted localities, and are always small and inconspicuous. Their abundance in these favored localities indicates that small mammals, even though almost invisible in the fossil record, swarmed underfoot during much of the time when the dinosaurs were dominant.

The Puerco formation, laid down some 70 million years ago, is the oldest formation in which the mammals make a respectable showing, both in size and abundance. It marks the beginning of the Age of Mammals. When Cope began describing these fossils in the 1880s, it was recognized that their discovery was one of the most important events in the history of paleontology. Since Cope's time, a new geologic epoch, the Paleocene, has been set up to include the Puerco and related formations, and to stand as the oldest epoch of the Cenozoic. As it has turned out, the Puerco (or Nacimiento) beds are the world's most important repository of lower Paleocene fossils, and mammals of this age are almost un-known from anywhere but the Rocky Mountain West.

In the rocks of the Puerco, Cope's collector David Baldwin found several kinds of primitive mammals that had survived from the Mesozoic, the Age of Reptiles. These primitive mammals are in modern paleontology called multituberculates, after the strange molar and premolar teeth, which have a large number of points and ridges, instead of the relatively few such structures on the teeth of most modern mammals. Cope had little idea as to the relationships of these mammals; he called them "?Marsupiala," recognizing at least the fact that they were primitive. With a geo-logic life-span of over 100 million years, from Jurassic to Eocene, the multituberculates must, using the criterion of longevity, be reckoned the most successful group of mammals. The secret of their success lay in the fact that they seem to have been the first group of mammals to become herbivores. They evolved the tooth pattern later exploited by the rodents—heavy curved gnawing in-cisors in front, then a toothless gap, and then a series of large, complicated grinders. Judging from skeletal remains, some were tree-dwellers. Some of the multituberculates became gigantic com-pared to contemporary Mesozoic mammals, reaching the size of a woodchuck. Teeth and jaws of the multituberculates are abun-dant in the Puerco, then become rare and disappear in the Eocene, as their more advanced competitors, the rodents, take the stage.

Mammals living today differ from the most nearly related group of vertebrates, the reptiles, in having milk glands, fur, and also in giving birth to "living" young, except for the platypus of Australia and echidnas of Australia, Tasmania and New Guinea, which still lay eggs somewhat in the manner of their reptilian ancestors. It cannot be judged with certainty from the teeth and skeletons just what were the "soft" mammalian characteristics of the multituberculates. The best guess would seem to be that they

Nacimiento Badlands in the San Juan basin of
northwestern New Mexico. In the rocks of this
formation there have been found most of the
world's supply of fossils of mammals that
represent the beginning of the Age of Mammals.

were furry, warm-blooded creatures that fed their young milk, but
still had the primitive characteristic of being egg-layers, which, it
can be surmised, proved fatal in the face of competition from the
more advanced placental animals which began to diversify in the
Paleocene.

In addition to such holdovers from the Mesozoic as the multituberculates, there were placental mammals in abundance. Cope found the most common placental mammal in the Puerco to be *Periptychus,* which he described as being as large as a collared peccary (an American relative of the pig, about 3 feet long), a giant among mammals in these early times. He said of it that it was unlike any known mammal, having a long tail, thick at the base, walking flat-footed like a bear, and having a short neck, like an elephant. Its teeth were fitted for plant-eating, but modern studies show that its five toes were fitted with claws, rather than hoofs. The group to which this animal belongs, the extinct condylarths, represents one of the early attempts of the placental mammals to take up a herbivorous diet.

The first of the placental mammals (those with the young fed through an umbilical cord, born at relatively large size, and not carried in a pouch, as are the more primitive marsupials) were small carnivorous animals. Because of their size they fed mainly on insects, hence are called insectivores. These primitive mammals are still in existence, represented by such abundant creatures as the shrews and moles. From the insectivores of the late Mesozoic and perhaps early Cenozoic there descended all the varied groups of placental mammals, including the primates (the group to which man belongs) and both flesh- and plant-eating animals. In the Paleocene there were several groups of mammals that represented evolutionary attempts in the direction of hoofed, herbivorous mammals from the clawed, meat-eating insectivores. The condylarths were such a group, and the modern hoofed mammals such as the deer, horses, and sheep probably are descended from them.

Along with the large, new-style herbivores of the Paleocene, there appeared carnivores to match. Like the herbivores, they evolved from the insectivores.

The change from insectivore to carnivore is a relatively small one. The teeth are reduced in number, with a tendency for crushing molars to be eliminated, particularly when the diet is predominantly meat (muscle) that has only to be sliced up. The legs become modified for speed and strength. One experiment in this direction led to a group of predators called the creodonts, which appeared in the Paleocene, flourished in the Eocene, then persisted as a few stragglers into the Pliocene. They were unprogressive, small-brained types, which gave way early in the Tertiary to the order Carnivora, the "true" carnivores, which also appeared in the Paleocene, from different insectivore ancestors.

The great variety of carnivores now alive are apparently descended from a single stock of insectivores. With their appearance there began the race between predator and herbivore, between the hunter and hunted, that dominates much of the evolutionary history of mammals during the Teritary. Each became larger and more powerful, the herbivores generally ahead in speed or in sheer bulk, the carnivores depending on agility and cutting weapons. In both a premium was placed on intelligence—the cooperation of hunting packs in dogs, carefully planned stalking in the cats, and the herd organization of the grazing mammals—and throughout the Teritary there is an increase in brain size in most groups of mammals.

The oldest Paleocene rocks give us a look at the beginning of the Age of Mammals. The last of the Cretaceous rocks give us a look at the end of the Age of Reptiles. Between them lies the so-called Mesozoic-Cenozoic boundary. In several places in the Rocky Mountain West there are thick layers of sedimentary rock that are so homogenous, so much alike throughout that they have been given a single formation name, but which nevertheless contain both the last of the dinosaurs and placental mammals like those described by Cope from the Puerco formation. That is, the formation belongs to both the Cenozoic and the Mesozoic eras, to both the Age of Mammals and the Age of Reptiles. Such a formation is the Denver formation which lies in the piedmont of the Colorado Front Range.

A few miles west of Denver, at the foot of Table Mountain, and along the edge of some rather elegant suburbs, lies a very small patch of badlands which are the delight of adventure-minded children. From the top of one of the barren ridges one can look west into a landscape like that of the bandit's hideout of a western movie, to the east over a terrain of rooftops that fades into a horizon of yellow-black smog. With one's eyes closed, one can almost imagine that an Indian village lies to the east, for over the suburbs floats a chorus of frustrated barking of dogs penned up in a thousand back yards. These badlands, carved into the Denver formation, are not rich in fossils. A most careful search is needed to find a few bone scraps, but the vertebrate fossils that have been found have attracted worldwide attention from the fraternity of geologists.

Over the years, a number of vertebrate fossils from the region near the Table Mountain Badlands had accumulated. Marsh himself had a dinosaur skull fragment (he mistakenly called it a buffalo horn-core) from the area. Also, a few mammals similar to those found by Cope in the Puerco were found in the same rocks. But in no instance were fossils of both dinosaurs and Puercan mammals found close enough together to be able to say which was above the other—that is, which was older, which younger. It was assumed by some geologists that both were mixed, and that there was no clear-cut boundary in time between dinosaurs and large placental mammals.

In the 1930s and 1940s the problem was attacked systematically, with special attention to the Table Mountain Badlands. Here it was shown that dinosaur remains were always below the Puercan mammals, with about fifty feet of barren sandstone separating them. It was therefore assumed that here could be seen the beginning of the Age of Mammals, and conventions of geologists have been taken to one of the hillsides of these badlands to be shown the Mesozoic-Cenozoic boundary. And if they did not believe this one, there were other places in the Rocky Mountain West that also are claimed to show in detail this landmark in geologic history.

The significant aspect of the Mesozoic-Cenozoic boundary in the Table Mountain Badlands and that of other favorable localities is that the sedimentary rocks in which it lies show a record of continuous deposition. There are many places where Tertiary sediments are in contact with Cretaceous sediments, but usually there is a discontinuity that indicates a gap in the record of millions or tens of millions of years. At the Table Mountain locality there are alternating layers of clays and sandstones, indicating minor uplifts and periods of quiet, but nothing to indicate a long temporal gap. Sometime during the interval when a few-score feet of the Denver formation were being deposited, with no visible evidence of an abrupt change in the environment, there died the last of the dinosaurs that lived in the wide river valleys east of the newly forming Rocky Mountains. Very likely we can see before us sediments deposited during essentially the whole time that the Mesozoic was giving way to the Cenozoic.

Why, after having been in existence for nearly 100 million years, did the mammals discard their character as small furtive creatures and become, within the 35 million years of the Paleocene and Eocene periods, the rulers of the earth? Did they stumble upon some revolutionary new biological invention? It would seem not. Judging from the teeth and bone found in the rocks, there were placental mammals in existence well before the end of the Mesozoic. It is therefore likely that the complete galaxy of major mammalian inventions—fur, warm blood, live birth at an advanced stage, and milk glands—was present, that these fundamental characteristics of the mammals evolved under the shadow

A scene in the miniature Table Mountain Badlands near Denver. The black arrow below and to the left of the summit of the lightcolored ridge marks what is sometimes given as the Cenozoic-Mesozoic boundary in this formation.

of the dominant reptiles. It would appear that only the quantitative improvement of mammalian characteristics, rather than the appearance of qualitatively new ones common to placental mammals, could have taken place during the Cenozoic.

Probably the most significant difference between reptiles and mammals is the higher intelligence—the ability to profit from experience—of the mammals. Intelligence is correlated mainly with increased brain size. Within the different groups of mammals, brain size has generally increased during the Cenozoic, but even the earlier mammals usually had larger brains than their reptilian contemporaries.

It is interesting that many of the other characteristics of mammals contribute directly or indirectly to the evolution of larger brains. The warm blood of mammals is important mainly as a device for maintaining a constant body temperature. Given the methods of heat regulation available to a mammal, it is easier for the animal to maintain a constant temperature if that temperature is usually higher than that of the environment. The fur is, of course, an important factor in maintaining this high temperature. The chief advantage of the constant body temperature is that it creates the proper internal environment for the accurate functioning of the central computer for the body—the brain. Apparently the different chemical processes that go on in the brain have different temperature characteristics, so that their coordination is destroyed if the normal operating temperature is abolished. The mammalian brain is quite sensitive to temperature changes, and becomes incompetent in fever or hypothermia. Constant temperature thus was a necessary condition for the evolution of the large and complex brain.

The close link between mother and offspring established by the evolutionary origin of milk glands also produces a situation that favors the evolution of large brain size. There is the establishment of a parent-offspring group, a family, in which the experienced parent can teach the young, or the young profit from emulation of the parent. Thus it becomes possible to take advantage of variation in the direction of increased brain size, creating a situation in which natural selection acts relatively swiftly on the evolution of a better brain. Throughout the mammals, as opposed to the reptiles, parent-young communication, is a prominent feature of life.

If superior intelligence was a mammalian characteristic even during the Age of Reptiles, then perhaps it was some change in the environment that got the Age of Mammals underway. This is the most generally accepted explanation. The change in the envi-

144

ronment was a biological change—the disappearance of the major reptilian groups—which was probably a result of changes in the physical environment. According to this view, before the mammalian revolution could take place, there had to be a harvest to clear away the old order. Mammals could then become larger (which in fact they did at the beginning of the Cenozoic), and thus even more intelligent. The brain of a mouse can accomplish little by way of learning. It requires an appreciably large mammal, with a correspondingly large brain, to take good advantage of the potential for increased intelligence that exists in mammals.

But in all fairness, it must be admitted that we really do not know the extent to which reptilian competitors of the mammals were cleared away near the Mesozoic boundary. It is difficult, for example, to imagine that the lumbering horned dinosaurs that died off at this time were direct competitors of the mammals. The causes of the mammalian revolution remain much of a mystery.

# 13

# MARSH
# AS PARTISAN

DURING THE YEARS 1874 and 1875 Cope was, within the confines of the coterie of vertebrate paleontologists, making history with his discovery of the Eocene and Paleocene of New Mexico, and with the publication (in 1875) of his *The Vertebrata of the Cretaceous Formations of the West*. These two years were also important years for Marsh, but for quite different kinds of reasons. They marked turning points in his professional life. Also, rather fortuitously, Marsh became, in the eyes of the public, perhaps the most well known scientist in America.

In 1874 work began on the Peabody Museum at Yale, and Marsh had to be in New Haven much of the time to supervise construction of the new building. This was the first of his growing administrative responsibilities that were, after 1874, to keep

146

him out of the western fossil fields, except for occasional brief trips to check on the work of his numerous hired field parties (in 1874 he had twelve such parties at work). His last significant field work is thus described in the section "Scientific Intelligence" of the *American Journal of Science* early in 1875:

*Return of Professor Marsh's Expedition.*—Professor Marsh returned to New Haven, Dec. 12th, after an absence of two months in the West. The object of the present expedition was to examine a remarkable locality of fossils, discovered during the past summer in the Bad Lands south of the Black Hills. The explorations were very successful, notwithstanding extremely cold weather and the continued hostility of the Sioux Indians. The latter refused to allow the expedition to cross White River, but a reluctant consent was at last obtained. They afterward stopped the party on the way to the Bad Lands, attempted a night attack on their camp, and otherwise molested them, but the accompanying escort of United States troops proved sufficient for protection. The fossil deposits explored were mainly of Miocene age, and, although quite limited in extent, proved to be rich beyond expectation. Nearly two tons of fossil bones were collected, most of them rare specimens, and many unknown to science. Among the most interesting remains found were several species of gigantic *Brontotheridae,* nearly as large as Elephants. At one point these bones were heaped together in such numbers as to indicate that the animals lived in herds, and had been washed into this ancient lake by a freshet. Successful explorations were made, also, in the Pliocene strata of the same region. All the collections secured go to Yale College, and will soon be described by Professor Marsh.

Apparently what brought Marsh to the already rather well-known Big Badlands was his growing interest in the titanotheres,

147

or Brontotheridae. These elephant-sized relatives of the horses flourished in the Oligocene of the western United States, and in places their huge bones were so abundant that they whitened the ground, forming veritable bone yards. At the peak of their evolution, their horned skulls were a yard long. The group reached their climax and became extinct during the time the sediments of the Big Badlands were being laid down. The first fossil described from the badlands was a titanothere, and they had been repeatedly collected since, but usually only fragments were taken, and there still were many new genera and species to be described. Marsh had a taste for large, rare, and expensive fossils—he had also specialized on the largest mammals of the Eocene, the Dinocerata—and now began to accumulate what was to be in its time the world's best collection of the titanotheres.

Even in the mid-1870s there still remained a western frontier, with more or less hostile and dangerous Indians on the other side. After their first round of defeats in the Sioux war, the Sioux were in 1868 given reservation land in South Dakota, together with less formally defined areas to the northwest. With rumors of gold in the Black Hills, scientific interest in them waxed strong, and in 1874 General George Armstrong Custer ramrodded a scientific party through the Sioux country into the Black Hills with an escort of a thousand troops. Marsh had been asked to go, but declined, instead sending George Bird Grinnell, a student who had been on earlier expeditions with him. This invasion of the sacrosanct Black Hills by a race the Indians knew to be mad for gold began to trouble the peace that had reigned since 1868, and with the influx in the early winter of 1874 of off-reservation Sioux who had been hunting along the upper Yellowstone and Bighorn rivers, the possibility for open warfare developed in the Sioux country.

The Army had now developed an extraordinary interest in fossil collecting in the badlands, and again asked Marsh to come out

148

for a bone hunt, and were again refused. But a third request, made by Colonel T. H. Stanton and General Ord, finally brought Marsh, on a cold November 4, to the Red Cloud Indian Agency, which lay somewhat south of a line between the Big Badlands and the Black Hills. Here Marsh collected another adventure.

It is recorded that some of the higher Army brass went fossil hunting with the professor in the badlands, including General L. P. Bradley, Colonel Stanton, and Major A. S. Burt. On the foray of early November, there was also a company of troops as an escort, commanded by Lieutenant W. L. Carpenter. The Sioux found it hard to believe that Marsh was not after gold, and at first refused permission for the expedition to pass through the Reservation to the badlands. However, after a display of typical Marsh eloquence, and at the price of a firm promise to Chief Red Cloud to take to Washington certain complaints about food and supplies, a reluctant consent was granted. Nevertheless, the behavior of the Indians made it clear to Marsh that they really did not intend to let him go, so in the middle of the night he ordered his party to proceed. Stealing through the camps of sleeping Indians, they were not discovered until daybreak, when they were kept under surveillance by Red Cloud's men.

At the collecting ground, in the face of an impending snowstorm, and given additional incentive for speed by word that the hostiles from the hinterland intended an attack, perhaps that night, they frantically pulled fossils out of the rock, and piled them in heaps. But Marsh decided that they should stay on until the next day, in order to be able to pack the fossils properly. He won the gamble, and left some twenty-four hours before a war party descended on the empty camp, looking for him.

A few months after Marsh returned to the East, he went to Washington to attend the meetings of the National Academy of Sciences, the most prestigious and select of American scientific societies. Now, a cross that Marsh had been bearing for some two years was the fact that his young colleague Edward Drinker Cope had been a member of the Academy, while he himself was not. But in 1874, Marsh was elected to the Academy by a vote of 37 to 1; everyone of course knew the origin of the single dissenting vote. In his luggage on this trip to his first Academy meeting in Washington, early in 1874, Marsh carried samples of defective foodstuffs and tobacco given him by Red Cloud as evidence of mistreatment of the Indians by the Indian agent. Academy affairs finished, Marsh took these specimens first to the Commissioner for Indian Affairs, then, dissatisfied with the reception given him by this official, on the next day confronted President Grant himself with the evidence.

In some way doubtless known to Marsh the details of the meeting with the Commissioner were leaked to the press. As a result, a presidential advisory board on Indian affairs called Marsh in for consultation. On his own initiative, Marsh brought along a reporter from the New York *Daily Tribune,* a powerful and lively newspaper hostile to the Grant administration and infiltrated with Yale influence. The affair now flamed into widespread newspaper publicity, and the rotting, moldy specimens of foodstuffs brought back from the Sioux country by Marsh became more famous than the fossils he had dug from the rocks of the badlands.

The man who, quite unwittingly, provided the most effective publicity for Marsh was an unfortunate career politician, Columbus Delano, who was at the time the head of the Indian Bureau. Probably out of ignorance rather than malice, he wrote, in a widely publicized letter defending the bureau, of "certain reports put in circulation by a Mr. Marsh, relative to the Indian service at Red Cloud agency." Marsh had as many connections with the sources of power as a politician—through innumerable generals, establishment scientists, and businessmen—and the uproar in the press that greeted this reference to "a Mr. Marsh" was to inundate Delano, and eventually lead to his resignation.

A sample from one of the editorial efforts of the time shows what a field day was offered the journalists by Marsh's appearance in this political fight.

There is something fascinating to the average intellect in the way in which this climax has been reached. The Professor with his party of retainers and a small cavalry escort, trying to penetrate the remotest wilds of our territory, and caring little for the red man unless he might chance to be found in a fossil state; the encounter with the unwilling and unscientific savages in a state of activity not in the least suggestive of fossils; the tedious "talk" about the council fire; the final conviction of the Professor that in order to get at his beloved hipparions and pterodactyles he must covenant with the legitimate owners thereof; then the circumlocutions and evasions of the Washington officials, and finally the formal appeal to the President—all these combine to make a passage of departmental history that shall be a warning to future Secretaries of the Interior and Indian Commissioners.

The imputation of worldly innocence to Marsh could only be made by someone writing either in ignorance or for artistic effect.

Nevertheless, a taste of the reality of politics in the corrupt Grant administration must have come as a shock even to Marsh. One encounter with Delano is thus described in *The Nation* for September 16, 1875:

The investigation of the Indian frauds seems, as far as can be made out from the scattered telegrams which describe the evidence, to be substantiating the charges brought by Professor Marsh. Meanwhile, Mr. Delano has been making another revelation of the character of the men whom Grant retains while "under fire." Meeting Mr. Marsh at breakfast in a Washington hotel, Mr. Delano asked the latter when he "was

going to cease attacking him," and upon Mr. Marsh's reply-
ing, "Probably when you cease attacking me," poured out a
flood of abuse upon Mr. Marsh, calling him a "liar" and a
"poltroon," and heaping upon him every sort of insulting ep-
ithet which he had at his command. During all this, Mr.
Marsh, fortunately for himself, was able to keep his temper
[another account says Marsh sat down and calmly took
notes], and finally Delano, after exhausting his somewhat extensive vocabulary, left the room. The scene is described as a
strange one "even in Washington." There has been one
place, and only one, in the country, and that some years ago,
where such a scene would not have seemed strange or anything out of the usual course of politics—and that was in
New York when the city was governed by Boss Tweed.

While Marsh was presenting the complaints of Red Cloud to
the authorities, the question of the sale of the Black Hills by the
Indians came up, and a delegation of Sioux chiefs arrived in
Washington to negotiate. With the arrival of Red Cloud, he and
Marsh were called before one of the investigating committees for
a review of the charges that Marsh had made to the Indian Commission. Here Marsh got a sharp setback when Red Cloud, perhaps confused by the government-supplied interpreters, failed to
confirm some of the charges that Marsh had made on his behalf.
This encouraged the pro-administration to launch a powerful
counterattack, through the newspapers friendly to them, in which
Marsh was handed out a good deal of personal abuse. One of the
charges, that Marsh was in it for the publicity, was probably not
far from the truth, if it be granted that it was only a subsidiary
motive.

Perhaps confident that Marsh was now in a fatally weak position, a committee asked him to put his charges in writing.
Marsh's reply was, in effect, "I'm glad you mentioned that." He

had, with characteristic foresight and thoroughness, already written and quickly had printed a 36-page pamphlet, and had written a carefully composed open letter to President Grant, in which the charges were laid out and documented in systematic fashion. The pamphlets he sent not only to the committee, but also to some 1,500 prominent citizens of the country. It probably was this surprise attack that turned the tide. Before the year was out, Grant announced the resignation of Delano, a committee report signed by Professor George Atherton of Rutgers recommended that the agent in charge at the Red Cloud Reservation be removed, and, shortly after, the Commissioner for Indian Affairs himself resigned.

In later years Red Cloud and Marsh remained fast friends, and the chief visited Marsh in New Haven, where he no doubt became acquainted with the western memorabilia in the Wigwam, the reception room of the Marsh mansion. The treasure of fossils in the Peabody Museum apparently made no impression on him, but it was reported that a visit to the Winchester rifle factory brought on a smile.

# 14

# THE BEAUTIFUL JUDITH

IN CENTRAL MONTANA, isolated, dome-shaped mountain ranges surround the traveler with a pleasing vista. These rise above a floor of Cretaceous rocks, some of the rocks deposited in the Cretaceous Sea, others in the lush, dinosaur-infested swamps and river valleys that emerged from the sea at the close of the Mesozoic. Generally these rocks form the surface of a plain, but north of Lewiston, as one approaches the Missouri River, the ground suddenly falls away under one's feet, and at eye level, stretching away for miles to the north, are summits of a tumbled mass of small mountains of Cretaceous rocks, whose canyons and ravines lie five and six hundred feet below. These are the Judith River Badlands, discovered by Lewis and Clark in 1805 and named for Clark's Judith River, which flows nearby.

Since going up the Missouri River by boat was one of the easi-
est ways for the earliest travelers to reach the western mountains,
the Judith River Badlands, startlingly picturesque as seen from
the river, are often described in western travel literature of the
early 1800s. Their first scientific explorer, if we except such early
transients as Meriwether Lewis, was Ferdinand V. Hayden who,
surrounded by entire mountain ranges whose geology was still
completely unknown, studied the badlands and adjoining regions
in the 1850s. In a report addressed to the American Philosophical
Society in 1859, he says:

> Near the mouth of the Judith River, not far from the sources
> of the Missouri, in Lat. $47\frac{1}{2}°$, Lon. 109°, is a wild, desolate
> and rugged region which I have called the "Bad Lands of the
> Judith," in contradistinction to those of White River. No
> portion of the Upper Missouri country exhibits the effects of
> erosion and denudation on so large a scale, and to add to the
> picturesque effect of the scenery, the variegated strata are dis-
> torted and folded in a wonderful manner by the action of the
> subterranean forces that have elevated the mountain masses
> in the vicinity. The surface of the country occupied by the
> deposit I am about to describe is cut up into ravines and can-
> yons, with nearly vertical sides, rising to a height of 400 to
> 600 feet above the bed of the river, with scarcely a tree or a
> shrub to greet the eye of the explorer. A few scattering pines
> cap the summits of the hills and draw a scanty nourishment
> from a thin dry soil, but it may be regarded for the most part
> as an inaccessible desert suited only as a retreat for the buf-
> falo and mountain sheep.

The aspect of the Judith River Badlands that one finds most
pleasing, apart from their gigantic size—the relief is about three
times that of the Big Badlands—is the forest of pine on the summits of the peaks and tablelands, and the picturesque trees cling-

ing to the crags on the sides of the canyons. The badlands are now the resort of the deer hunter, and roads and trails follow along the winding ridge tops that separate the canyons. Anyone following the ridge tops eventually finds himself stranded at overlooks high above dry rocky canyons or the Missouri River itself. Only two roads in the area descend, by carefully picked routes, to the river. The Missouri here is wide, running smoothly and swiftly, and is flanked by forests of cottonwoods. Toll-free ferry boats at the ends of the narrow dirt roads carry automobiles across, on demand, to a near-wilderness on the north side of the river. A little known segment of American life haunts the river— a flotilla of the boats of fishermen and retirees.

When Cope in 1875 reviewed the vertebrate fossils thus far known from the Cretaceous rocks of the West, he was intrigued by the several species of dinosaurs that had been discovered by Hayden in the Judith River area and described by Joseph Leidy. Accordingly, he organized an expedition to these badlands for the season of 1876. His companion was to be the well-known professional collector Charles Sternberg.

When Sternberg met Cope at the Omaha railway station, Sternberg found him so weak—from confining desk work, he thought —that he reeled from side to side as he walked. Yet, after a few days in the field, he was climbing the steepest cliffs, and traversing the most dangerous ledges, even though, as his companion said, "he was United States Paleontologist, and worth a million dollars." Sternberg presents, in his *Life of a Fossil Hunter,* a vivid picture of the hard-driving Quaker scientist at work. A party of Sioux warriors, fresh from their bloody victory over Custer at the Little Bighorn, camped nearby, frightening away the cook and scout of the expedition, but Cope persuaded the rest of the party to remain. One particular horse of the team that drew their wagon was famous for his stubbornness. Already irritated by the desertion of the two men, Cope repeatedly knocked the animal to the ground with blows from a whip handle, and finally had the horse running to the traces in his eagerness to get into harness. Sternberg tells of the mad dash to catch the boat that was to take Cope home down the Missouri—Cope had stayed until the last hour of the last day on the collecting grounds:

> I knew the uselessness of trying to combat his iron will, but I pleaded with him against the folly of attempting to thread in the darkness those black and treacherous defiles, where a single misstep meant certain death. I begged him to wait until daylight. We were, to be sure, hungry and thirsty, and food, water, and shelter were to be had only at the river, but sleeping in the saddle blankets without supper was, I urged, preferable to running the risk of being dashed to pieces.
>
> He paid no attention to what I said, but dismounting, led his horse into the canyon. He had to cut a stick to shove in front of him, as his eyes could not penetrate the darkness a single inch ahead. I cut another to punch along his horse, which did not want to follow him.
>
> Sometimes when we had climbed down several hundred feet the end of the Professor's stick would encounter only air, and a handful of stones thrown ahead would be heard to strike the earth far below. Then we had to turn and climb back through the deep dust to the top, and circling a canyon, plunge down on the other side.
>
> Once we got down to the river four miles from the prairie, and thought that our journey was over, as we could see the lights of the station just across the river. But when we had watered our thirsty horses and started down for the landing, we found our way blocked by a huge ridge with a towering precipice impinging on the river; and we had to drag ourselves back over those four long, hard miles to the prairie, and start again. I freely confess that I should have been will-

A general view of the Judith River Badlands.

ing to lie down in the dust just where I was, and let the horses look out for themselves, but Cope's indomitable will could not be conquered. Back we climbed to the top, and down we went into the next ravine.

I have never known another man who would have attempted this journey.

When Cope went to the Judith country, the alternative to going upriver on one of the infrequent shallow-draft steamboats was to take train to the southeastern corner of Idaho, then go by stage some six hundred miles to Fort Benton, which was on the Missouri about fifty miles northwest of the badlands. The stage was a fast one (when the driver was properly drunk, "we rushed and tore and jumped and bounced"), changing the team of four or six horses every 15 miles or so. Cope wrote to his wife, whom he had left in Ogden, of his conception of highwaymen, assuring her that they never harmed unresisting passengers, but went about it thusly: "They present the muzzle of their guns for the inspection of the stage people, then order all out and hands up in the air, when they go through pockets etc." Cope had $120 in cash which he hid in a pants leg, and opined that in Helena he could cash a money order if he first got a shave.

At Fort Benton, Cope bought wagon and team, and hired a cook and scout. He wrote to his wife that he was starting to get his western appetite, that the "old man" was coming on pretty strong, and that he had gone through two droves of horses looking for good ones—driving, riding, and examining them, and bargaining to where he got them for $65 each. He went overland to the Judith River, riding through vast grasslands and expansive scenery. Montana was well-named, he had said; the snow-covered Bear Paws were to the north, the Little Belt to the south, in the east was Table Mountain; and more intimately, as they came opposite the mouth of the Judith, the miniature mountains of the badlands.

From the information at hand (he talked to the governor of Montana at Helena, and some government survey men), Cope estimated that the Sioux, after the battles along the Little Bighorn in southeastern Montana, would not get as far as the Judith River country until October, and that tribes now in the area (many of them hereditary enemies of the Sioux) would be peaceful. It turned out that he was right, but only a few days after he left, the military post on the Missouri where he embarked for home was overrun, and the soldiers killed. Indians of such tribes as the Crow, the Piegans, the Blood, and the Gros Ventres, were encamped along the river bottom, and visited the bone hunters. Once when Cope entertained several Crow chiefs at dinner, he astounded them by taking out his false teeth and putting them back; one Indian rode several miles to ask for a repeat performance. Cope met such characters as the Mountain Crow war chief

Bear Wolf, who claimed 26 Sioux scalps and the theft of 900 horses. One night an Indian crept into camp, thinking that it was the headquarters of the illicit whisky dealer in the area, and was very nearly shot by one of the party.

Up until the time when the cook and scout deserted, Cope's field party was an especially congenial one—the best he ever had, he thought. The cook, Austin Merrill, was chosen for a fat face, which to Cope denoted a love of good eating, and Cope thought he had made an excellent choice. Their scout and hunter, James Deer, brought in ducks, fish, sage hens, and young bighorn sheep, which the cook worked up in elaborate fashion. Sternberg, however, complained about the results. Where Cope had remarked merely that there was "all sorts of cookery, to the detriment of our dreams," Sternberg writes that

> Every night when we returned to camp, we found that the cook had spent the whole day in cooking. Exhausted and thirsty—we had no water to drink during the day (all the water in the Bad Lands being like a dense solution of Epsom salts),—we sat down to a supper of cakes and pies and other palatable, but indigestible food. Then, when we went to bed, the Professor would soon have a severe attack of nightmare. Every animal of which we had found traces during the day played with him at night, tossing him into the air, kicking him, trampling upon him.
>
> When I waked him, he would thank me cordially and lie down to another attack. Sometimes he would lose half the night in this exhausting slumber. But the next morning he would lead the party, and be the last to give up at night.

In the evenings Cope read from the Bible, and was gratified to find that the men listened respectfully, for he still remembered, in his letters, a field trip to Colorado a few years before when an especially worthless cook and teamster had scrubbed their teeth while he read from the Bible.

160

One of the difficulties of collecting in the Judith River Bad-lands was that they were too steep and the scale too vast. Both Cope and Sternberg exaggerated their size, speaking of cliffs 1,200 or 1,000 feet high, but along the Missouri, the cliffs are 800, and in the higher reaches of Dog Creek, in the heart of the badlands, 400 feet high. A 45° slope of crumbling shale, just steep enough that a plunge quickly accelerates beyond the point of no return, is one thing when perhaps a slide of only 30 feet or so lies beneath, as in ordinary badlands, but quite another when there is a spacious 500 feet underneath, interrupted by stone ledges so narrow that they would only give a few additional bounces to the descent. The canyon walls of the Judith River formation are of the kind the cynical climber describes thusly: in the uncontrolled descent first your hat comes off, then your shoes, and the rest of your clothes are flung off wildly; and what remains is best found by watching the ravens.

Sternberg tells of following along a ledge just below the summit, prospecting the shale slope above it for fossils, when he came to a gap caused by a block of the ledge falling away. He was so high, he says, that the trees below looked like seedlings. He was in the habit of using his pick to check minor slips, so had no fear in crossing the gap. But apparently he had forgotten that hard sandstone here underlay the shale, and when the slip occurred, he was horrified to find that the pick bounced off with splendid resilience, and he began an accelerating plunge. His life story went through his mind in fractions of a second. While his conscious mind was turning out this lengthy rerun, complete with the appropriate emotional sensations, his more practical subconscious somehow directed his body back to the ledge from which he had come, where he lay weak and trembling for the better part of an hour before he could resume his work.

Besides the objective physical danger, another fault of the Judith River beds is that the exposures are so nearly vertical that little surface area is exposed, and the complex of rounded slopes that exposes such tremendous areas in other badlands is not present. And finally, conditions of preservation are such that the bones are broken and scattered. In a layer of rock at the summit fragments of teeth and bone of dinosaurs are abundant, but complete skulls and skeletons are rarely found.

Collecting and describing fragmentary fossil remains was, however, Cope's specialty. He probably described hundreds of species of fossil mammals and reptiles on the basis of a specimen he could pick up in one hand, creatures whose complete form would only be known sometime in the future. Not that he refused to collect and study more complete material when available, but he was willing and able to do good diagnoses from very limited evidence. Traveling light and fast, with a sharp eye out for novelties, and publishing his results immediately Cope, according to a tally made in 1900, described 1,115 of the 3,200 species of vertebrate fossils then known from North America. Actually, he had described a larger number than this as new, but some of his names became synonyms, having been described already.

Marsh also, early in his career, tended to move light and fast, and publish quickly, but this phase lasted only a few years. Later he concentrated more on getting complete skeletons, especially of large and spectacular animals, and published exhaustive, bulky monographs. Added to this, he became less active scientifically, spending more time in administrative work, and in socializing and, perhaps, dozing in men's clubs. As a result, in his lifetime he described less than half the number of new species as did Cope, 496 in all.

Cope's two-month-long exploration of the Judith River Badlands was noted in the *Proceedings* of the Academy of Natural Sciences of Philadelphia for 1876: "Prof. Cope stated that he had recently returned from an exploration of the Judith River beds of the Upper Missouri, which were discovered by Dr. Hayden in 1855. Attention was given to the relation of this formation to the

A glimpse of the Missouri River in the Judith River Badlands.

underlying marine cretaceous beds, and to the respective faunae of the two as compared with that of the early eocene period." Descending the badlands from summit to canyon was to go back in time, from sandstones laid down by streams flowing from the newly emerging highlands that signaled the end of the Age of Reptiles, down into thick layers of shales deposited in the floor of the ancient American Mediterranean Sea. In the uppermost rocks, Cope collected 18 specimens of dinosaurs, some of them represented by hundreds of specimens. (Of one, he wrote, "This abundant species of herbivorous dinosaur has left its shed teeth in many localities of the Fort Union horizon.") In the stream deposits he also found clam shells, primitive fishes related to the gar pikes, salamanders, turtles, and crocodiles. In the underlying marine shales were sharks and sea-going reptiles (good specimens, in contrast to the fragmentary dinosaur remains above) related to those he had found years before in the Smoky Hill Badlands of Kansas.

At Cow Island, near the collecting grounds, Cope in early October loaded his 1,700 pounds of fossils aboard a river steamer, leaving Sternberg to collect until the first winter snows drove him from the field. On the way downstream, the crew burned a cord of wood an hour (gathered en route), with the steam used mainly for engines that pried the craft off sandbanks, by means of long wooden levers. At the mouth of the Yellowstone the boat was commandeered by General Hazen of Fort Buford to carry troops in pursuit of the Sioux led by Sitting Bull, who had now reached the river some hundred miles up stream (it was, however, released in favor of another boat).

Cope continued his collecting activities by bringing aboard a number of Sioux skulls and skeletons. The boat's captain accused him of "immolating" the dead, the rumseller "made the loudest protests, mingling oaths and sentimental stupidities in equal proportions," and the clerk ventured the observation that no one would get the bones of *his* wife, buried "in some Arkansas swamp," and Cope was forced to disembark the bones. (Cope applied his standards evenly. When his own coffin was to be carried to the grave, it was nearly or quite empty. By Cope's request, his skeleton was already in the drawers of a collection, the brain bottled up in a laboratory, and the rest in ashes.)

Sternberg was invited to spend the winter of 1876–77 at Cope's farm in Haddonfield, where a barn loft was converted into a workshop, and also at the home on Pine Street in Philadelphia. His account of life there continues his character portrait of Cope:

I boarded with a Mr. Geismar, Professor Cope's preparator, but I had a standing invitation to eat dinner every Sunday with the Professor and his wife and daughter, a lovely child of twelve summers.

I shall never forget those Sunday dinners. The food was plain, but daintily cooked, and the Professor's conversation was a feast in itself. He had a wonderful power of putting professional matters from his mind when he left his study, and coming out ready to enter into any kind of merrymaking. He used to sit with sparkling eyes, telling story after story, while we laughed at his sallies until we could laugh no more.

In later years, Sternberg collected for Cope in the John Day Badlands of Oregon, and the Texas Redbeds, although not in his company. While working for Cope in Texas, in 1897, he received a message from Annie Cope of her husband's death. "I had lost friends before, and had known what it was to bury my own dead, even my firstborn son, but I never sorrowed more deeply. . . . One thing is certain—as long as science lasts, and men love to study the animals of the present and the past, Cope's name and work will be remembered and revered."

# 15

# SUPER-DINOSAURS

ALONG THE EASTERN front of the mountain ranges of the Rocky Mountain West is the Dakota hogback, the first of the foothills, a long ridge broken by canyons emerging from the higher mountains that is crowned by ledges of hard sandstone and conglomerate. This Dakota formation (a convenient name left over from the older geology; a variety of local formation names are used by the modern specialists) is of middle Cretaceous age, and represents the time before the American Mediterranean Sea flooded the mid-continent. Between the Dakota hogback and the main range of mountains there is invariably a wide valley and, usually, along the inner edge of the valley are soil and rock ledges of a flaming red color that is the mysterious chemical result of the climate of the Permian and Triassic. Lying underneath the ledges of the Dakota hogback, and extending out to the redbeds, is the pastel-colored Morrison formation, of Jurassic age, generally so soft and easily defeated by erosion that its green, purple, and tawny clays are converted to soil and covered with vegetation. But in favorable, properly arid localities the Morrison is weathered into naked badlands. In such exposures of the Morrison are found the bones of the greatest creatures that ever walked on earth, the super-dinosaurs of the Jurassic.

Dinosaurs were reptiles, with a small brain and, no doubt, with a scaly skin. Some were herbivores, others huge and agile carnivores that must have produced some of the most spectacular violence in the history of terrestrial life—before the advent of man, anyway. The largest of the Jurassic herbivores are believed to have been swamp dwellers. So huge were their bodies that it is unlikely they could move about for long periods of time unsupported by water, and the nostrils, placed high up on the head, are those of an animal that spends much of the time submerged, with eyes and nose above the surface of the water.

The reptiles came into existence in the Carboniferous period, perhaps 300 million years ago, evolving from the amphibians, which were air-breathing but perhaps mainly aquatic animals. By the end of the Paleozoic, some tens of millions of years later, the reptiles already had become dominant over the land, with great numbers of ox-sized reptilian plant eaters (which were not dinosaurs) grazing on the uplands. Toward the end of the Triassic, these first successful reptiles, and the last of large, crocodile-sized amphibians became extinct or much diminished in numbers. During this period a new group of reptiles was slowly fashioning the equipment that was to gain them the title of "ruling reptiles," a group that includes the dinosaurs, the flying dragons or pterodactyls, and the modern crocodiles and alligators, as well as some rather obscure extinct forms. The initial invention that founded the group was an improved method of locomotion, in which the hind legs became progressively more important, until finally some of these reptiles became agile, speedy bipeds. Even those ruling reptiles that are completely quadrupedal usually show traces of a bipedal ancestry.

One of the most bizarre consequences of freeing the front legs from the obligation of running and walking was the evolution of the winged reptiles, the pterosaurs or pterodactyls, and of birds.

As to the origin of birds, it is guessed that some of the smaller swiftly running bipedal reptiles had flaps of skin stretching from the arms back to the sides of the body, which served at first to lighten the animal when running, in a manner as to increase speed, and later even to make possible short gliding flights, which would improve chances to elude a pursuer. Some of these reptiles, by the conversion of scales into feathers, evolved into birds— birds are structurally much like the ruling reptiles, and have in fact been called "glorified reptiles."

Fossils of pterodactyls are found in the Jurassic and Cretaceous. The earlier types are smallish, some hardly larger than sparrows, but they became giants in the Cretaceous, and Cope and Marsh found pterodactyls with wings spanning more than 25 feet in the chalk of the Smoky Hill River valley. In a few localities in the world, bone fragments of the Cretaceous pterodactyls are found by the thousands. These finds are in marine rocks, and it is thought that these kinds of pterodactyls are found in sediments that were apparently deposited hundreds of miles from the coastline. Since these animals were not able to swim, they must have been extraordinarily good fliers. As in the modern albatross, the flight muscles were relatively small, compared to those of most birds, so that they, again like the albatross, must have relied mostly on gliding flight. Albatrosses fly for hours on end without flapping the wings, using as an energy source the differential velocity of wind currents near and well above the water. Perhaps their distant relatives, the pterodactyls, also had mastered the skies above the high seas in this way.

The word dinosaur (from the Greek, "terrible lizard") was

Como Bluff, Wyoming, site of one of the world's
richest known dinosaur beds. Elk Mountain,
a well-known landmark along the old Overland
Trail, is in the background.

coined for some fossil reptiles discovered in Europe. But careful
study of the innumerable skeletons discovered since showed that
the word covers a variety of diverse kinds of animals. Some types
structurally similar to the large kinds are small, chicken-sized reptiles. Also, there are two rather distantly related groups of ruling
reptiles involved, with quite different structures. There are no
good common names for these two groups of dinosaurs. The technical names are Ornithischia, referring to the bird-like pelvic
bones, and the Saurischia, with an ordinary reptile-like pelvis.

In spite of the constant repetition of these facts in the textbooks, no author ventures a detailed analysis as to what the biological, that is, the functional significance of this difference in

structure might be. The "bird-hip" dinosaurs never reached the gigantic size of the other group, and all were herbivores. They did not become dominant until the Cretaceous, near the end of the reign of the dinosaurs. Saurischians include both carnivores, some of them the most impressive engines of destruction that ever trod the earth, and the swamp-dwelling herbivores called sauropods, which were the super-dinosaurs. The latter reached their climax in the Jurassic, when the Morrison formation was deposited, then gave way to the smaller "bird-hip" plant-eating dinosaurs during the Cretaceous. Carnivorous dinosaurs of the saurischian group continued their evolution beyond the Jurassic, producing the gigantic *Tyrannosaurus* of the Upper Cretaceous.

During most of the 1870s, when Cope and Marsh were doing their pioneer work in the western fossil fields, the dinosaurs were of little more than academic interest. The new species were described from isolated teeth and skeletal fragments, and the information they yielded merely rounded out what was already known about the dinosaurs already discovered in Europe. But in 1877 an expatriate English clergyman living in Golden, a town at the base of the foothills west of Denver, struck a spark that ignited the Cope–Marsh powder keg to produce a display of dinosaurs that amazed the world.

A few miles south of Golden is the small foothills town of Morrison, which is the type locality for the Morrison formation. Lying just above this formation is the Dakota sandstone, here forming a strong ledge at the top of a hogback which extends north-south along the eastern front of the mountains. On a March day in 1877 Arthur Lakes, the clergyman, then teaching in a sectarian school in Golden, was, in company with H. C. Beckwith, a United States Navy captain, looking for fossil leaves in the Dakota when, on the hillside below the ledge, he discovered a huge fossil vertebra embedded in rock. He sent a sketch of the bone to Marsh, who replied with an offer to identify it, if he could see the

Some of the best-known Cope dinosaur quarries near Canon City lie around the base of a hill called the Nipple.

specimen. Lakes wrote that he first wanted to look for more bone, and in fact did find a thigh bone more than a foot in diameter. Marsh had not replied to Lakes' second letter, but Lakes nevertheless sent him 1,500 pounds of dinosaur bone.

At the same time, Lakes innocently lit the fuse for an explosion by also sending Cope some specimens. Along the way, Marsh had sent $100 to Lakes for the the specimens, and on July 1 published in the *American Journal of Science* a description of one of Lakes' dinosaurs, which he estimated to have been 50 or 60 feet long, and therefore to be the largest land animal yet known. On

A portion of the wall of a small building
near Como Bluff constructed of scraps of
dinosaur bone.

July 20, Cope had made some remarks on the Lakes material before the American Philosophical Society, but Lakes, with Marsh's money in his pocket, wrote Cope that the specimens were to be sent to Marsh, so Cope did not publish his paper.

However, Cope was not left long behind in the race for the biggest dinosaur. Also in March of 1877, another Colorado schoolteacher, O. W. Lucas, superintendant of schools for Fremont county, while collecting plants along Oil Creek northeast of Canon City, found some large bones which he sent to Cope. Cope described the specimens in late August, noting that one of the vertebrae sent him indicated a dinosaur bigger than the one from Morrison recently described by Marsh.

Dinosaur bones had been sold in curio shops in Canon City (usually as petrified wood) for years before their discovery by Lucas, and even one of Marsh's ace collectors, David Baldwin, of

Puerco fame, had seen the big bones lying on the ground early in 1877, and had written Marsh, without result. Apparently it was the letter from Lakes telling of specimens sent to Cope that galvanized Marsh into action.

Both Cope and Marsh were now describing bones of the sauropods, the massive amphibious dinosaurs of the Jurassic that dwarfed the Cretaceous dinosaurs that had so much impressed the early paleontologists in Europe. One of the 6-foot-long thigh bones sent to Marsh was probably what is now called *Brontosaurus,* with modern estimates giving a length of 67 feet and a weight of thirty tons to the larger specimens. *Brachiosaurus,* also known from the Morrison, holds the record for size among this group of dinosaurs, and therefore among all dinosaurs and all land animals. Where much of the length of *Brontosaurus* comes from the excessively long whiplike tail, the brachiosaur is comparatively short-tailed, yet still had a length of 80 feet. With its stout body, it probably weighed something like fifty tons. Quite recently, a brachiosaur from the Morrison of western Colorado has been discovered which, by a preliminary estimate, is 100 feet long, and may have weighed eighty tons.

The dinosaur quarry at Morrison, which was operated by Marsh, was a small one, dug into a steep hillside into sharply dipping strata of rock. Also, the bones were in a hard sandstone layer of the generally soft Morrison formation, and difficult to get out. The excavation produced an overhang which one day caved in, an accident that could easily have killed the entire crew. Marsh transferred the bulk of his activities to Canon City, where Cope's hired party was already digging bones. There was room for all at the Canon City locality. Here the strata were nearly horizontal, there were huge areas of soft, easily accessible exposures of the Morrison shales, and dinosaur bone was everywhere. Even today, after a hundred years of exploration, one can still see scraps of bone littering the ground near some of the old Cope quarries.

The *Wunderjahr* of the dinosaurs was not yet over. In mid-August of 1877 Marsh got a letter from the Laramie Station of the Union Pacific Railroad, signed with a pair of fictitious names, offering to "sell the secret" of a fossil bed. The men gave the measurements of gigantic bones they had seen, and went on to say that "We would be pleased to hear from you, as you are well known as an enthusiastic geologist, and a man of means, both of which we are desirous of finding—more especially the latter." The men were W. E. Carlin and W. H. Reed, station agent and section foreman at Como, about fifty-five miles northwest of Laramie. They spoke of a vast boneyard, so close to the railroad track that the fossils could be hauled to the station by wheelbarrow, and one where, Williston said, the bones "extend for *seven* miles, and are by the ton."

Como has been twice deserted, once by the railroad, whose line was long ago relocated several miles farther south, and recently by Highway 40, now left as a minor road in favor of the wide Interstate 80, which touches the Medicine Bow range some distance to the south, and which is known among the fraternity of truck drivers as the "Ho Chi Minh Trail," on account of ferocious winter winds that pile up snowdrifts twenty and thirty feet deep and make it dangerous to follow. The fossil beds themselves are in the northern lee of Como Bluff, a long, low Dakota ridge that extends in an east-west direction, facing the Triassic and Permian redbeds along Rock Creek. The colorful Morrison shales under the ridge form a wide band of subdued badlands of soft, nearly horizontal, easily worked rock. In 1877, the bones seem to have been scattered about like logs on a forest floor. Along the highway is a small museum whose walls are built of dinosaur bone. Today, Como Bluff is a plundered and deserted graveyard, with the skeletons of dinosaurs spirited away to museums all over the world, and antelope roam undisturbed over the windswept hills. Only near the eastern end of the Bluff are signs of fossil hunters—

recent digging after the inch-long jaws of Jurassic mammals in the famous Quarry 9. Most of the world's supply of these mammals, whose bones, from the standpoint of the work needed to find them, are worth many times their weight in gold, have come from this quarry.

After hearing from Carlin and Reed, Marsh sent his assistant S. W. Williston, who later became a world-renowned authority on fossil reptiles, to take charge of the digging. Como Bluff in its entirety turned out to be by far the richest dinosaur locality yet known, although one of the quarries at Canon City produced more dinosaurs than any single quarry at Como. Williston supervised the extraction of thirty tons of bones for Marsh during the first year, and wrote "I doubt not that many thousands of tons of bones will yet be exhumed." Williston says of the Como Bluff quarries,

> By far the most commonly, extensive deposits, or "quarries," are found containing remains of numerous individuals mingled together in the most inextricable confusion, and in every conceivable position, with connected limb bones standing nearly upright, connected vertebrae describing vertical curves, etc., precisely as though in some ancient mud holes these huge monsters had become mired and died, and succeeding generations had trodden their bones down, and then left their own to mingle with them.

In these quarries, men toiled like Lilliputian miners, laboring with picks and ropes at bones that towered above them. One of the early diggings was eighty feet long and forty feet deep.

After seeing the Como Bluff field, Williston expressed his astonishment that the fossil beds had so long been ignored by Marsh and others. Hayden and King had long before mapped the formation in areas where the bones, so big they could scarcely be lifted by a man, lay strewn over acres of ground. But actually,

Trapped in a backwater of some early Mesozoic
stream, the bones of these reptiles at the Dinosaur
National Monument are sheltered and admired
by certain large-headed mammals of post-
Pleistocene times.

Marsh had been there first. He writes in his *Dinosaurs of North America,* published only a few years before his death:

> The first known specimen of Sauropoda from the West was secured by the writer in August, 1868, near Lake Como, in Wyoming Territory [this was on Marsh's first trip West, when he was after live salamanders in the Lake]. This fossil, an imperfect vertebra belonging to the genus since named *Morosaurus,* was found in the upper jurassic clays, in the horizon now known as the Atlantosaurus beds. . . . This locality has since become one of the most famous in the entire Rocky Mountain region, and the writer has secured from it remains of several hundred dinosaurs.

*Morosaurus* was not described by Marsh until 1878, when the big dinosaurs from Morrison and Canon City had begun to come in, so that it must be said that Marsh, even if he had picked up a dinosaur vertebra at Como in 1868, entirely missed the significance of his find.

Williston urged Marsh to make haste in signing a contract with Carlin and Reed. The men had already accumulated thousands of pounds of bone, and were in a position to sell them to anyone. Also, Williston learned that Cope already knew about the locality. A man named Brown had early that year written to the Smithsonian Institution about the large fossils at Como, and the authorities there had informed Cope, who wrote Brown asking for specimens. Williston got this information to Marsh before Carlin reached New Haven to negotiate, and the contract was signed. It turned out that Carlin was both lazy and treacherous. In a little over a year he deserted Marsh for Cope. Reed, by contrast, was courageous, hard-working, and loyal, working faithfully for Marsh over a period of years in spite of the abusive neglect dealt out to him by Marsh.

When Williston had to leave Como for a time during the winter of 1877–78, Reed was left in charge, Carlin not being back yet, and quickly proved his competence. He wrote to Williston: "I wish you wer hear to see the bones roll out and they are beauties. . . . it would astonish you to see the holes we have dug." Reed discovered a new quarry on the other side of Rock Creek, about a mile from the railroad. He asked Marsh for money to hire a horse to carry fossils, but Marsh did not deign to reply, and Reed that spring had to carry incredibly heavy loads on his back across the dangerously swollen creek.

In April of 1878 Williston wrote to Marsh from Como of an ominous visitor who called himself "Haines"—a heavy set, sullen man of about forty who walked with a limp. He claimed to be there selling groceries, but kept asking about fossils. Carlin had thought the man to be Cope himself, noting that when he told the man that Cope was a "damned thief," the man had "sneered." But Williston got a specimen of the man's handwriting, and decided it couldn't have been Cope, because the writing was legible. Nevertheless, they kept a lookout for Cope spies.

Carlin himself was a Judas, and by the beginning of 1879 had defected to Cope, leaving Reed to work alone in the bitter Wyoming winter. Reed wrote to Williston that it was "meerly H——, H——, H——." Carlin was the station master, and could crate up fossils for Cope in the comfort of the station room, while Reed had to work out on the exposed freight platform. When Reed finished a quarry, he smashed the remaining bones so that Carlin could not get them. He had constantly to be on guard against trespassers. When two strangers appeared one day at one of his quarries, he retaliated by moving to the top of the quarry and digging out dirt and rock which fell onto the men below. They ordered him to leave, "but I was not quite ready to go yet," and after four days of digging and having Reed cover their work up again, the men left. Reed complained that they were doing a lot of talking down at the station, but that did not hurt him at all, or

178

The famous Marsh quarry near Canon City
lies on the tilted platform just above the cliffs
in the lower center of the photo. Collectors
at first threw unwanted bone scraps over the
cliff into the canyon below. Later Marsh
ordered them back to retrieve the fragments.

even "scare me much either." When Marsh heard of the incident, he sent Lakes up from Morrison to strengthen his contingent.

Carlin left the field, and Cope replaced him with two brothers from Michigan named Hubbel. Among the specimens they sent him was a nearly complete skeleton of the large bipedal carnivo-

These exposures of the Morrison formation
near the shelter at Dinosaur National
Monument show the strongly tilted strata that
provide the dramatic backdrop to the bones
actually excavated and on exhibit.

rous dinosaur, *Allosaurus,* which now is one of the most prized
exhibits of the American Museum of Natural History in New
York.

In early August of 1879, Cope arrived at Como Bluff to inspect
the fossil beds, but stayed only a day. Marsh's group had been
warned, and had gone into a frenzy of patrol activity, trying to oc-
cupy all the quarries simultaneously. Lakes met Cope, and made

this entry in his diary: "The Monstrum horrendum Cope has been and gone and I must say that what I saw of him I liked very much his manner is so affable and his conversation very agreeable. I only wish I could feel sure he had a sound reputation for honesty." Apparently Marsh had been successful in making it an article of faith throughout the West that Cope was a "damned thief." The mammal-jaw Quarry No. 9 was discovered just before Cope's arrival, but although Cope asked about a mammal jaw (from another quarry) that Marsh had published, he apparently learned nothing of the secret of the new quarry.

Lakes and Reed did not get along, so they worked independently in different parts of the Bluff. Lakes spent much of the winter of 1879–80 digging alone in a quarry that he eventually got down to a narrow trench at a depth of forty feet. He was out of the eternal Wyoming wind, but the temperature dropped to 20° or 30° below zero, and the walls had to be braced against cave-ins. He struck a spring of ice water, and had to bail with one hand while digging bones with the other—more like fishing for eels than fossil hunting, he said.

By the summer of 1881 Como Bluff was overrun by bone hunters. Marsh responded to the pressure during the next few years by sending out more collectors. He had the habit, either as a result of administrative stupidity or as a calculated device for stimulating competition among his collectors, of not subordinating the new employee to one already hired. This led to perpetual conflict among his men. In 1883, this practice nearly resulted in gunplay among the Marsh employees. One of his men wrote him that "a man working for you by the name of Brown [probably the same man who in 1877 wrote to the Smithsonian about the Como Bluff fossils] assaulted me at the station with two revolvers and wanted me to fight him." The man declined the challenge, on account of having a family.

Harvard University had sent collectors to Como Bluff, and by

William Harlow Reed, a formal portrait (left) and with fossils encased in plaster at Como Bluff (right). The dinosaur leg bone in the foreground was 5 feet 8 inches long and was taken up in four sections, with two men required to lift each one. Reed sustained the Marsh effort in these fossil beds for many years under extremely adverse conditions. (Courtesy of the Western Research Center, University of Wyoming)

1889 the University of Wyoming also was there. Marsh kept Quarry 9 going until 1889, when he finally terminated operations at the Bluff. In all, Marsh bagged a total of 26 new species of dinosaurs from Como Bluff, a remarkable achievement, especially so when it is taken into account that many of them were represented by tolerably complete skeletons. These were taken from both the Morrison formation and the underlying Sundance, which is present at Como Bluff. He got 6 new species from the site near the town of Morrison, and 8 from Canon City. From Quarry 9 at

Como Bluff, he got 45 new species of Jurassic mammals, a lion's share of the known North American species.

Marsh prepared hundreds of plates illustrating the skeletons of the dinosaurs he had collected, and in 1896 published a 100-page summary of what was known about North American dinosaurs as a preliminary to later more exhaustive monographs which, however, he did not live to complete. This work was, of course, done with the assistance of extremely competent technical help both in the laboratory at New Haven and in the field. The aging Professor Marsh, in his *Dinosaurs of North America,* wrote to a great extent of the good old days that never were when he said, of his role in the discovery of the dinosaurs:

> To discover and bring together these remains, representing several hundred individuals, from widely separated localities and various geological horizons, has been a long and laborious undertaking, attended with much hardship, and often with danger, but not without the pleasure that exploration in new fields brings to its votaries. These researches, especially in the West, have been continued by the writer more than a score of years, and have led him across the Rocky Mountains a still greater number of times.

As has been said previously, Marsh retired almost completely from field work after 1874, three years before he became much interested in dinosaurs, and made only occasional excursions into the field to check on the work of his subordinates. His assistant John Bell Hatcher, who spent years in the field collecting dinosaurs for Marsh, has given his view of Marsh's contribution to the work on Hatcher's speciality, the horned dinosaurs of the Cretaceous. Marsh had named the formation in eastern Wyoming where Hatcher worked the Ceratops beds. On the basis of discoveries made in the Judith River beds by Hatcher, in eastern Wyoming by Hatcher, and by others west of Denver, Marsh said that these beds extended all along the eastern front of the Rockies, and had been carefully explored. With a statement that he had personally examined the principal sites, he implied that he was responsible for this exploration.

In one of the first of his own publications, Hatcher reviewed Marsh's efforts toward the elucidation of the Ceratops beds, then went on to say: "This constitutes Professor Marsh's *field work* in the *Ceratops beds*. In a total of three and one-half days field work he seems to have found sufficient time to 'carefully explore' the geological deposits of the *Ceratops beds* and to trace them for 'eight hundred miles along the eastern flank of the Rocky Mountains,' besides making numerous other observations of scientific interest."

After the time of Cope and Marsh, the Morrison formation continued to be a gold mine of dinosaurs. Bone Cabin Quarry, northwest of Como Bluff, so named because a sheep-herder had built a cabin with a foundation of dinosaur bones, yielded 50 partial skeletons from a single quarry. Far to the southwest, near the Colorado–Utah boundary, the site that was to become Dinosaur National Monument was discovered. Here the visitor can see, in what is one of the most impressive displays of fossils in the world, the skeletons as they lie in a slab of near-vertical rock. The fabulous Morrison, deposited in immense river valleys that received sediment from highlands somewhere to the south, extends even into New Mexico, and there also dinosaurs are found.

One of Reed's campsites near Como Bluff (above) and Reed (below) with a dinosaur leg bone from Como Bluff. (Courtesy of the Western History Research Center, University of Wyoming)

# 16

# "DAWN HORSES" AND BIRDS WITH TEETH

$T$HE ONLY WAY TO prove by direct evidence that organic evolution has produced the immense variety of living things that now inhabit the earth is to travel back in time to observe the forms of life that existed in the past. So far, the only vehicle known for such an exploration is paleontology. Yet, when Charles Darwin in 1859, with his *Origin of Species,* convinced the scientific world that evolution had occurred, paleontology did not effectively support his theory. To the leading geologists of the time, the opposite was true, since the fossil record seemed to show that novel groups of animals appeared suddenly in the fossil record, without identifiable ancestors.

Darwin was forced to rely on indirect evidence which, however, was so compelling that his theory won the day. Darwin realized that the absence of a continuous record of change in the data of paleontology was an important weakness in his theory, but answered the difficulty by noting the vast extent of geologic time, and the exceedingly imperfect and fragmentary nature of the known fossil record, which represents only a few pinpoints of information from the immense theater of life on earth. He predicted that future geologic exploration would resolve many of the obstacles that the paleontology of his day had placed in the path of his theory.

To a great extent it was Cope and Marsh and their followers who made Darwin's prophecy come true. In a sketch of the history of paleontology, H. F. Osborn writes: "After a long period of gradual revelation of the ancient life of Europe, extending eastward to Greece, eastern Asia, and to Australia, attention became centered on North America, especially on Rocky Mountain exploration. New and unheard of orders of amphibians, reptiles, and mammals came to the surface of knowledge, revolutionizing thought, demonstrating the evolution theory, and solving some of the most important problems of descent." Darwin was an older contemporary of Cope and Marsh during their most active years, and there exists a presentation copy of the *Origin of Species* from Cope's library, and a letter from Darwin to Marsh congratulating him on the discovery of toothed birds, which helped fill in the gap between birds and reptiles.

Darwin was a reclusive invalid who shrank from the commotion aroused by his new theory, which was widely held to be inimical to the public order, and he never defended it on the lecture platform. His champion was the aggressive, vocal, and witty British paleontologist Thomas Henry Huxley. In 1876 Huxley came to America for a lecture tour on evolution, and visited Marsh in New Haven. Huxley wrote to his wife:

My excellent host met me at the station, and it seems as he could not make enough of me. I am installed in apartments which were occupied by his uncle, the millionaire Peabody, and am as quiet as if I were in my own house. We have had a preliminary canter over the fossils, and I have seen some things which were worth all the journey across. . . . We are hard at work still. Breakfast 8.30—go over to the Museum with Marsh at 9 or 10—work til 1.30—dine—go back to the Museum to work till 6. Then Marsh takes me for a drive to see the views about the town, and back to tea about half-past eight. He is a wonderfully good fellow, full of fun and stories about his Western adventures, and the collection of fossils is the most wonderful thing I ever saw. I wish I could spare three weeks instead of one to study it.

At the time, one of Huxley's pet subjects was the evolution of the horse. Most of the scientific work on the subject had been done by the erratic but brilliant Russian paleontologist Vladimir Kovalevsky. Kovalevsky and Huxley had shown that several genera of Old World fossil mammals, the oldest not at all resembling a horse, could be arranged in a graded series that led by small steps to the modern horse. Huxley knew that Marsh had a good collection of the American relatives of these animals, but he was amazed at the size and completeness of the collection. It seemed to him, he said, that Marsh was a wizard who could with a wave of the hand conjure up a fossil, brought in by an infallible assistant, to illustrate any kind of horse that Huxley might imagine to have existed as transitional between the known forms.

In fact, the scheme for the evolution of horses worked out by Huxley and Kovalevsky was incorrect. Their evolutionary sequence consisted of a series of isolated steps, without connecting links, and when more fossils were found, they did not fit into the progression. Marsh, as early as 1874, had 30 species of horses from the western Tertiary deposits, and got more in later years. The North American fossil horses, he found, could be arranged into a different and smoother progression than that postulated for the Old World genera. It later became evident that North America had been the center for the evolution of horses, with only occasional branches of the evolutionary tree extending into Eurasia, which gave only a fragmentary view of the evolutionary history of the group in that continent.

Both Cope and Marsh saw that the key to understanding the evolution of horses lay in the Eocene fossils from Wyoming and New Mexico, but only Marsh was able to convert this insight into a commodity of real educational and publicity value. Cope's brief papers on the subject failed to point up the drama inherent in the subject. The casual reader would not gather from his terminology that horses were even present in older Tertiary times, since he referred the earlier forms to other families. His technical diagrams of the phylogeny of the group were uninspiring.

When Huxley visited Marsh, he naturally impressed upon him the importance of the paleontology of the horse group, since he based one of his own public lectures on evolution upon the subject as an unusually informative example of evolution in action. He roused Marsh to a high pitch of interest in the fossil horses, and each set the other on a new round of thinking about it. After talking to Marsh, Huxley revised his lecture on the spot, and in the lecture, given shortly after, he made the prediction that a yet older fossil would be found in America that had a more primitive foot structure than anything yet known among the horses. He and Marsh dreamed up the name Eohippus for this imaginary animal. Some weeks later, Marsh found this animal in his collection, and named it *Eohippus,* the "dawn horse."

When Marsh a few years later illustrated his scheme of the evolutionary history of the horses, he used straightforward, easily understood diagrams of foot and tooth structure which, embellished

189

with more up-to-date information, are still one of the mainstays in teaching evolution theory.

The bones and teeth of horses are common in the Tertiary rocks of the West. It is the fossilized teeth, flint-hard and resistant to weathering, that are most often found. During the 45 million years since the first horses appeared in the Eocene, the cheek teeth have changed from small crushing teeth, about as large as the tip of one's small finger, to tall, thumb-sized teeth crowned with sharp ridges equipped to grind the most abrasive vegetation. The expert finds an almost inexhaustible store of information in these complex teeth—he can give the name of the animal that possessed them, say much about its mode of life, and can give the geologic age of the rocks from which they were taken.

In the Western United States, the horses have a continuous fossil record from the Eocene through the Pleistocene, and during this time they changed continuously along several branching lines of evolution. The various branches died away at different times, only one persisting until the end of the Pleistocene. Because of the structural changes made as time progressed, it is possible to give relative ages to the fossils. So that the horses provide what are called index fossils—their presence in a formation identifies the age of the formation. The foot structure of the horses also underwent comparable evolutionary change, so that the foot bones, too, can be used in determining geologic age.

Taking both tooth and foot structure into account, paleontologists have been able to trace a continuous line of descent leading down from the last group of horses known in North America (these were Pleistocene species almost identical with existing horses of Eurasia, which have been introduced by man into the New World) back through the Tertiary to an Eocene animal that looked much more like a small dog than a horse. There are no appreciable gaps in the sequence. This trip through 45 million years of time shows an animal that changes, sometimes rapidly, sometimes slowly, and shows conclusively that the modern genus *Equus* evolved, through a number of other genera, from the Eocene "dawn horse." The sequence is by far the longest and most continuous series known for an actively evolving group of organisms. It provides the kind of direct, introconvertible evidence that makes of evolution a fact rather than a theory.

Darwin said not only that evolution had taken place, but that it took place by natural selection, in which nature selects from the variable population of each generation those individuals that give rise to the next. Natural selection means the survival of those variants fitted to the environment, implying adaptation, and the kinds of evolutionary changes that can be seen in the feet and teeth of horses during the Tertiary are clearly of kinds that have adaptive meaning. They are related to changes in the environment that took place in the interior of the North American continent during the Tertiary—from lush warm forest lands to the modern intemperate prairies. This meant a change from the soft leaves of shrubs and herbs to the prairie vegetation, which is abrasive on two counts: the grasses, as an adaptation which discourages animals from eating them, contain microscopic globules of silica (silicon dioxide) which are harder than glass; and second, the vegetation close to the ground is likely to be well supplied with dust and sand, which also generally contain silica. Teeth fitted for grazing on grasslands have open roots, which makes possible continual growth to make up for wear, and also have a hard cement layer added to the dentine and enamel layers of the grinding ridges on the crown. In North America, such teeth appeared, by gradual improvement of the older types, during the Miocene.

There also were environmental changes that affected the evolution of the feet. Predators appeared in early Eocene that matched the first horses in size and speed. The evolutionary reaction of the horses was also to increase size and speed. This meant a reorganization of foot structure from the sprawling multitoed primitive

191

foot to one where a single monolithic toe bore the weight. There are a number of intricate structural changes involved, including one arrangement used by many of the Miocene and Pliocene horses whereby a pair of lateral toes were retained which helped absorb the shock of impact of the foot on the ground. The high speed, single-toed foot, capable of carrying the weight of a large animal, is of course practical only on the hard ground of the plains environment, which became increasingly widespread during the Tertiary.

Thousands of teeth of some species of horse have been collected from a single locality, so that they represent in a general way a single population. Careful study shows that they represent just the kind of random variation that Darwin postulated to have been necessary for natural selection to have occurred. Some teeth have characteristics typical of the average for a previous geologic time, and some those which will be characteristic of the future.

The nature of the fossil record of the horses therefore not only shows conclusively that evolution took place, but shows also that the explanation given by Darwin, that it took place through the agency of natural selection, is probably true, or at least it is the best explanation now available.

Marsh gained both fame and notoriety from his discovery of another "missing link," the birds with teeth. He was praised by Darwin for the discovery, and ridiculed by enemies in the United States Congress who protested the use of the taxpayer's money in a search for such elusive objects as the teeth of birds. In a public lecture given in 1887 for the American Association for the Advancement of Science, Marsh has this to say of the toothed birds:

The classes of Birds and Reptiles, as now living, are separated by a gulf so profound that a few years since it was cited by the opponents of evolution as the most important break in the animal series, and one that doctrine could not bridge over. Since then, as Huxley has clearly shown, this gap has been virtually filled by the discovery of bird-like Reptiles and reptilian Birds. *Compsognathus* and *Archaeopteryx* of the Old World, and *Ichthyornis* and *Hesperornis* of the New, are the stepping stones by which the evolutionist of today leads the doubting brother across the shallow remnant of the gulf, once thought impassable.

In 1861 the impression of a single feather was found on a piece of slate of Jurassic age in Bavaria. It represented the oldest known bird, and was given the name *Archaeopteryx*. That same year, a skeleton, the size of a small crow, which was surrounded by a set of feathers, was discovered in the same formation, and eventually was also considered to represent a species of *Archaeopteryx*. In 1872 a better skeleton, complete with head, was found. To this day, these are the only reasonably complete skeletons known, and only two other partial skeletons have been found.

*Archaeopteryx* was variously regarded as a feathered reptile or a lizard-tailed bird, but it is now classified as a bird. At the time that Marsh discovered his toothed birds, the fragments of skull present in the first specimen of *Archaeopteryx* had been overlooked, and the second specimen was not yet cleared of matrix, so that it was not realized that the jaws were toothed. Marsh tried to buy the second specimen (the first was already owned by the British Museum), but only succeeded in driving the price up to 20,000 marks, far beyond his purse, but a price paid by the Berlin Museum. Marsh says that he saw the teeth of the British Museum specimen in 1878, long after he had studied the toothed birds of Kansas.

Marsh in 1880 published a sumptuous volume on the toothed birds of Kansas, called *Odontornithes: A monograph on the extinct birds of North America.* He gives a typically Marshian Wild-West introduction:

The first Bird fossil discovered in this region was the lower end of the tibia of *Hesperornis,* found by the writer in December, 1870, near the Smoky Hill River in Western Kansas. Specimens belonging to another genus of the *Odontornithes* were discovered on the same expedition. The extreme cold, and danger from hostile Indians, rendered a careful exploration at that time impossible.

In June of the following year, the writer again visited the same region, with a larger party, and a stronger escort of United States troops, and was rewarded by the discovery of the skeleton which forms the type of *Hesperornis regalis,* Marsh. Various other remains of *Odontornithes* were secured, and have since been described by the writer. Although the fossils obtained during the two months of the exploration were important, the results did not equal our expectations, owing in part to the extreme heat (110° to 120° Fahrenheit, in the shade) which, causing sunstroke and fever, weakened and discouraged guides and explorers alike.

A considerable part of these Cretaceous deposits still remained unexplored, and in the autumn of 1872, a third expedition through this territory was undertaken by the writer, with a small party. Additional specimens of much interest were secured, including the type of the genus *Apatornis,* and one nearly complete skeleton of *Hesperornis,*—an ample reward for the danger and hardship we incurred.

The specimens thus secured by these various expeditions have since been supplemented by important additions, collected in the same general region by different parties equipped and sent out by the writer, who could no longer give his personal supervision to work in that field. The fossil Birds procured in this region since 1870, by these different expeditions, include remains of more than one hundred different individuals of the *Odontornithes.* These are all in the

194

Museum of Yale College, and form the material on which the present volume is based.

To represent Marsh's finds of 1870 and 1871 as the "discovery" of the toothed birds is not quite accurate, since at the time he did not have the head of *Hesperornis*, and therefore did not know anything about teeth. Actually, the first of what Marsh called "birds with teeth" was discovered by Professor Benjamin F. Mudge, an antislavery petroleum chemist who had been run out of Kentucky before the Civil War and come to rest temporarily at the Kansas Agricultural College at Manhattan, Kansas. Another Kansas geologist, Samuel W. Williston, writes of Mudge's find,

> He [Professor Mudge] had been sending his vertebrate fossils previously to Professor Cope for determination. Learning through Professor Dana that Professor Marsh, who as a boy had been an acquaintance of Professor Mudge, was interested in these fossils, he changed the address upon the box containing the bird specimen after he had made it ready to send to Professor Cope, and sent it instead to Professor Marsh. Had Professor Cope received the box, he would have been the first to make known to the world the discovery of "Birds with Teeth."

Marsh got these specimens in 1872. But history must also reject this claim, since modern research on *Ichthyornis,* the bird sent to Marsh, shows that there is no conclusive evidence that the teeth described by Marsh actually belonged to the bird skeleton. (To add another twist, Marsh at first described the teeth as those of a small reptile, before reversing himself and associating them with *Ichthyornis.*)

*Ichthyornis* was a delicate, long-winged bird, standing about eight inches high, that probably resembled a modern tern in appearance and habits. The other important bird of the Kansas chalk, *Hesperornis,* was a large swimming bird, whose skeleton stretched 6 feet from beak to toe. Like the modern penguins, it was at home in the waters of the high seas, its rudimentary wings probably acting as flippers to help steer while the creature was driven swiftly through the water by the powerful legs. Unlike the penguins or any other modern bird, its jaws were well equipped with teeth. Marsh got fossils of approximately 50 individuals of *Hesperornis,* a tribute to his tenacity as a collector.

# 17

# PRINCE OF COLLECTORS: JOHN BELL HATCHER

Marsh trained, as hired employees, two of the leading vertebrate paleontologists of the generation that followed him—Samuel Wendell Williston and John Bell Hatcher. Two other paleontologists of equal standing were William Berryman Scott and Henry Fairfield Osborn, both largely self-motivated and self-trained in vertebrate paleontology, but who were friends and younger colleagues of Cope.

Williston became an authority on both fossil reptiles and on a group of living insects, the Diptera, or two-winged flies, an anomaly which was the result of Marsh's refusal to let Williston do research on fossil vertebrates while an employee. Scott and Osborn, associated with Princeton University and the American Museum of Natural History, respectively, became specialists on fossil mammals, Osborn in addition becoming director of the museum and a well-known writer of nontechnical books on evolution, paleontology, and the history of science. John Bell Hatcher stands apart as a legendary hero of vertebrate paleontology—he died at forty-three, just as he was finishing a career as the most strenuous and skillful fossil hunter ever known, and entering what promised to be an equally impressive career in paleontological research.

Hatcher was a small man, and had been a sickly child, educated at home by his father, a farm laborer and part-time school teacher. As an adolescent he gathered strength, and worked as a coal miner in Iowa. With the money saved he enrolled in Yale College and graduated in 1884, at the age of twenty-three. While working in the mines he had become interested in the fossils associated with the coal beds, and had made a small collection, which he showed to Marsh. Upon graduation, he presented himself to the professor, announcing that he was ready to collect fossils, anywhere, anytime, for any salary. Marsh was impressed, and within weeks Hatcher was in Kansas, digging rhino skeletons from the Pliocene rocks about a hundred miles north and east of the Smoky Hills Badlands.

This fossil bed, near the town of Long Island, came to be known as the Sternberg quarry, and is one of the best-known bone quarries in the world. It and nearby localities contained the bones of huge land turtles and a variety of Pliocene mammals, including mastodons, but the quarry is best known for the abundance of a rhino, *Teleoceras*. Skeletons of this stubby-legged animal, built like a hippo, and so fat that its belly must have nearly dragged on the ground, were there by the hundreds. Sternberg discovered the quarry in 1882 when, one day, sleepy in the heat, he let his team wander at will. He ended up near trees and water in a shady draw, whose walls were bristling with rhino bones.

The owner of the land came upon Sternberg at work digging fossils. After asking him to leave, without result, the owner traveled far and wide in search for a justice of the peace who would issue an order for Sternberg's arrest, but was unsuccessful. In 1884 Marsh got access to the quarry by hiring Sternberg who now, with money in his pocket, hired the owner to help dig the overburden away from the fossil beds.

Hatcher arrived on the scene in July, burning with desire to prove himself as a bone hunter. Within two days Hatcher began to display the trait that was to be manifest for the rest of his short life—he was a difficult man to work with. He wrote Marsh that he would not be able to send a report on his work unless he were given permission to work independently of Sternberg's group, and ventured the opinion that Sternberg was doing a poor job of excavating fossils. Soon he was asking Marsh not to judge his work by that of Sternberg, who was, he said, a careless man, "in a hurry about taking out and packing the specimens." Hatcher solved the problem when Sternberg was away on a trip to town by hiring the owner's son to help dig, and moving to the side of the ravine opposite Sternberg's operation.

The kindly Sternberg describes the incident in this way:

That year, 1884, in which I explored the quarry at Long Island, was a memorable one, not only because we secured a large carload of rhinoceros bones, but also because we had with us Mr. J. B. Hatcher, who afterwards helped to build up three great museums of vertebrate paleontology,—the museums of Yale and Princeton and the Carnegie Museum. With the last he was connected at the time of his death in 1904, just twenty years after he had made his first collection of vertebrate fossils with me. A bright, earnest student, he gave promise of a future even then by his perfect understanding of the work in hand and the thoughtful care which he devoted to it. I have always been glad that I had the honor of being his first teacher in the practical work of collecting, although he soon graduated from my department, and requested me to let him take one side of the ravine while I worked the other. He employed Mr. Overton's son with a plow and scraper, and got out a magnificent collection with no further instructions from me.

At the end of the summer Marsh visited the Sternberg quarries, and must have been enormously impressed by what he saw. Hatcher had made a grid map showing the position of the bones as they were taken out, and even with this time-consuming operation, was getting out huge quantities of bone. The largest shipment of fossils yet to reach the laboratory at New Haven was made in late November, when 117 large wooden boxes (250 to 1,000 pounds or more per box seems to have been the size of the crates sent by Marsh's parties) were dispatched. But there was no rest for Hatcher. In December he was off to the redbeds of Texas, in the north-central part of the state, in search of Permian vertebrates. Here, in weather fiercely cold, Hatcher was adrift with team and wagon in a desolate region where settlements were fifty miles apart. Marsh sent his pay in small amounts, making Hatcher wait for weeks on end at isolated post offices for checks that never came on time.

By the end of March, 1885, Hatcher was back at the Sternberg Quarry, and in less than two weeks he was able to write Marsh that he had already dug out 726 rhino bones, including four skulls and some of the very rarely found small bones that lie at the base of the tongue. After working through the summer in Kansas, Hatcher spent the winter at the laboratory in New Haven. Marsh could now, by reason of his association with the United States Geological Survey, funnel money from the federal government into his collecting operations. Although the specimens collected were supposed to belong to the United States National Museum, they actually went to Marsh for his exclusive use as long as he wanted them. With large sums of money now available, Marsh could indulge in his penchant for the large and spectacular (but he was also fond of the small and rare), and sent Hatcher to Nebraska to add to his collection of titanothere skulls and skeletons.

The titanotheres (in the technical literature, often referred to as the brontotheres, the generic name *Brontotherium,* invented by Marsh, now being regarded as better than *Titanotherium*) in Oligocene times reached a height of 8 feet at the shoulder. After an evolutionary career of 15 or 20 million years, beginning early in the Eocene and centering mostly in North America, they became extinct, probably because they never evolved the improved tooth structure needed to handle the harsh vegetation that became increasingly prevalent in the interior of the continent from late Oligocene times onward. So abundant were these animals that a layer of the White River group was named the Titanotherium bed by Meek and Hayden in 1857.

Working out of Chadron, in northwestern Nebraska, Hatcher collected nearly 25,000 pounds of titanothere bones during the summer of 1866, working from early May into October. That winter he was laid up in a hospital in New Haven with inflammatory rheumatism, but in March was again in the field, this time in the Hat Creek country of eastern Wyoming. In three months he took out 11 titanothere skulls. Moving on to the Oligocene of South Dakota, he got another 13 skulls, 3 in a single day.

Marsh planned an elaborate monograph on what he called the brontotheres (the "thunder beasts") and prepared 60 plates for the project, besides publishing a number of short preliminary papers establishing the general outlines of their structure and the fact that they had common ancestry, near the beginning of the Eocene, with the horses. He pushed his collectors relentlessly to get abundant and complete material.

In 1886 Hatcher was commissioned to find the rest of a partial

John Bell Hatcher. (From
*American Geologist,*
1905)

skeleton that had been brought in by another of Marsh's collectors eleven years before, and had been made the type specimen of
a new species, *Titanotherium robustum.* Hatcher found the skeleton as ordered; "About six miles northwest of the town of Chadron, in Dawes County, Nebraska, on a small branch of the west
fork of Dry creek," he said. Hatcher goes on to describe the collection of titanotheres assembled by Marsh for the monograph, referring to "the large collection either made or purchased by the
writer . . . now numbering nearly 200 complete skulls and many
more or less complete skeletons." Neither Marsh nor Hatcher
lived to write the monograph. After their deaths the Geological
Survey turned the project over to H. F. Osborn. In 1929, the
work appeared in two volumes, entitled *The titanotheres of ancient Wyoming, Dakota, and Nebraska.*

Hatcher spent part of the winter of 1886 in the East, collecting

The Lance Creek country of eastern Wyoming
is studded with low outcrops of upper
Cretaceous rock, deposited while the American
Mediterranean sea was cleared away by the
slow uplift of the new Rocky Mountain system.
This is the region where Hatcher gathered his
unmatched collection of the gigantic skulls
of the horned dinosaurs.

dinosaur bones along the Potomac near Washington, D.C., under
the noses of the government geologists who did not even know
whether the rocks were Tertiary or Cretaceous; he commented
that there was a good deal of "fireside geology" in Washington.
Early in the spring he was at Chadron, then at Hat Creek. Titanotheres now began to bore him, and he set his sights on the Judith River beds, no doubt hoping to improve on the record of the
collectors who had been there before him. For once he was de-

feated. Like Hayden, Cope, and Sternberg, he found only fragmentary specimens, of which he brought back about a ton.

Hatcher's Judith River trip, however, was a momentous one for the development of paleontology during the next decade. Hatcher found part of a dinosaur skull with horns which Marsh recognized, and soon published, as representing a new family of dinosaurs, the Ceratopsidae, or horned dinosaurs. Cope had earlier found fragments in the Judith, which he described as a new species of dinosaur without having much idea of what the animal looked like, which several years later he realized were Marsh's ceratopsians. On the way back from the Judith River Badlands to the titanothere beds, Hatcher got a vivid insight into the nature of the horned dinosaurs from a story told at a ranch in eastern Wyoming, in the Lance Creek country. One of the cowboys had found a skull with "horns as long as a hoe handle and eye holes as big as your hat" high up on the bank of a ravine. He had put a lariat on one of the horns, broken the horn off, and rolled the skull, estimated to weigh a ton, crashing and splintering into the bottom of the ravine.

Back at New Haven, the Ceratops from the Judith, Hatcher's story of the huge skull in Wyoming, and the fact that Marsh had the year before described a huge "bison" horn from a formation that should have been too old for bison, set Marsh thinking. He had the horn core at the Wyoming ranch sent to him, and found that all three finds pertained to a single group of horned dinosaurs. Next spring he sent Hatcher after the Wyoming skull, and early in May his collector wrote, "The big skull is ours."

Hatcher was married in 1887, and established a home at Long Pine, in north-central Nebraska, situated conveniently to the fossil beds, where he was to labor for many years. Marsh embarked on a great ceratopsian hunt in 1889, with Hatcher and several aides, financed by the federal government, as the troops in the field. Ceratopsian skulls are truly gigantic. Together with the armor frill at the back of the skull which protected the shoulder and throat, the skulls are two yards long. The squat body (about 8 feet high at the hips) and rather short tail bring the total length to hardly more than 20 feet, so that the ceratopsians were only medium-sized dinosaurs, perhaps each weighing about ten tons.

Hatcher's collecting ground for these reptiles was the Lance Creek beds, uppermost Cretaceous in age, of Niobrara (then Converse) County, in eastern Wyoming. Today this is a vast ranchland, with narrow dirt roads winding off to nowhere that tempt one beyond the limits of the ordinary gasoline tank. By 1892, after tremendous expense and labor, Hatcher had collected 31 more or less complete skulls in this area. The largest skull weighed nearly 7,000 pounds, and had to be hauled by wagon forty miles to the rail line.

Fellow bone hunters thought Hatcher had a sixth sense that led him to exposures of rock that contained fossil bone. His uncanny skill was based in part on a close study of rock that enabled him to imagine from the appearance of the rock the current flow in long-vanished streams, or reconstruct an eddy where a floating carcass might have come to rest and been buried. In a paper entitled "The Ceratops Beds of Converse County, Wyoming," he writes:

> In many instances, it has been possible to determine the direction of the currents which succeeded in burying the bones, and thus prevented their decay. For instance, on one side of a bone the matrix will be made up entirely of sand, while on the opposite side the stem and leaves of plants have been dropped, and now partially lignitized, form a considerable portion of the matrix. This arrangement of the materials of the matrix shows the direction of the current to have been from that side containing only sand, and toward the side containing the plants. So shallow were the waters, the bone itself became an obstacle sufficient to produce an eddy

Rocks of Miocene and Oligocene age abound in the Hat Creek country of eastern Wyoming and adjacent parts of South Dakota and Nebraska. The lower levels of these badlands are famed especially as a hunting ground for titanothere skulls. Hatcher for many years collected in this area.

on its lower side, in which the leaves and other vegetable materials accumulated, and sank to the bottom.

Marsh and his assistants toiled for years at finding and preparing specimens and trying to understand the structure, classification, and probable mode of life of the horned dinosaurs. Marsh died without publishing more than preliminary papers on the group. Hatcher then took up the work. So massive were the skulls and skeletons that it was inconvenient to assemble all the specimens in one laboratory (by now the fossils belonging to the United States National Museum had been removed from the Peabody Museum, and other institutions had begun to build up large collections of fossil vertebrates), so that Hatcher had to travel from museum to museum to do research. The Geological Survey paid him for the work, which took up the last two years of his life, but Hatcher spent most of it on preparators, draftsmen, and clerical help, leaving only a few hundred dollars for himself. The monograph, entitled *The Ceratopsia,* was published three years after his death. A foreword by H. F. Osborn says that Marsh contributed 204 plates and no manuscript, and that Hatcher was responsible for most of the text. He writes that "I trust that this volume may prove to be a lasting monument to the rare and noble spirit of John Bell Hatcher."

As at Como Bluff, Marsh wanted Hatcher, at the Lance Creek locality, to concentrate on both the huge reptilian remains and on the minute teeth and tiny jaws, scarcely more than an inch long, of the Mesozoic mammals to be found there. Cope had published four years previously (1882) an account of mammals discovered by his collector Jacob Wortman in the Upper Cretaceous. As has been discussed in an earlier chapter, mammals were in existence during much of the Mesozoic, an era dominated by the reptiles. Although they seem to have been quite abundant, especially toward the end of the Mesozoic, most were very small, and were preserved as fossils only under extraordinarily favorable conditions, so that they have been rare in collections. Their 100-million-year history before the age of mammals began is thus shrouded in darkness, making all the more valuable the pinpoints of light provided by the Jurassic and Cretaceous mammals that have been painstakingly gathered since their discovery early in the nineteenth century.

Marsh had described most of the world's known Jurassic mammals on the basis of finds in Quarry 9 at Como Bluff. He now stressed, in his instructions to Hatcher, the importance of finding mammals in the Cretaceous Lance Creek formation. Hatcher found the first mammal jaws during his second year of collecting the ceratopsians. When Marsh got the specimens, he ordered Hatcher to stop work on the dinosaurs and concentrate entirely on the mammals. Evidently he had great expectations for Hatcher wrote him: "You seem to think that Laramie mammals are everywhere abundant out here and that all that is necessary is to go out and scoop them. . . . They are very rare and about two teeth represents an average patient day's work." But as the summer wore on, Hatcher improved his techniques, and was able to send more than 800 teeth. It was here that he worked out his well-known "anthill" method of collecting these minute fossils, which he described in later years when he was working as an independent investigator:

The small mammals are pretty generally distributed, but are never very abundant, and on account of their small size are seen with difficulty. They may be more frequently found in what are known as "blow-outs" and are almost always associated with gar pike scales and teeth, and teeth and bones of other fish, crocodiles, lizards, and small dinosaurs.

These remains are frequently so abundant in "blow-outs" as to easily attract attention, and when such a place is found careful search will almost always be rewarded by the discovery of a few jaws and teeth of mammals. In such places the ant-hills, which in this region are quite numerous, should be carefully inspected, as they will almost always yield a goodly number of mammal teeth. It is well to be provided with a small flour sifter with which to sift the sand contained in these ant-hills, thus freeing it of finer materials and subjecting the coarser material remaining in the sieve to a thorough inspection for mammals. By this method the writer has frequently secured from 200 to 300 teeth and jaws from one ant-hill. In localities where these ants have not yet established themselves, but where mammals are found to be fairly abundant, it is well to bring a few shovelfuls of sand with ants from other ant-hills, which are sure to be found in the vicinity, and plant them on the mammal locality. They will at once establish new colonies, and if visited in succeeding years, will be found to have done efficient service in collecting mammal teeth and other small fossils, together with small gravels, all used in the construction of their future homes. As an instance of this I will mention that when spending two days in this region in 1893, I introduced a colony of ants in a mammal locality, and on revisiting the same place last season [1895] I secured in a short time from the exterior of this one hill 33 mammal teeth.

Paleontologists have in recent years come to the search for mammals of the Upper Cretaceous with modern mass production methods, which include screening wet and disintegrated matrix. At one locality in the Hell Creek formation of northeastern Montana, 26,000 teeth and a thousand partial or complete mammalian jaws were recovered, along with bones from the rest of the skeleton, in ten weeks of field work. It was estimated that each pound of rock, and there were millions of pounds of fossiliferous rock at the locality, contained on the average 4 teeth or jaws. About 20 species of mammals were represented, some of them, curiously, of kinds thought to be restricted to the early Paleocene. The mouselike primitive multituberculates, by far the commonest of the mammals in the fossil bed, must have been as common in the Upper Cretaceous as are the wild mice that swarm in the meadows of today, unnoticed by the ordinary observer.

The conviction grew upon Hatcher that Marsh was deliberately keeping him in the role as a field technician, when he was meant for better things. One of his fellow workers in the field, whom he felt to be no more than his equal, at best, was sponsored by Marsh for a doctorate at Yale, while Hatcher was excluded from the academic side of paleontology. Accordingly, in 1893 he left Marsh to become Curator of Vertebrate Paleontology at Princeton, where he was associated with W. B. Scott, a friend of Cope.

While at Princeton, Hatcher conceived and carried out plans for an ambitious exploration of Patagonia. These desolate plains, swept unceasingly by some of the most powerful winds on earth, had been a testing ground for the young Charles Darwin, who made strenuous explorations there in 1833. Along the coast Darwin collected bones of mammals of exotic kinds that for most of the Tertiary were confined to their ancestral home in South America, among them ground sloths as big as elephants and Volkswagon-sized armadillos. The fact that these animals belonged to the same groups of animals that were typical of the modern South American fauna—only a few species had spilled over into North America when the two continents were joined near the end of the Tertiary—indicated to Darwin that there must be some kind of hereditary connection between the extinct and living animals of a region. This was one of the pieces of information that went into the creation of his theory of evolution.

After the time of Darwin, two Argentinians, Carlos and Florentino Ameghino, made extensive collections of these strange Patagonian fossils. They exhibited a selection of them at the Paris Exposition of 1878. Cope was in Europe that year, and besides presenting papers at the British Association for the Advancement of Science, went to Europe for the meetings of the French Association and to buy and sell specimens. He was captivated by the spectacular Ameghino collection, which he obtained by making a down payment of half of the total price of $2,500. Cope did no re-

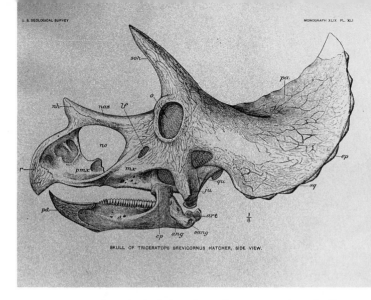

SKULL OF TRICERATOPS BREVICORNUS HATCHER, SIDE VIEW.

A technical drawing of a ceratopsian skull, used by Hatcher in his monograph on this group of horned dinosaurs. (From the U.S. Geological Survey Monograph 49, 1907)

search on the collection, which remained in storage in a cellar for more than twenty years. After its purchase by the American Museum, the great sloths, armadillos, and sabertooths became prized exhibits.

The Ameghinos were out of the mainstream of paleontological research, and although Florentino described many new species, his interpretations seemed rather bizarre to his Northern Hemisphere colleagues. This, together with the fact that their collecting activities had barely touched the vast fossil beds of Patagonia, gave the region high priority as a target for exploration, in the mind of Hatcher.

Possibly because he was to some extent outside the academic community at Princeton, not having a doctorate, and holding only the appointment of assistant in the Department of Geology, Hatcher assembled support for his Patagonian expedition on his own, without working through the university. When he ran out of money in the course of the expedition, he used his own. The expedition began in March of 1896 and ended in the late summer of 1899. During all but four months of this time, Hatcher was in the field, usually traveling with a companion—O. A. Peterson during the first and last years, A. E. Colburn the second.

The results of the expedition were published in a sumptuous set of volumes (eight volumes, the last divided into three heavy books) paid for by J. Pierpont Morgan. Hatcher and his assistants collected, in addition to the vertebrate fossils which were the prime object of the expedition, birds, aquatic invertebrates, and plants. Hatcher wrote only the 300-page introductory volume, entitled *Narrative and Geology.* In this he aimed to delineate the entire sweep of the natural history and ethnology of Patagonia, which he accomplished mostly on the basis of his own observations. The photography of the *Narrative,* done by himself, is superb.

Without money for proper equipment, the explorers worked under trying conditions, without adequate transport and usually without a tent. Hatcher suffered from his perennial rheumatism, and once was helpless for six weeks. During five consecutive months of travel they did not see another human being. In this wild country, well back from the coastline, guanaco were always in sight, and deer so tame that a herd would stand only a few feet away, watching a recently shot companion being cut up for meat.

Hatcher left Princeton after returning from Patagonia, and W. B. Scott eventually wrote up the vertebrate fossils that were collected. A botanist described the plants in three volumes.

The oil geologist James Terry Duce has written in the *Atlantic Monthly* an account of some of the activities of the hard-bitten Hatcher in Patagonia:

One trick Fate played on the Patagonians was to send a rather subdued-looking American scientist from Princeton to collect fossil bones. . . . He came for a few months, stayed three years, and taught the Patagonians poker. The professor passed through every hamlet from Bahia Blanca to the Straits; the lessons were always the same . . . but as a rule the loose change of the community passed on to the bone hunter to be spent on science. When the famous night finally arrived on which Hatcher was to leave San Julian the whole countryside dropped in to exact revenge. The game started early and was one of those friendly Western games with everyone's six-shooter on the table. The stacks of pesos in front of Hatcher climbed up and up until he was almost hidden behind them; the whistle of the steamer sounded down the harbor. Hatcher announced that he must go. Someone suggested that they would not let him. He picked up his gun and his pesos and backed through the door with a "Good night, gentlemen." No one made a move. The wind whooped round the eaves and Patagonia went back to its sheep-shearing with a wry smile on its face.*

In 1900 Hatcher became Curator of Paleontology and Osteology at the Carnegie Museum of Pittsburgh. During the summers of 1900–1903 he led student expeditions to the West. He was very successful as a teacher in the field, much admired by the students for his skill and energy. While he was at work during the summer of 1904 on the Ceratopsia monograph, he was stricken with typhoid, which proved fatal to a constitution weakened by years of working at the limit of endurance.

* *Atlantic Monthly,* September 1937, p. 372 (by permission).

# 18

# THE TRIUMVIRATE: HAYDEN, POWELL, AND KING

Cope and marsh worked in the shadow of three government-sponsored geologic and geographic surveys that dominated the scientific exploration of the American West from 1867 to 1879. Each of these surveys was created and headed by powerful and ambitious individuals whose actions influenced the careers of Cope and Marsh. These men were Ferdinand V. Hayden, John Wesley Powell, and Clarence King. All three were scientist–administrators who combined years of adventurous field work on the Western frontier with the most exacting political and administrative work in Washington. They were innovators and visionaries who did much to shape the expansion of the United States into the western half of the continent.

Before the Civil War, the governments of the wealthy and long-established eastern states had sponsored scientific exploration of their territories, but with the opening of the vast and sparsely settled lands of the trans-Mississippi West, the federal government became the most effective instrument for the explorations needed to support the military and economic aims of the growing nation. The earlier federally sponsored explorations were general-purpose surveys—primarily topographical, but with geology, botany, and meteorology appended to make for well-rounded geographical exploration. The survey to determine the boundary with Mexico that was begun in 1849, following military operations against that country, published a number of volumes which are classics in the literature of Western natural history. Between 1853 and 1856 five surveys were run through the West to determine the best route for a railway to the Pacific. In the thirteen large volumes of the *Pacific Railroad Reports* there is much geology and biology in addition to purely topographical information. This period of general surveys lasted through the time of the Civil War.

After the Civil War, science had grown to the level where specialized surveys were needed to carry out exploration in proper fashion. On March 2, 1867, Congress enacted legislation that established two surveys in which, although the term "geographic" was included in one of the titles, the primary aim was geology: Hayden's *Geological and Geographical Survey of the Territories,* and King's *Geological Exploration of the Fortieth Parallel.* On July 11, 1868, Congress authorized the War Department to issue rations to Professor Powell's group of twenty-five men who had already, under the sponsorship of the Smithsonian Institution, been exploring the Colorado River. Over the next few years this modest appropriation grew into a commitment to support a continuing survey of the Canyon Lands—southwestern Wyoming, central and southern Utah, and adjacent portions of Nevada and Arizona.

Powell's group came to be called the "Geological and Geographical Survey of the Rocky Mountain Region."

At the close of the Civil War Hayden was a veteran of long service as a surgeon in the Union Army and of nearly seven years of geological exploration of the Western frontier. When he left the Army in 1865 Hayden accepted an appointment as professor of geology and mineralogy at the University of Pennsylvania, a position he held for seven years. However, his main interests lay in the West, and he spent every summer in the field.

After working in the badlands of Dakota and Nebraska for the Philadelphia Academy of Science in 1866, Hayden was commissioned, on recommendation from authorities of the Smithsonian Institution, to make a geological survey of Nebraska Territory. The first year he had an appropriation of $5,000. Later his domain was extended to include all the Territories, and he worked for eleven years from Montana to New Mexico. His staff grew to a small army of packers, cooks, surveyors, and scientists, and in 1872 his appropriations peaked out at $115,000. When his Survey terminated in 1878, nearly $750,000 had been spent or committed for exploration, mapping, and the publication of some fifty volumes of reports.

Hayden saw himself as a publicist for the wonders of the American West. He directed his reports mainly toward the swarm of would-be settlers and homesteaders who wanted to leave the Midwest and East, but there was a large market for information about the American West in Europe. To the British, Colorado, in particular, was a mecca, and in the 1870s it was infiltrated with Englishmen. The publication of Hayden's *Atlas of Colorado* in 1878 was an international event.

From the beginning, Hayden and his scientists spoke in favor of the theory that cultivation of the arid plains lying east of the Rockies would increase the amount of rainfall. This won him popular support, but the scant scientific evidence he could provide did not much impress the scientific community. Hayden gained the reputation of making rapid but superficial surveys, and as a propagandist with a good ear for what would please the public. With the publication of annual reports which contained much material written in popular style, he became the best-known public scientist of the 1870s, and because of his influence among Congressmen who represented western interests, one of the most powerful.

In June of 1871 there appeared in the new *Scribner's Monthly* a feature article on the Yellowstone geyser basin by Nathaniel P. Langford, illustrated by the artist Thomas Moran. Moran had never been to the region, and made the drawings from descriptions provided by Langford. Hayden saw the publicity value of this spectacular region, quickly rerouted his survey party working in southern Wyoming, and took a thirty-man expedition to the Yellowstone, which included Moran and the pioneer photographer of the western mountains, William Henry Jackson. The following winter, Hayden led a fight to establish the Yellowstone as a national park, propagandizing members of Congress with the paintings and photographs made during the expedition. Early in 1872 Yellowstone became the first national park, with Langford as its supervisor. In 1876 Hayden published *The Yellowstone National Park, and the Mountain Regions of Idaho, Nevada, Colorado, and Utah,* whose 15 chromos of water-color sketches by Moran have made it the most beautiful and prized of the volumes to result from the western explorations of the 1870s.

Actually there were not three, but four surveys in the field during the 1870s. The fourth was the "Geographical Survey West of the One Hundredth Meridian," sponsored by the War Department, and headed by Lieutenant George M. Wheeler, of the Corps of Engineers, and charged with making inquiries into geology and natural history as well as the topography of the land. Wheeler was a loyal Army man, not an individualist of the type

One of the Hayden Survey camps in the heart
of the Colorado Rockies. Hayden is at the left
of the group. (W. H. Jackson photo, U.S.
Geological Survey)

of Hayden or King or Powell, yet the Wheeler Survey, with the
Army behind it, was aggressive both in the field and in the political arena of Washington. The Wheeler and Hayden Surveys were
constantly at odds in Colorado; some areas were surveyed twice
and the peaks given duplicate names. When, in 1874, Congress
took up the question as to whether there should be four simulta-
neous surveys with overlapping jurisdiction, it asked President
Grant for his opinion. After consulting Hayden, Powell, the Secretary of War, and the Chief of Engineers (King had completed
his Survey), Grant decided that the Surveys should be consolidated into a single agency with the Army in charge. However,
nothing was done for the next four years.

Hayden had a number of prominent scientists associated with
his Survey, often without pay, but benefiting because they had ac-

cess to specimens collected by the Survey, could get escort for field work, and could get Hayden, accused by his enemies of having the Government Printing Office at his disposal, to publish their writings. One of Hayden's star scientists was Cope. The largest volume published by the Survey was the so-called "Cope's Bible," a summary of the Tertiary vertebrates so bulky it has to be wrestled off the library shelf, and generally has a broken binding as a result. As vertebrate paleontologist for Hayden, Cope could and did give himself the prestigious title of paleontologist for the government. When the question of the reorganization of the Surveys came up in 1874, Cope was for good reason a status-quo man.

The fact that Cope was in the Hayden Survey led to friction between Marsh and Hayden. Cope had kept up a barrage of criticism of Marsh's scientific work in reports published by the Survey. Sometime late in 1873 Marsh asked Hayden to get Cope to desist. Hayden replied that Cope wrote only of scientific, not personal, matters, that he could do nothing, and that Cope and Marsh would have to settle such disputes between themselves. A few months later, the conflict took a more serious turn, as indicated in a letter to Marsh from Hayden:

> My dear Marsh.
> Your name is being used extensively here at this time by certain parties to sanction a statement that the survey of which I have charge is a fraud, etc. It is working to your disadvantage. Is the use of your name in such a connection authorized by you? Please write or telegraph me on receipt of this at my expense. I wish to make use of your reply for your own good.

The letter was written only two days before Marsh's nomination came up at the National Academy of Sciences, and Marsh could hardly take this as other than a threat to blackball him there. Accordingly he waited until after the Academy meeting was over (where he was elected to membership unanimously, except for a dissenting vote by Cope), and contemptuously answered Hayden that he had recognized the nature of the threat, and had intentionally made no reply, "leaving it to you to act as you saw fit." The fantastic misjudgment of Marsh's character and the emptiness of Hayden's threat was a bad omen for the future, when the question of the fate of the various Surveys was to be decided.

John Wesley Powell was, like Hayden, a veteran of the Union Army. A combat engineer, he served with distinction and gallantry, and rose to the rank of major. His right arm was shattered at the battle of Shiloh and later was amputated, but this did not hold him back from a vigorous life as an explorer in the West after the war was over.

Powell was the son of an abolitionist preacher, and grew up in southern Illinois. As a boy, he was friends with the local intellectual, George Crockham, a well-to-do farmer, a member of the Underground Railway, and an amateur scientist and owner of a private museum. When the young Powell was stoned on the streets and driven from the public school by pro-slavery hoodlums, he took refuge with Crookham, where he continued his education. He drifted away from his family, his father being a fundamentalist who was antagonistic toward science. While Hayden, with a doctor's degree was exploring the Upper Missouri country, Powell wandered up and down the Mississippi, collecting plants and animals on his own, and getting scraps of education at one college and another. He taught in country schools, and eventually came to rest as a school principal in southern Illinois before enlisting in the Union Army as a private.

Out of the Army in 1865, Powell got a post as professor of geology at Illinois Wesleyan University, and the next year moved on to Illinois State Normal University. He began politicking in the state legislature for funds to set up a state natural history mu-

The Hayden Survey near the junction of the
North Platte and Sweetwater rivers in Wyoming.
Hayden is sitting at the rear center of the
group. (W. H. Jackson photo, U.S. Geological
Survey)

seum, with himself as curator. He got the money, and organized
an expedition for the summer of 1867 to the Big Badlands of
South Dakota. At Council Bluffs General Sherman, who was to
furnish him a military escort, advised against going into the Sioux
country, so Powell took his party of amateur naturalists and relatives to Colorado. This determined the whole direction of his life,
for his acquaintance with the Colorado mountains drew his attention to the geographical problem of the Colorado River.

The following summer Powell and his naturalists and relatives were back again in Colorado to collect minerals, flowers, and animals to stock the cabinets of the Illinois Museum. They made the first ascent of Longs Peak, the one-armed Powell climbing up the final 700-foot slab of the Home Stretch, which is now marked with paint spots to show hikers a more or less foolproof route to slide down or scramble up the smooth granite slope. Late in the summer they camped on the headwaters of the Colorado River. Here they met Samuel Bowles, a reporter for the Springfield *Republican,* and told him of their plans to go by boat down the Grand Canyon of the Colorado. Bowles gave high praise to Powell and his group, and pointed out that the Canyon of the Colorado was, on the official maps, a huge blank space of fifty or a hundred thousand square miles in extent. Powell, "single-minded as a buzz saw," had decided to fill in that blank space.

Powell's group that winter got as far as the valley of the White River of Colorado, where they built cabins for shelter. In the spring they advanced as far as the Yampa. Powell left the party to go to Washington for money, but all he could get was a promise of rations from the Army, some of which could be converted to cash. He had $2,000 from educational institutions in Illinois. With this he built boats and hired men, and in 1869 made the famed first passage of the Grand Canyon of the Colorado, a perilous boating expedition that lasted three months.

Clarence King, a man of brilliant personality, had a meteoric career that faded in his thirties. He is a scientist well known to the literati, on account of his friendship with Henry Adams, and nearly every biographer quotes the passage from *Education of Henry Adams:*

> King had everything to interest and delight Adams. He knew more than Adams did of art and poetry; he knew America, especially West of the hundredth meridian, better than any-

one; he knew the professor by heart, and he knew the congressman better than he did the professor. He knew even women; even the American woman; even the New York woman, which is saying much . . . he knew more practical geology than was good for him. . . . His wit and humor; his bubbling energy which swept everyone into the current of his interest; his personal charm of youth and manners; his faculty of giving and taking, profusely, lavishly, whether in thought or in money, as though he were nature herself, marked him almost alone among Americans. . . . One Clarence King existed in the world. Whatever prize he wanted lay ready for him—scientific, social, literary, political.

His image appears on a bronze plaque of American heroes on the door of the national Capitol, and a sunny California valley is named King's Canyon, yet he is little known, his memory being for a time suppressed because of his inability to conform with contemporary social standards, because of what one biographer called a defect in character.

King was the only one of the three Survey leaders to have a sound technical education, perhaps because he was the only one to come from a well-to-do family. He was a classmate of Marsh's in Yale's Sheffield School, and graduated the year before Marsh. That same year, mainly as an adventure, he went West with an emigrant train to California. There he volunteered to work with the new California State Geological Survey, headed by J. D. Whitney, soon became an indispensable member of the group, and for several years assisted in the first geologic exploration of the Sierra Nevada and of the Arizona Apache country.

At the age of twenty-five, King decided to set up his own geological survey, and to finance it with money from the federal government. He had come to California on the emigrant trail that was picked for the route of the first transcontinental railway, the

Union Pacific. This first intimate view of the West—the emigrants were three months on the way—together with the rich experience gained working for the California Survey, convinced him that a geologic transect along the 40th parallel, which on the average runs fifty to a hundred miles south of the railway, would be scientifically important, since it cut through an immense variety of geological features, and would be economically significant because of the chance of discovering mineral wealth near the railroad. Taking these factors into account, he considered it a sure-fire scheme to attract the support of Congress.

In the fall of 1866 King was in Washington petitioning the members of Congress to support his exploration. They were captivated by his brilliant and inspirational conversation. That spring, to the amazement of the Washington bureaucrats, Congress authorized an appropriation for his Survey, which was to be under direction of the War Department, and he was appointed geologist in charge. When the Secretary of War handed him his appointment, he said, "Now, Mr. King, the sooner you get out of Washington, the better—you are too young a man to be seen about town with this appointment in your pocket— there are four major-generals who want your place."

The King Survey had the highest degree of professional competence of the three Geological Surveys. King had something of the engineer's attitude toward geology, and made careful studies of the great gold and silver fields already being mined. He made a detailed study of the Comstock Lode, and was interested in chemical and physical studies that pertained to the origin of igneous rocks and mineral deposits.

Most providentially, while his Survey was in progress, there was reported a remarkable discovery of rubies and diamonds along the southern edge of his territory, in northwestern Colorado. A reconnaissance showed him at once that the geology of the area made it impossible that diamonds and rubies should be there, and a minute examination of their distribution showed that the ground had been salted with the gemstones. The swindle had already become a multimillion dollar enterprise, and King's exposé of the hoax gave his Survey immediate fame.

The geologic and topographic operation went like clockwork. King reached the western boundary of Wyoming in 1869, the year the transcontinental railroad was completed. Fieldwork was completed in 1873, but laboratory research and preparation of the eight volumes of reports and maps published by the Survey continued until 1880. Nearly $400,000 was spent by the King Survey.

With the inauguration of President Hayes in 1877 and the appointment of a new Secretary of the Interior, Carl Schurz, steps were taken to reform the administration of the public lands. Powell had all along taken the position that the government had to know what resources were on the public lands before it could determine their disposition, and had promoted the idea that a geologic survey was the proper instrument to produce this knowledge. Powell's idea had taken hold in Congress, but before coming to a decision they asked the National Academy of Sciences to give recommendations on the best way to survey and map the Territories of the United States.

At the beginning of 1878, Marsh was vice-president of the Academy, but when the president died in April, Marsh became acting president. Thus, when the charge was handed to the Academy by Congress, Marsh was the responsible officer, and thus became one of the arbiters of Cope's fate as vertebrate paleontologist to the United States.

Marsh appointed a six-man committee of Academy members, with himself as chairman ex-officio, to prepare a draft, which was adopted by the Academy late in November by a nearly unanimous vote, with the only dissenter being Cope. The proposal was along the lines of Powell's thinking (Powell was not yet an Academy member), and not accidentally so, since Powell had sent to the committee copies of his newly published "Report on the Lands of the Arid Region of the United States." It recommended that there be one agency responsible for topographic mapping and another, to be called a geologic survey, which would determine the geologic structure and resources of the land. It recommended also that the Wheeler, Hayden, and Powell Surveys be discontinued (the field work for the King Survey had already been completed).

When the Academy proposal came up before the House early in 1879 it was opposed by a large western bloc allied with Hayden, but after considerable maneuvering, a bill which consolidated the existing Surveys into a single organization, the United States Geological Survey, became law in March of 1879. Hayden, alone of the three contenders, pushed a claim to be made director of the new Survey, and Cope interceded with Schurz on Hayden's behalf. Powell and Marsh both jumped into the fray, supporting the nomination of King. Behind the scenes there was an avalanche of vituperative complaint against Hayden. The paleontologist J. S. Newberry wrote to a congressman,

Hayden has come to be so much of a fraud that he has lost the sympathy and respect of the scientific men of the country and it may well be questioned whether he and his enterprises should be generously assisted as they have been. In former times he was an energetic and successful explorer, and although his individual work had little scientific value, he has been the means of causing much good work to be done by others. Of late years, however, he has come to be simply the political manager of his expedition, has spent most of his time in Washington where he has in some way accumulated a handsome property.

Powell wrote to another congressman that Hayden was "a charlatan who has bought his way to fame with Government money

John Wesley Powell led geological expeditions into Colorado and Utah in 1867 and 1868. He served as director of the U.S. Geological Survey from 1881 to 1884. (From his *Explorations of the Colorado River of the West*, 1875)

and unlimited access to the Gov't. Printing Office." And from Harvard, Charles Eliot, the president, wrote to President Hayes, of Hayden: "I have often heard his ignorance, his scientific incapacity, and his low habits when in camp, commented on with aversion and mortification. He has never shown that he is himself either a geologist, a topographer, a botanist, or a zoologist." Hayden was brushed aside, and King was appointed in April. Marsh congratulated Powell on the success of their campaign, and

The always dapper Clarence King (to the left
of the tent ridge pole) at the camp of the U.S.
Geological Exploration of the 40th parallel,
near Salt Lake City. (T. H. O'Sullivan photo,
in New York Public Library)

invited him to the next meeting of the Academy to present a
paper.

As the new director, King gave Hayden and Powell appoint-
ments in the Survey, with Hayden sinking into taciturn obscurity,
and Powell being groomed to succeed King, who had planned to
hold the directorship only long enough to organize the Survey.
Cope was left with nothing except a commitment from the government to publish a lengthy report on the Tertiary vertebrates
which he had begun while with the Hayden Survey.

King was a man with expensive tastes. He kept a valet, collected art objects, belonged to exclusive clubs, and indulged in expensive food and drink. His salary, as director, of $6,000 a year was a negligible contribution to his financial requirements. He had always leaned toward applied geology—of his list of twelve forthcoming publications presented during his brief tenure as director, only three were in theoretical or basic geology—and he felt he could get rich as a mining engineer and promoter. Accordingly, making arrangements with Powell to take his place, he slipped almost unnoticed out of office late in 1880. Powell was director for the next fourteen years.

The triumvirate of the West had varied destinies. Hayden, fifty years old at the time of the dissolution of his Survey, lived an uneventful life until his death in 1887. Powell, forty-seven when he became director, guided the new Survey along a path of a creative contribution to the development of the western public lands. When he resigned as director, he devoted himself to the Bureau of Ethnology as a student and friend of the American Indians.

One of his protégés, Lester Ward, hired as a paleobotanist but actually a theoretical sociologist (he later became a professor of sociology at Brown University), influenced him in his old age toward philosophy. Powell summarized his philosophical thinking in 1898 in a book entitled *Truth and Error,* which he dedicated to Ward. It was a "cranky" book—Ward thought it a bit touched —dealing with what Powell called the "five-fold properties of matter" in a way that no one could understand. Also, in old age he complained of a wife who talked too much.

King published no more scientific work after leaving the Survey. He plunged into strenuous mining ventures, one day prowling through the tunnels of a desperately dangerous, half-drowned mine, the next consulting with a financial wizard on a multimillion dollar project. He became locked in contradictions that were insoluble, that froze his mind into paralysis. To make the Mexican silver mines profitable, he had to force small armies of men to work under intolerable conditions for next to nothing. Yet his sympathies lay with the working men. His financial backers, while aware of his high level of engineering skill, scorned him for his inability to drive his laborers to the limit. He failed as a promoter; he did not win riches.

And King had a liking for dark-skinned women, to the continuing wonderment of Henry Adams. In 1887 he fell in love with a beautiful brown-skinned and kinky-haired woman, regarded as a Negro, named Ada Rivers. He married her in an illegal ceremony of his own devising, calling himself James Todd (he only revealed to her his real name on his deathbed), and had by her five children. Hoping for an inheritance from his socialite mother, he kept the liaison a profound secret, maintaining his family in an apartment in a shabby neighborhood.

He began to have attacks of amnesia. Once he was arrested for creating a disturbance, but remembered nothing of the incident. He was hospitalized in a mental institution, and spent some months convalescing in Cuba with Henry Adams, where he took a lively interest in the Cuban revolutionaries of that period and in the local geology. A fulminating attack of tuberculosis warned him that the end was near. He made arrangements for his wife and children to move to Canada, and himself went to Arizona, where he died in 1901, penniless, and with only a doctor and a brother-in-law in attendance.

# 19

# COPE
# AS FINANCIER

The DECADE OF THE 1880s brought good news for Marsh, but was disastrous for Cope. These were years in which Cope, without place and with his inherited fortune melting away, watched his archenemy climb to the pinnacle of power; yet Cope remained cheerful, hopeful, and happily combative, continuing his travels in the mountains of the West, carrying on a brilliantly varied research program, and keeping up a continuous harassment of Marsh. "Vanity and hatred stained Marsh's career, but they utterly corroded Cope's," wrote one author, but Osborn, who knew Cope, discounts any sick brooding, and speaks of "Cope's thoroughly humorous Celtic attitude towards it [the conflict with Marsh], namely: that he was thoroughly enjoying the fight for its own sake."

The Marsh–Powell coalition that was put together in 1878

PHENACODUS VORTMANI, COPE, ½

One of Cope's prize Eocene fossils was this
*Phenacodus,* a genus that lies near the ancestry of
the hoofed mammals that survived the tertiary.
The specimen is 32 inches long. (From
"Cope's Bible," 1884)

lasted for fourteen years, ten of them coinciding with Powell's
tenure as director of the United States Geological Survey. The
Survey was politically sensitive because it was the only government agency responsible for the scientific study of the vast public
domain that lay between the eastern front of the Rocky Moun-

tains and the Sierra Nevada. The Survey was thus an agency that had great potential for determining the disposal of these lands, since knowledge is the necessary preliminary to action. Large corporate interests were the natural destiny of the varied western lands, which were utterly unsuited for the small independent homesteaders of the type that had settled the rainy plains and forests that lay east of the 100th meridian. They exerted constant pressure on Congress to make sure that it was private enterprise, unfettered by government supervision, that was to develop this land. Consequently, the devotion of Marsh to the well-being of the Survey was important to Powell, because of Marsh's high standing in the scientific establishment and his influence through Yale associations with prominent members of the political and business communities. In return, Powell was able to give Marsh the position of vertebrate paleontologist to the Survey (he was appointed in 1882) and to supply him with funds for field work and laboratory research.

During the ten years that Marsh held his post in the Survey, he was given nearly $150,000 for research, which enabled him to employ a total of fifty-four staff members, some for a short time, others, such as J. B. Hatcher, for a number of years. Of these, thirty-seven were field collectors. Marsh was paid $4,000 a year salary, but he put all of this back into the research and field work. The fact that much of his staff was now on the federal payroll did not much improve their lot. They were paid only when Marsh submitted vouchers to the pay officer in Washington, and he did this only when there were no other more important matters to claim his attention. He apparently never got it through his head that there were people in existence who had to get the trifling sums involved at a definite time.

In the days when photographic techniques were not much used, the preparation of drawings and lithographic plates was a large item in the budget for the preparation of paleontological

233

monographs, which must be elaborately illustrated. Marsh got funds for these from the Survey, also.

As a member of the Yale faculty Marsh had access to the *American Journal of Science* for quick publication of notes and short papers. To match this, Cope had in 1878 bought a controlling interest in the *American Naturalist,* which was thus at his disposal for publication, but it was a drain on his resources.

With the fall of Hayden, Cope was cut off from government funds to support his research, and seeing Marsh move ahead on a wide front, realized that his personal fortune was not big enough to make him a respectable competitor. The collection, preparation, and study of vertebrate fossils at the degree of sophistication now attained in paleontology had become an expensive affair. Cope therefore decided to use what money remained of his patrimony to win a fortune by mining silver and gold.

Cope seems to have had no talents as a businessman, but he no doubt thought the fact that he was a scientist and therefore presumably could think logically, that he knew something of geology and was widely traveled in the West, were preeminent qualifications for making him a mining investor. It was clear that he had no idea of the fantastically high level of competence of men who devote their lives to the art of taking money away from someone else. The few hundreds of thousands of dollars that Cope was able to throw into the arena of mining speculation in the 1880s must have been a choice morsel for the professionals.

The published record of Cope's mining venture consists of fragments of correspondence between Cope and his wife Annie (whom he calls Mamma) and his daughter Julia, now in her late teens (whom he calls Mammani). These are still of the sparkling, affectionate, and richly descriptive kind that was characteristic of Cope's letters to his intimates. Cope had entangled several of his relatives and friends in his enterprise: he intended to invest Julia's money for her ("I would of course be glad to look after Ju-

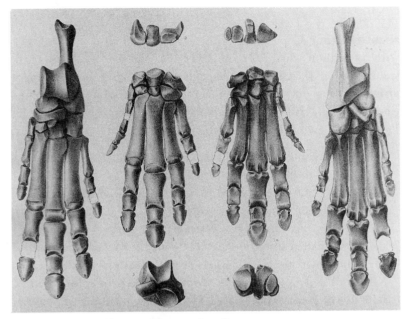

The feet of the Eocene *Phenacodus,* from western
Wyoming are of a type so primitive as to be ancestral
even to those of "Eohippus," the Dawn Horse. (From
"Cope's Bible," 1884)

lia's money"), and wrote to his wife "Grande had gone to $8 and
Plata to $5 which is a pretty good profit on what thee paid viz;
$2.50 and $1.60." And others, "I would write to Mary about
the Grande, but I do not know her address. She must be scared
at the proceedings of the stock robbers, who put the price
down by telling falsehood," and "I have written bros. Phil. and
J. B. Cope somewhat in detail."

Most of Cope's mining properties were silver mines in Lake
Valley, in southwestern New Mexico. This field was opened in
the late 1870s, and was the home of the Apaches, who were still
troublesome evictees when Cope was there in the 1880s. Huge
amounts of gold and silver were taken out. In one mine, begun

about the time Cope arrived, an ore vein led into a cave filled with $3 million worth of pure silver chloride. He was there each summer from 1881 to 1885, inspecting and buying mines, supervising drilling operations, and doing administrative work, sometimes as a high-ranking officer. Some extracts from his letters from Lake Valley give the flavor of the mining activities:

> I have gotten used to looking down deep shafts—and you have to get used to it—and have got so far as to go down with my foot in a loop of rope, and holding the rope in my hands, while one man turns the windlass. . . . The mines at Lake Valley have to be protected by a company of soldiers. . . . I was called upon to address them. I made a speech and they cheered me. . . . There is a good deal of valuable ore here, and it is now being developed on the principles I first laid down. New exposures of it are being made every day.

Cope described what he called a typical day's work: in the morning a visit to the most important and interesting mines to see how the work progresses, whether the ore veins get thicker or thinner; after lunch a look at cores from the diamond drill which they are using for underground exploration; and "We then wind up on some of the hill sides and pick up fossils." For the truth of the matter is that Cope kept up a steady round of collecting and observing in many phases of natural history, including vertebrate paleontology, while supposedly trying to get rich.

On his way home from the mines one season he sent to his daughter a box of New Mexico flowers: "I am told that when soldered air-tight that they will keep green for a long time. I have put in 20–30 species nearly all with pretty flowers, but none very large. They belong to many orders, some of which I do not know." At a mine in Idaho, workmen living in one of the shanties had two barrels used for holding water; "In these I found dead Mammals which had tumbled in and could not get out. I got five species: one gopher, two kinds of rats, a shrew, and a small kind of skunk all complete." He took advantage of the opportunity to collect minerals: he lists the contents of one box sent home as pyrolusite, manganite, cerargyrite, embolite, and vanadinite. His search for mines merely widened his range of field activities, which now extended from Idaho to the heart of Mexico.

Extracts from a series of letters to his wife will give an idea of his expectations and disappointments.

[August 11, 1881] After seeing what I have, I have no doubt of the great value of the four properties at this place. They are *all* good, probably the best in all New Mexico.

[July 18, 1883] The Sierra Grande meeting turned out otherwise. . . . They made me President! So we are rid of a disgrace and it is left for me to save the reputation of several members of the society of Friends. . . . we will have honesty at the mines at last.

[August 5, 1883] The mine is looking and doing well, but we have 4 law suits which threaten to absorb all or nearly all our profits for sometime yet!

[September 10, 1883] We will not go to the poorhouse yet awhile.

[October 1, 1883] Once in a while a little ore is still stolen, but not as in the palmy days of Wright appointees. Then all hands got $120,000 by stealing. . . . Had the management continued much longer in the hands of the robbers, I should have lost ⅔ of what I am worth. The danger from that is now past but it will take me a little while to recover financially.

[April 10, 1884] With mines it is either everything or nothing. I went in hoping to increase my income. I did so for a while; then it fell to nothing.

By 1886 Cope had to give up his stocks, which had become nearly or quite worthless. In that year he wrote his wife: "I found that certain things had occurred in connection with the company who will put them into tedious litigation for a long time, which will use up any profits that will be made out of the ore."

The next few years saw Cope scrambling for dollars. In 1888 he wrote his daughter that he was thinking of selling a duplicate collection of shells, boasted that he had received $10 for an article in a magazine, and had another due for publication. He advertised in the United States and Europe some plaster casts of an especially fine Eocene mammal in his collection, "but I have no replies as yet."

During the first year of his career as a businessman, Cope did little paleontological exploration himself, but had seven hired parties in the field, led by such well-known collectors as Wortman, Williston, Cummings, and Baldwin. Among the more important results of these explorations was a large collection from the Eocene of the Big Horn basin of western Wyoming, made by Wortman.

The next year, 1882, after visiting mining properties in Idaho, Cope took a side trip to southeastern Oregon in search of vertebrate fossils in Pleistocene sediments around the margins of the desert lakes of this region. During the Pleistocene the climate of the area lying in the rain shadow of the Sierras and Cascades was much wetter than now and these lakes, like the Great Salt Lake to the south, were larger than at present, and the surrounding countryside was green and teeming with life. In modern times, precipitation dwindled to the point where many of the rivers are without channels to the outer world, so that there is interior drainage, with the rivers ending in salty and brackish lakes without outlets. As the lakes became smaller, they left wide margins of Pleistocene lake sediments in which are found the bones of water birds that swarmed on the lakes and of the mammals that inhabited the shoreline.

The first large collection of Pleistocene fossils from the Oregon desert was made for Cope by Sternberg in 1877. Cope himself collected there in 1879, and his return in 1882 was made on the strength of a rumor that a new bone bed had been found some distance to the south of the original discovery.

Fossils were first discovered at a dried up lake bed in the Silver Lake area. Sternberg spent three weeks at this locality, sifting through the windblown sand for bones of mammals and birds. There were ducks and swans of extinct species, and a grebe apparently the same as the one that still swims on the lakes of the area. Sternberg found bones of a flamingo, which at first was taken to mean that the climate of the late Pleistocene had been semitropical, but since flamingos today are found at high latitudes in South America, even in the cold lakes of Patagonia, it is not likely that temperatures differed much from those of today.

That the surrounding country was a forest, rather than desert, is shown by the fossils of beaver, including the giant beaver, an animal the size of a half-grown bear. There also were mammoths, a number of kinds of horses, all much like the modern horse, and some camels, that combined the characters of the modern camel and llama. Beautiful obsidian points made by the Indians were scattered among the bones.

In 1882 Cope spent a couple of weeks in the Oregon desert, with team and wagon furnished by the United States Army, but was disgusted to find the report of fossils at the new locality was erroneous. Even a previously known locality failed him. He writes: "For 3 days I hunted in vain over these naked flats to find where the wind had broken it up and exposed the fossils at that place. The fossils are all concealed so far, but some day I think they will come to light in numbers."

Early in 1883 Cope was hard at work finishing up the monograph on Tertiary vertebrates ("Cope's Bible") which was to be published with funds left over from the defunct Hayden Survey. By the end of summer he was ready for another bone hunting expedition, and near the end of August wrote his wife: "I am today in a room of an old Fort, now used as a Hotel at this place [Little Missouri, Dakota]. . . . I have arranged with some people here to hire me a team and I am going off tomorrow to explore the country with a guide 30 miles S., where the badlands are said to be especially bad." These were the badlands along the Little Missouri River of North Dakota, now the site of a Theodore Roosevelt Memorial Park (Roosevelt's headquarters for hunting western big game was here). The rocks are of Upper Cretaceous age, capped here and there by Oligocene sediments. For two weeks he diligently sought after dinosaurs and primitive mammals in the Cretaceous rocks, but with little result. One day he rode half a mile through a forest of fossil tree stumps, and on the summits of some buttes, found Oligocene rocks where he collected 13 species of mammals, with rhinos abundant and a scattering of three-toed horses, sabertooth cats, and a giant relative of the pig.

For the whole two weeks Cope lived on venison and on buffalo meat from the last of the great buffalo herds. Camp life agreed well with the forty-three-year old Cope; he writes that "I acquired the usual tremendous appetite . . . . I never felt better. . . . This kind of work suits me amazingly and I only wish mining matters had permitted me to remain longer and to have explored down the Little Missouri."

A few weeks later, Cope was camping in the mountains of New Mexico, in Socorro County, enjoying the scenery and looking for fossils. A man took him to a "buffalo" skull, which proved to be a fossil rhino. Cope hoisted the skull onto his saddle and in a short time had it on its way from a nearby railway station to his museum at Pine Street in Philadelphia. This was in mid-October.

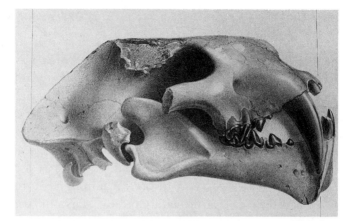

Skull of the saber-tooth cat, from the John Day
of Oregon, measures just short of 11 inches.
Famous among bone hunters as having been found
perched on the summit of a 40-foot-high rock
spire. (From "Cope's Bible," 1884)

By November Cope was in Monterrey, Mexico, in the first of
his yearly trips to that country during his mining phase. He was
after coal mines, geologic scenery, and objects of natural history.
He also enjoyed the human scene; "The women are often very
pretty," he writes his wife, "and have very pleasant manners. I
was not however smitten by any of them." His malaria recurred,
with a temperature of 105, and to his usual quinine-morphine-
belladonna mixture he added niter.

With few fossils to be found in Mexico, Cope concentrated on
collecting live reptiles and amphibians. He had led a double scientific life from near the start of his career, and in his twenties
had a worldwide reputation as a herpetologist and as an ichthyologist. He wrote the first comprehensive account of the herpetology of North America, and a leading modern journal of American
herpetology and ichthyology is called *Copeia*.

During his travels in the West after fossils, he also collected
living fishes, reptiles, and amphibians, giving names and de-

scriptions to the new ones. (There is a story that he once saw on the desk of a colleague a new reptile, which was being described by its owner. Cope's retentive memory enabled him to write up a description of the animal as soon as he got home, which he quickly published as a new species.) His Mexican collections were published in a series of papers called "Contributions to the herpetology of tropical America" which appeared during his mining years.

Even by 1884, two years before his mining venture collapsed, Cope had realized that he could not beat Marsh in "cornering the old bones market." He had to give up his hired collectors, and in March of 1884 he wrote his wife that "On my way home I will stop at Columbia Missouri and see if the University still has an idea of buying my collection. I am very sorry to put it in such an out of the way place, but if they have more enterprise there than elsewhere they will get it."

During the mining years, Cope continued to be far more prolific of scientific papers than his rival Marsh, even though Marsh could keep his hired science factory going. He published from forty to seventy-five papers each year, some of them fairly ambitious reviews of major groups of animals. Cope was anything but a single-minded man of business.

# 20
# REVENGE

After his failure as a mining promoter, Cope tried everywhere, and without success, to find a job. In a letter to his wife he says, "I wrote to Prof. Baird about securing a place made vacant by Mr. Stejneger in the Smithsonian, but I found the place did not exist," and in 1888, "The application I made for a position at the N.Y. American Museum of Natl. History has also been declined." He even considered a post as president of the new Stanford University, and tried to get a position as paleontologist for the Geological Survey, even though Marsh was already a member of the Survey. He gave lectures of all sorts for hire, including religious and philosophical discourses, and wrote popular articles for magazines.

Cope made plans and negotiated, without success, to set up a new science institution which would give employment to himself. He propagandized for one such establishment in the pages of the *American Naturalist:* "We have colleges and universities enough in most of the States, but there has not yet been established a single school where knowledge is produced, which corresponds in scope with the numerous institutions where it is taught." He thought that an endowment of a million dollars would be enough to support the six departments needed to cover all fields of knowledge. To keep out administrators, he said that the charter of this precursor of the modern graduate school should require "that the position of director should be forfeited by that one who should not produce some original work of merit every year or two."

Year after year Cope was in Washington to lobby Congressmen for an appropriation that would pay him to write a concluding volume to his "Bible." At times he seemed close to success, but he failed. In 1886, he wrote to his wife, *"My bill was thrown out* on a technicality, no doubt in the interest of Powell. . . . We will have to live very cheaply for a year." But that poverty was to some extent relative for Cope is shown by this comment, in a letter of 1887, "If I get the appropriation I will not have to sell the Labradorite [a beautiful and valuable stone] table this year at least."

During the latter part of the 1880s the Geological Survey was periodically under fire from Congress, mainly because of the socialistic leanings of Powell. Since farming in the arid region, where precipitation amounted to only fifteen inches or less per year, was impossible without irrigation, Powell said that settlers should band together in small groups to develop irrigation facilities for common use, somewhat in the manner that the Mormons had settled the irrigable lands of Utah. In his classic "Report on the Lands of the Arid region of the United States," Powell says of the lands suited for grazing:

The great areas over which stock must roam to obtain subsistence usually prevents the practicability of fencing the lands. It will not pay to fence the pasturage fields, hence in many cases the lands must be occupied by herds roaming in common; for poor men cooperative pasturage is necessary, or communal regulations for the occupancy of the ground and for the division of the increase of the herds. Such communal regulations have already been devised in many parts of the country.

Powell was an admirer of the pioneer American anthropologist Lewis Morgan, who furnished some of the underpinnings for the work of Marx and Engels, and said in a lecture before the Anthropological Society, "individualism is transmitted into socialism, egoism into altruism, and man is lifted above the brute to an immeasurable height."

Although Cope on occasion made halfhearted attempts to get assistance from Powell, in general he thought that his best chance for getting Congress to give him money was to inflame prejudice against Powell, and to discredit the Survey. In 1885, a year when the situation was especially critical for Powell, Cope, with the help of his mining engineer F. M. Endlich, and a friend, Persifor Frazer, got together a lengthy attack on Powell and Marsh which was circulated privately among the members of Congress. Cope, however, did not succeed in bringing down Powell, who successfully defended his position until 1892. The sapping operations conducted by Cope may have weakened his defense, but the proximate causes of the downfall of Powell and Marsh involved factors much more fundamental than the squabble between Cope and the federal geological establishment.

In 1885 Cope had begun seriously to gather ammunition to destroy Marsh. This he did by cultivating Marsh's laboratory assistants in the hope that he could turn them against their employer.

The large staff that Marsh had assembled included (besides the field collectors, technicians who prepared the bones, and artists who drew them) a number of assistants who in fact, if not in practice, had the status of academic colleagues entitled to publish their own papers in vertebrate paleontology and to rank as co-author with Marsh on some of the papers that came from the Yale laboratory. The first of these hired intellectuals, and the most indispensable to Marsh, was Oscar Harger, an undersized, scholarly, semi-invalid with an enlarged heart. Harger had worked his way through Yale College to a bachelor's degree in mathematics in 1868 by doing statistics for an insurance company. Poor, and lacking in drive, he could not progress to independent standing, and fell under the domination of Marsh, who owned him from 1870 until his death, at forty-four, in 1887.

Harger was Marsh's eyes and brain. Marsh, after his student days, read little in vertebrate paleontology; Harger read everything. Harger could relate the facts discovered in the laboratory to the contemporary world of paleontological research, and he provided sound judgment that helped Marsh to convert the work of the laboratory into the standard scientific commodity, publication. In his gentle way, Harger yearned to be a part of the scientific community by writing and publishing on his own or with Marsh as co-author, but Marsh was adamant in keeping him an invisible subordinate. Two of the Yale professors begged Marsh to give Harger scientific freedom, and even the president of Yale, Timothy Dwight, knew the case of Harger, whom he called a "kindly and gentle spirit," but Marsh was unmoved.

Samuel Williston came to the Yale laboratory from Kansas in 1876. A strong and independent spirit who achieved careers in medicine, entomology, and administration, as well as paleontology, he got what he could from Marsh by way of training and money, then, about the time of his friend Harger's death, criticized Marsh in language that fairly smoked with rage, and left Marsh's laboratory to become a staff member of the Yale Medical School. He was nine years on the Marsh payroll, during which time he got both an M.D. and a Ph.D. He eventually became professor of geology at the universities of Kansas and Chicago.

When Marsh became vertebrate paleontologist for the federal government in 1882, he got funds to expand his laboratory. Remembering the Prussian laboratories of his student days in Europe, where a single professor ruled as undisputed autocrat over assistants who loved to be subservient to capricious and arbitrary authority, Marsh imported three laboratory assistants from Germany—Max Schlosser, Otto Meyer, and Georg Baur. Marsh bungled the job. Two of the three left him soon after their arrival, and the other, Georg Baur, was a monumentally bad choice for an assistant, since he came from a long line of aristocratic German professors.

Baur negotiated an agreement with Marsh to be allowed to publish under his own name, and during the six years he was at Yale published seventy-five papers. The only hold that Marsh had over him was to keep him in a state of carefully modulated poverty. Like a coal miner in a company town, Baur was continually in debt to his employer, and it took a good deal of maneuvering for him to get clear of Marsh and find another job. One of his final publications based on his experiences in the Yale laboratory was an exposé of Marsh published in the *American Naturalist*. Convinced of his own superiority over Marsh, he tore the reputation of his one-time employer to shreds in a paper that is perhaps unique in American scientific literature. Later, while paleontologist at the University of Chicago, Baur's health collapsed. Always unstable, he became insane and died in a German asylum at the age of forty-four.

To join this love feast there came, in the mid-1880s, Edward Drinker Cope. He lurked about the laboratory at New Haven, taking the assistants aside for confidential chats, and trying to get a look at the fossils that Marsh was working on, to the point where Marsh had to forbid visitors access to the laboratory. Cope wrote his wife that "I want to stop over a day in New Haven and see Dr. Baur"; to Osborn that "I spent a day at New Haven, recently, with Baur and Williston"; and he consorted with Baur at scientific meetings.

By 1885 Cope had made good progress in bringing disaffection in the Marsh laboratory to a head. He was particularly concerned about the problem of getting Baur out of hock, and wrote to Osborn:

> The 4 men at Yale are anxious to publish in both Europe and America their statement, and I naturally am willing that they should. There is however one difficulty. Dr. Baur who is as important as any of the four & furnishes a good deal of the backbone, is in Marsh's debt some $650 and he can do nothing till that is paid as he is a married man. I want to find someone to lend him the money or part of it, because if it is paid out of his wages, he cannot pay it till next April, which will be too late for the paper to be of any service in the investigation. Although I am entirely impecunious, I have taken upon me to try & raise $200 of this amount.

Cope asked Osborn to contribute some money, pointing out that "The publication of the paper will be a blessing to American Science generally, for the demoralizing effect of Marsh's success is incalculable. . . . He has completely suppressed my work." Cope sums up the results of his researches into the operation of Marsh's laboratory by saying that Marsh is "more of a pretender than even I had supposed him to be. . . . It is now clear to me that Marsh is simply a scientific-political adventurer who has succeeded, in ways other than those proceeding from scientific merit, in placing himself in the leading scientific position in the country." The modern scientist will recognize this as a rather judicious portrait of some of his own scientific competitors.

Probably Cope made use of the material from his scientific espionage when he circularized Congress with the scandal sheet on Marsh and Powell in 1887, but it did not come to the surface until the winter of 1889–90. That fall Cope got a small foothold in the domain of security with an appointment as professor of geology and mineralogy at the University of Pennsylvania. However, this gave him little more than a bare living—there was little for field work, research, and publication in the style to which he was accustomed.

The only large financial asset remaining, after he had sold his mining stocks for what they would bring, was his collection of fossils, into which he had poured nearly $80,000 of his own money, besides increasing their value with years of work getting them into the literature, and making types of many of them. As he wrote his wife, "My entire future in a financial sense . . . depends on that collection so far as I can see now."

Cope was stunned to receive, in December of 1889, a demand from the Secretary of the Interior, John W. Noble, that he turn over to the United States National Museum (and thus to Marsh) his entire collection of vertebrate fossils from the Tertiary and Cretaceous formations of the West, on the grounds that they were government property, since Cope had been a member of the Hayden Survey. The Secretary acted on the recommendation of Powell, who doubtless was egged on by Marsh. Powell was fully aware of the way in which Cope built up his collection, and of the fact that Cope had been an unpaid "volunteer" for the Survey. The move was pure malice, perhaps made with the knowledge that Cope would be able to defend himself against the manifestly unfair claim, but only after providing a good deal of fun for his tormentors.

Cope reacted promptly, although the revenge he exacted may have been something short of what he first had in mind, since he wrote to Osborn, "When a wrong is to be righted, the press is the best and most Christian medium of doing it. It replaces the old time shot gun & bludgeon & is a great improvement." Cope decided to give the scandalous information he had accumulated about Marsh and about Powell's Survey over the past twenty-eight years to the press. He had for all this time kept a drawer of what he called "Marshiana"; and since Marsh immediately produced a return barrage of equally slanderous tales about Cope, Marsh must have kept ready for use a store of "Copeiana," most likely kept locked in a steel safe.

The instrument for Cope's revenge was to be a young journalist for the New York *Herald* named William Hosea Ballou, whom he had known for several years. When Cope laid out his project before Ballou, the journalist must have thought the squabble had great possibilities for publicity, since Marsh was well known, and criticizing the Powell Survey was always good copy. When he saw Cope's article, he must also have seen that the attack was very ill advised, since Cope took on too many people at once: Marsh, a majority of the National Academy of Sciences, and the entire United States Geological Survey. But he apparently did nothing to dissuade Cope, and before publication took the article to both Marsh and Powell in the hopes of setting a lively dispute going from the very beginning.

Cope's article appeared January 12, 1890, prefaced by a fake interview scene contrived by Ballou.

I saw Professor Cope at his residence, No. 2102 Pine Street, Philadelphia, a few days ago. He was engaged in making new species of new fossil animals but he cheerfully put aside his work when the nature of my call was made known to him. He is a man not over forty-five years of age and of distinguished appearance.

"What is the origin, Professor, of this war against the Geological Survey?" I asked.

"It may be found in the outrageous order I have received from the Secretary of the Interior to turn over my collections to the National Museum at Washington. I have not more than a bushel of specimens belonging to the government and to those it is welcome. The fact is, I sent out my own collecting parties and secured my collection at an expense of about $80,000 of my own money, to say nothing of the value of all the time I have expended upon them."

"Who is the author of the order?"

"Why to be sure, who but Major Powell. The object of this absurd order to place my collections in the National Museum is to gain control of them, so that my work may be postponed until it has been done by Professor Marsh of Yale College, and this in spite of the fact that the preliminary work has been already published by me, and that the truth is sure to come out at some future time."

In the article Cope recited an extract from his long list of Marsh's technical errors, such as calling a dinosaur bone a buffalo horn, along with more serious but more esoteric errors which could not have much impressed the lay reader. He pointed out mistakes made by the amateur and self-taught geologist Powell. He accused Powell of packing the Academy with supporters of the Survey, and of buying influence by hiring Congressmen's sons and college professors in the Survey. He claimed that Marsh's scientific writings were stolen from other authors without acknowledgment, and those not stolen were written by his hired assistants. Cope then presented some of the testimony gathered from Marsh's employees. Among them was a letter written to him by Williston in 1886, which he had then predicted would cause "great execution" when used at the proper time.

I wait with patience the light that will surely be shed over Professor Marsh and his work. Is it possible for a man whom all his colleagues call a liar to retain a general reputation for veracity! . . . I do not worry about his ultimate position in science. He will find his level, possibly fall below it. There is one thing I have always felt was a burning disgrace—that such a man should be chosen to the highest position in science as the president of the National Academy of Science while men of the deepest erudition and unspotted reputation are passed by unnoticed. Professor Marsh did once indirectly request me to destroy Kansas fossils rather than let them fall into your hands. It is necessary for me to say that I only despised him for it.

The assertion of Professor Marsh that he devotes his entire time to the preparation of his reports is so supremely absurd, or rather so supremely untrue, that it can only produce an audible smile from his most devoted admirers. I have known him intimately for ten years. During most of the time while in his employ I never knew him to do two consecutive, honest days' work in science, nor am I exaggerating when I say that he has not averaged more than one hour's work per day. He is absent from the Museum fully half of the time, and when in New Haven he rarely appears at the museum till two o'clock or later and stays but an hour or two, devoting his time chiefly to the most absurd details and old maid crotchets. The larger part of the papers published since my connection with him in 1878 have been either the work or the actual language of his assistants. At least I can positively assert that papers have been published on Dinosaurs which were chiefly written by me. . . .

Professor Marsh's reputation for veracity among his colleagues is very slight. In fact he has none. . . . Those who know him best say—and I concur in the opinion—that he has never been known to tell the truth when a falsehood would serve the purpose as well. Those are strong statements to make of one holding such a position as he does, but I state them the more freely from the fact that everybody here [Yale College] concurs in them. He has no friends here save those who do not know him well.

When Marsh saw the advance copy of the newspaper article, he confronted Williston, and extracted from him a modified disclaimer, which only allowed that it was published without Williston's permission, not that the statement was false. As the newspaper said, "Next Professor Williston was mysteriously moved and wrote to the *Herald* that his letters concerning Professor Marsh were mostly written some years ago, under exasperating circumstances, before he had become connected with Yale College" [as a professor of anatomy].

Georg Baur also took part in the onslaught. Cope published a series of articles by Marsh's assistants in the *American Naturalist,* which were then bound into a pamphlet designed to serve as a companion volume to the newspaper articles. Baur's contribution was published in March, and gave an overview of the whole dispute, being entitled "A review of the charges against the paleontological department of the U.S. Geological Survey, and of the defense made by Prof. O. C. Marsh." Following is an excerpt.

I will now give a short review of the charges made against Professor Marsh, and of his defence, based on an experience of nearly six years, during which I was an assistant of Prof. Marsh, paid by the U.S. Geological Survey.

1. In the New York *Herald* of January 12th, Prof. E. D. Cope, of the University of Pennsylvania, stated, "The collections made by Prof. Marsh, as the vertebrate paleontologist of the Geological Survey. . . . are all stored at Yale College, with no assured record as to what belongs to the Government and what to the college."

To this Professor Marsh replied that "every specimen belonging to the government is kept by itself, and no mixing with the Yale Museum collections is possible." Prof. H. F. Osborn and Dr. O. Meyer have sustained this fully, and I am glad to say that great care is taken at the Yale Museum in this regard. But this is irrelevant to the question raised by

Prof. Cope, for, of course, the labeling is entirely in the hands of Prof. Marsh, without any control from the Geological Survey. In this connection there is one thing that I can not quite understand; how it is that the splendid specimens of horned dinosaurs became the property of Prof. Marsh, and not of the government. Can Prof. Marsh pay his collectors this month out of his own pocket, and the following out of the pocket of the government?

2. The next statement made in the *Herald* is, that these collections "are locked away from the people, and no one is allowed to see them, not even visiting scientists." This Prof. Marsh admits is in part true.

He says, that "visiting scientists of good moral character are always welcome." Now I may mention, that a scientist of "good moral character," well known in this country and in Europe, wanted to see the material of the Dinocerata shortly after the volume on this order had been published. When he arrived at New Haven he was told by Prof. Marsh that he was sorry not to be able to show him the material, since it had been boxed up lately and was inaccessible. The fact is, that the whole material was spread on a large table in the room where the conversation took place. By the order of the professor the fossils had been covered up with cloth the day before.

To the dispute as to how much Marsh relied on the work of his assistants, Baur addressed these comments:

The fact is that a great part of the descriptive and general part of most of Prof. Marsh's papers is the work of his assistants. Prof. Marsh asks them questions, the answers of which he either immediately puts down in black and white, or he makes out a list of questions to be worked out by his assistants, for instance: "What are the principal characters of the skull of the Sauropoda?" or, "What are the relations between the different groups of Dinosaurs?" and so on. The assistant, if not yet fully familiar with these questions, begins to work; he goes over the whole literature, a thing rarely done by the Professor, and studies the specimens in the collection. After this is done, the Professor receives the notes of the assistant, or he asks questions, writing down the answers he receives. In this way he accumulates a great quantity of notes, written in his own handwriting, or in that of the assistant. By comparing and using these notes it is easy for him to dictate a paper to any person who can write. This person, of course, when asked, can testify that the work was dictated by Prof. Marsh, without telling a falsehood.

Baur gave a vivid picture of the master at work on really important questions. Marsh had finished the main body of the work on the Dinocerata monograph, and wanted to write a conclusion that placed the whole subject in perspective. He invited Baur to his home on a Sunday for a conference. After various pointed questions, which settled some important matters, Marsh asked him how the ungulates, the group to which the Dinocerata belonged, were to be classified. Baur gave him a classification that had been proposed by Cope. It became clear that Marsh had never taken the trouble to read Cope's paper, but was happy enough to use the classification, without credit, although he changed Cope's names to those of his own liking.

The primary function of a scientific leader like Marsh is to exercise sound judgment as to where to borrow from others (and whether or not to acknowledge it); that is, he has to know how to recognize a good idea, rather than create it. The creation of ideas is generally left to the solitary thinker. Scholarly brooding is utterly foreign to the scientific entrepreneur, who has to move quickly and aggressively in order to prosper in the scientific market place. Marsh's sound judgment on scientific matters was his most valuable trait.

Baur described a pathetic scene in the Marsh laboratory. Marsh had written a laudatory review of his own book on the Dinocerata and asked Harger, then Williston, to sign it. Both refused, and Marsh had to be content with the initials of the "lady typewriter."

Marsh and Powell were given space in the January 12 issue of the *Herald* to make a preliminary counterattack, then Marsh let loose the full barrage a week later, taking up an entire page of the newspaper. He began:

> The author of the recent attack upon me and my work is Professor E. D. Cope, and he has at last placed publicly on record the slanders he has secretly been repeating for years. Whether he makes the statements directly or conceals them in the form of an interview with himself or others they are his own. He has devoted some of his best years to its preparation and to the preparation of the public for it, and it may thus be regarded as the crowning work of his life.

Now was the chance for Marsh to publish what must have been one of his favorite stories, here given a headline by Ballou.

WRONG END FOREMOST

Professor Cope had described an extinct reptile from the cretaceous of Kansas, under the name *Elasmosaurus,* and his published description made this the most remarkable animal of ancient or modern times. Besides his original description, he had read a paper on the subject before the American Association, in which he explained the marvelous creature. In a communication published by the Boston

256

Society of Natural History in 1869, he placed it in a new order, *Streptosauria*. In the *American Naturalist* he gave a restoration of the animal, represented as alive. This was afterward copied in *Appleton's Cyclopedia*. Finally, an extensive description was published in the *Transactions of the American Philosophical Society*, Vol. XIV, in which a full restoration of this wonderful creation was given.

The skeleton itself was arranged in the Museum of the Philadelphia Academy of Natural Sciences, according to this restoration, and when Professor Cope showed it to me and explained its peculiarities I noticed that the articulations of the vertebrae were reversed and suggested to him gently that he had the whole thing wrong end foremost. His indignation was very great, and he asserted in strong language that he had studied the animal for many months and ought at least to know one end from the other.

It seems he did not, for Professor Leidy in his quiet way took the last vertebrae of the tail, as Cope had placed it, and found it to be the atlas and axis, with the occipital condyle of the skull in position. This single observation of America's most distinguished comparative anatomist, whom Cope has wronged grievously in name and fame, was a demonstration that could not be questioned, and when I informed Professor Cope of it his wounded vanity received a shock from which it has never recovered, and he has since been my bitter enemy. Professor Cope had actually placed the head on the end of the tail in all his restorations, but now his new order was not only extinct, but extinguished.

Actually, Cope had turned *Elasmosaurus* right end to twenty years before, in the *Transactions of the American Philosophical Society*, where he wrote,

The determination of the extremities of this species was rendered difficult from the fact that Leidy in his descriptions of Cimoliasaurus, reverses the relations of the vertebrae, viewing the cervicals as caudals and lumbars, and describing the caudals as belonging to another genus. Not suspecting this error, I arranged the skeleton of *Elasmosaurus* with the same relation of the extremities, and the more willingly as the distal cervicals present an extraordinary attenuation, even for this type, and also as the discoverer assured me that the fragments of the cranium were found at the extremity which is properly caudal. Viewed in this light many details of the structure were the reverse of those ordinarily observed among reptiles, whence I was induced to consider it as the type of a peculiar group of high rank. This view is, of course, abandoned on a correct interpretation of the extremities. Leidy detected the error in this arrangement, and the correction extends to Cimoliasaurus as well.

Cope had charged that Marsh's fame as the discoverer of the true evolution of the horse was won by plagiarizing from himself and Kovalevsky, the brilliant Russian paleontologist. Marsh countered with the observation that Kovalevsky was best known for being as great a thief of other people's specimens as Cope, and that "Kovalevsky was at last stricken with remorse and ended his unfortunate career by blowing out his own brains. Cope still lives, unrepentant."

Powell, like Marsh replied with carefully measured prose, and offered this free analysis of Cope's character:

I am not willing to be betrayed into any statement which will do injustice to Professor Cope. He is the only one of the coterie who has scientific standing. The others are simply his tools and act on his inspiration. The Professor himself has done much valuable work for science. He has made great collections in the field and has described these collections with skill. Altogether he is a fair systematist. If his infirmities of character could be corrected by advancing age, if he could be made to realize that the enemy which he sees forever haunting him as a ghost is himself . . . he could yet do great work for science.

The controversy went on through several editions of the *Herald,* with most of the gunfire coming from the Marsh–Powell camp. Cope tried to wind up the affair with

The recklessness of assertion, the erroneousness of statement and the incapacity of comprehending our relative positions on the part of Professor Marsh render further discussion of the trivial matters upon which we disagree unnecessary, and my time is too fully occupied on more important subjects to permit me to waste it upon personal affairs which are already sufficiently before the public. Professor Marsh has recorded his views *aere perennius,* and may continue to do so without personal notice by E. D. Cope.

Marsh had the final say, with a comment to the effect that like the boy who twisted the mule's tail, Cope now looked worse but knew more. However, the public image that Marsh had fashioned for himself also was considerably less handsome than when it had emerged from the hands of its creator.

While the newspaper war was going on, Marsh tried to get at Cope through the provost of the University of Pennsylvania, where Cope held his new professorship (Cope said that the administration tried to fire him.) The provost was at the time involved in a case of blackmail that had been successfully kept from the public. The paleontologist W. B. Scott in his memoirs writes that "Marsh wrote to the Provost, demanding that he silence Cope, on pain of having his own scandals aired. The *Herald*, getting wind of this, let the Provost know that he would have cause to regret any attempt to interfere with Cope's freedom of speech."

The year 1890 was a drought year, and Congress brought pressure on the Geological Survey to produce immediately plans for reservoirs and irrigation projects. Powell, however, thought that more basic research had to be done, and in spite of the unfavorable publicity brought the Survey by Cope's newspaper campaign, successfully warded off attacks that were designed to fragment the Survey and get the scientific jurisdiction of the public domain out of his hands. Then in 1892 came a financial recession, and the public clamor for the mythical homestead sites that were supposed to exist in the arid West brought renewed pressure to open these lands, and this time Marsh proved to be the weak link in Powell's armor.

In 1892 a Congressman from Alabama, Hilary A. Herbert, who had a perfect record for voting against every bill designed to protect the public domain, proposed in Congress that the funds for paleontology be cut from the appropriation to the United States Geological Survey. He had been influenced by conversations with Professor Alexander Agassiz of Harvard (son of Louis Agassiz, founder of the Harvard Museum of Comparative Zoology), who besides being a scholar was a wealthy mining engineer with holdings in railways and copper mines. Agassiz thought that the federal government should have nothing to do with basic research in such scholarly subjects as paleontology, that this could be left to private funding and to college professors who would do research for nothing to enhance their own prestige.

Agassiz gave Herbert plenty of ammunition for his attack on Powell, and also in some way Herbert became aware of Marsh's huge, elegant, tinted-paper, gilt-edged monograph on Odontornithes, the toothed birds, which had been published as a report of the King Survey of the 40th parallel, and brought it before Congress. Ignoring the fact (which had been made known to Herbert) that Marsh had paid for printing the deluxe volume with his own money, and had paid for the collecting and research that went into it, Herbert made "birds with teeth" into a catchword for a war on what was called the waste of government funds in research.

The strange alliance of Cope, reactionary Congressmen, and Professor Agassiz made Congress again go through the gamut of charges against Marsh and Powell that Cope had been making for the past ten years. This time Congress was able to move quickly and with effect. It was Marsh's turn to be stunned with bad news from Washington. On July 20, 1892, he got a telegram from Powell which read "Appropriation cut off. Please send your resignation at once."

# 21

# AFTER THE BATTLE

T HE LOSS OF HIS lucrative post with the United States Geological Survey, held for ten years, was only the beginning of the troubles that beset Marsh during the last years of his life. With the economic recession of the early 1890s, income from the Peabody fortune began to dry up, and Marsh had to mortgage his luxurious home, with its greenhouse full of rare orchids. He had to ask for, and was given, a salary for his professorship at Yale.

During the 1890s Marsh continued publication on his paleontological research, taking advantage of his superb collection to make complete restorations of dinosaurs, which he described in a number of separate papers. He brought much of this together in one of his major works, published in 1896, when he was sixty-five years old—the *Dinosaurs of North America,* with over 100 pages of text and 84 large lithograph plates. He introduces the work with the paragraph,

Among the many extinct animals that lived in the country in past ages, none were more remarkable than the dinosaurian reptiles which were so abundant during Mesozoic times. This group was then represented by many and various forms, including among them the largest land animals known, and some, also, very diminutive. In shape and structure, however, they showed great variety, and in many other respects they were among the most wonderful creatures yet discovered.

One of Marsh's friends has remarked on the pleasure with which Marsh each day began his work at the laboratory, and his success in imparting his enthusiasm to those about him. During the 1870s, when he began his explorations for western fossils, he was completely absorbed in his scientific work. In later years, administrative work and wider social interests took most of his attention, but even toward the end of his life he worked happily on his fossils.

Marsh even managed, in his sixties, to gather the money and energy to pursue another of his gargantuan collecting enterprises. To match his collection of Jurassic dinosaurs, he decided to make a collection of the trees of the Jurassic. The characteristic trees of this time were the cycads, primitive links between the tree ferns and seed plants, of which a few still live in the warmer parts of the world. Before Marsh's time these had been known mainly from fragmentary specimens. He learned of whole trees preserved in the rocks of the Black Hills of South Dakota, and set about getting every fossil in sight, eventually building up a collection weighing many tons which was by far the best in the world.

A letter to a friend written in 1897 from an international scientific congress in Moscow shows a literate and humorous, although perhaps somewhat cynical, Marsh:

The Russians, of course, were most numerous, but the Americans . . . were not far behind. From James Hall (86) who took in the Ural excursion and everything else, Banquets, Balls etc., without injury, to one small boy (80 years younger at least) and various forlorn damsels of forbidding aspect and uncertain age, America was amply if not wisely represented. You will soon get the particulars of it all, but I will not risk spoiling the story by trying to condense it here. Some of it will not soon be forgotten.

Emmons was my companion du voyage, but has left for Mt. Ararat. I wanted to go, hoping to find a bone or two from Noah's menagerie, but I have some that Noah never saw, awaiting me at New Haven, and I must hurry back.

In 1897 Marsh received the highest award that can be given a paleontologist, the Cuvier Prize, which is awarded once every three years.

Ten years spent working for the United States Geological Survey had produced a large hoard of fossil bones that belonged to the government, and when Marsh became ill in 1898 with an arterial disease, one of his first priorities in winding up his affairs was to organize his records so that the transfer of these specimens to Washington could be made. He had already sent several lots of these to Washington, and a month after his death in 1899, the rest were assembled by a representative from the government and one of Marsh's assistants, Hugh Gibb. Marsh had already sent over thirty tons, and the final lot weighed eighty tons and filled five freight cars. The monetary value of the collections was put at $200,000. It contained type specimens of 53 species. Since Marsh had described about 496 new species, something over 400 types must have remained at Yale. However, it should be remembered that Marsh was very

Cope in the "museum" in the frame house at 2102 Pine Street, Philadelphia. (Courtesy of the American Museum of Natural History)

active in describing new species before he became associated with the federal Survey.

In the deed of gift of his estate to Yale University, Marsh thus describes his personal collection of vertebrate fossils that went to Yale:

This is the most important and valuable of all, as it is very extensive, contains a very large number of type specimens, many of them unique, and is widely known from the descriptions already published. In extinct Mammals, Birds and Reptiles, of North America, this series stands preeminent.

This collection was pronounced by Huxley, who examined it with care in 1876, to be surpassed by no other in the world. Darwin, in 1878, expressed a strong desire to visit America for the sole purpose of seeing this collection. Since then it has been more than doubled in size and value, and still holds first rank. The bulk of this collection has been secured in my western explorations, which have extended over a period of nearly thirty years, during which I have crossed the Rocky Mountains twenty-seven times.

Besides this collection, and several other specialized collections relating to paleontology, there was a

*Collection of American Archaeology and Ethnology.* This collection is the best in the country in several branches of the science, being particularly rich in Central American antiquities, several thousand specimens in number and many of them unique. Some of these I obtained myself in Central America, and among the others is the famous de Zeltner collection, rich in gold ornaments, which I secured by purchase. The specimens from Mexico are also of great interest, and the series is a representative one. It includes the well-known Skilton collection.

In a cold February rain in 1899 Marsh walked from the New Haven railway station to his home. After coming to his office for a few days, he admitted to being desperately ill, and died at home of pneumonia.

Cope in 1889 began a successful though low-key career as a university teacher. His lectures, spiced with a diversity of personal experiences, were popular. He published syllabi of his courses, one becoming a textbook of paleontology, another of geology. He produced a steady stream of technical papers, mainly but by no means exclusively of a kind that summarized and generalized. Two were classic works on living animals— "The Batrachia of North America" and "The Crocodilians, Lizards, and Snakes of North America" (the last published posthumously).

In 1892, the fifty-two-year-old Cope got expense money for field work from the Texas Geological Survey, and happily set about making preparations for another trip to the West. He wrote to his wife, "I made a great haul in the lower trunk in the closet, under the stairs. I found saddle bags, canteen, fish net, gum blanket no. 2, shoes, and a good coat, which I took along."

He spent six weeks in northwest Texas, prospecting the Permian redbeds with little result, but getting a rich haul of Pleistocene mastodons, camels, horses, and sloths from the Mount Blanco region. He writes of the field with the same joyousness of his first expeditions to the West thirty years before: "The country is a perfect flower garden. I never saw such a variety of beautiful flowers." He is even tolerant of the small, hotly stinging sweat bee, "the 'shirt bee' as I call it from the place where it tries to stay; and makes a great fuss if your shirt is too tight." The insects were mad for water: "Two beautiful moths came to my mouth for a drink last evening and another has just now quenched his thirst in the same way." The mockingbirds that crowd into the scant forests along the watercourses for nesting sites sang, in the manner of mockingbirds, both day and night.

267

On the way back East, Cope stopped off at the Sioux Reservation in South Dakota for a dinosaur-hunting trip into the Cretaceous rocks along the northern boundary of the state. With team and wagon, he made his way north into the valley of the Moreau River. Led on by stories from the Indians that bones of giants lay strewn over the ground, he crossed over the divide of Grand River, driving through flower-spangled grass over high plains. As evening approached, they saw on the horizon the long, low hill where the giants lay. "At the hill were numerous bones of giants nearly entire; one could hardly walk without stepping on them. . . . So it was all around . . . bones everywhere." A terrific lightning storm blazed around them, lighting up the gloom and giving credence to the belief of the Indians that the hill was the tomb of giants killed by lightning bolts. In the flickering light Cope saw a yard-long skull of a dinosaur sticking out of the ground. He went to bed in the darkness "to dream of dinosaurs," and was up at 4:30 to walk alone through the wet grass and dig up the skull in the light of dawn.

Cope made his last fossil-hunting expedition to the West in 1894, hunting dinosaurs in South Dakota and seeing the geological sights in Texas and Oklahoma. That year his beloved daughter Julia was married, at the age of twenty-eight. Perhaps because of the need for money, in 1895 he sold his collections to the American Museum of Natural History in New York. The collection of American fossil mammals was sold as a unit for approximately $32,000. It contained 10,000 specimens in 463 species, most of them represented by type specimens. Three other collections—of North American fishes, amphibians, and reptiles, of the Pampean fossils, and of European fossils—brought nearly $29,000 for the 3,245 specimens. Impressive as it was the Cope collection was only a fraction as large as the private collection of Marsh, which was valued at well over a million dollars.

During 1896 Cope became trapped in his final illness, which he called cystitis, and was stricken with periods of agonizing pain alternating with periods of enforced rest. His wife was also ill, and they were often separated. His secretary at the university, Anna Brown, helped care for him. "If thee can not stand or walk much Miss Brown can get what is necessary," he writes his wife, and to his sister, "Annie [his wife] was with me parts of two days but she fell sick and had to go to bed."

Since he had sold his home during the financial storm of the 1880s, he lived in his museum at 2102 Pine, and spent his illness on a cot surrounded by piles of bones. Although he had a doctor, he also prescribed for himself, taking what he called "enormous" amounts of morphia, belladonna, and finally, to the horror of his friend Osborn, took formalin. Osborn made arrangements for surgery, which was the only thing that could save Cope. But according to W. B. Scott, just before the operation was to take place there was a temporary improvement in Cope's health, and he went off to Virginia on a "wild goose chase" after fossils, became desperately ill, and came home to die. Six men sat quietly around his coffin at his Quaker funeral, amidst the fossil bones, with a pet live tortoise and Gila monster moving steathily about the room.

After the time of Cope and Marsh, the fraternity of bone hunters increased, but not mightily, and today they are a decided minority among the paleontologists. Their work concerns mainly the theoretical aspects of both biology and geology. While other paleontologists have these interests, some of them are more directly concerned with applied science, especially oil geology. The paleontologists working with the microscopic shelled animals of marine deposits, and with plant spores and pollen grains, flourish by the thousands. These microscopic shells and pollen grains survive the crushing by the drills that

269

Marsh (center) at a garden party somewhere
in Europe, 1897. (U.S. Geological Survey,
portrait 406)

dig wells, and so are indispensable for oil exploration. Yet it is
the impractical dreamers who make the greatest impact on
human life; the material-minded at best provide the leisure
and shelter for the enjoyment of the fragile stuff of dreams.

Many millions of people each year see the dinosaur skeletons
that are to be found in the largest museums, and I have seen a
grown person spend a half hour or more musing over a huge
*Diplodocus,* her imagination obviously deeply stirred by the attempt to make a mental image of this creature in life. It is said

that the discovery of the dinosaur fields in the West, and the availability of large numbers of skeletons, completely revolutionized both the construction and philosophy of museums. At the Denver Museum of Natural History, the acquisition of a large *Diplodocus* skeleton in 1938 is supposed to have nearly tripled museum attendance, from about 300,000 a year to 800,000 a year and more.

An evaluation of the social roles of such complex and vivid personalities as Cope and Marsh, who have been the subject of a certain amount of censure, is probably both impossible and unnecessary, yet it is difficult to withold comment.

Some years ago a psychiatrist undertook a study of life on shipboard, in this instance on whaling ships with all-male crews that operated for long periods of time at sea. As a preliminary, he browsed around among groups of marine biologists, to get background on whales. He was astonished to find that a large proportion of the verbal activity of such groups consisted in the destruction of the reputations of absent colleagues (perhaps he had forgotten the behavior of his associates in his own field). Only the unusual person remained aloof from the malicious gossip. This leads to the rather trite observation that scientists are the same as everyone else, most of them requiring this particular kind of mental activity as part of their normal functioning.

At a level above the ordinary garden variety of malicious gossip is genuine rage, which probably is one of the most valuable forces in existence for producing quick, accurate, incisive, and original thinking. Both Cope and Marsh enjoyed the benefits of this emotion to an unusually high degree.

Finally, there is durable, intelligent, well-focused hatred, a long-range creative force as powerful as love. Here Cope and Marsh truly excelled. Even though dragging fantastic loads of what are generally called "human frailties," they managed to create on the way a new understanding of the earth and its life. No higher human achievement is possible.

# BIBLIOGRAPHY

GENERAL

Bartlett, Richard A. *Great Surveys of the American West.* Norman, University of Oklahoma Press, 1962.

Cope, E. D. "Vertebrata of the Tertiary Formations of the West," *Report of the U.S. Geological Survey of the Territories,* Vol. 3 (1884). (Often referred to as "Cope's Bible.")

Darrah, William Culp. *Powell of the Colorado.* Princeton, Princeton University Press, 1951.

Dupree, A. H. *Science in the Federal Government: A History of Policies and Activities to 1940.* Cambridge, Harvard University Press, 1957.

Goetzmann, William H. *Army Exploration in the American West 1803–1863.* New Haven, Yale University Press, 1959; re-issued in softback.

Hay, Oliver Perry. "Bibliography and Catalogue of the Fossil Vertebrates of North America," *Bulletin of the United States Geological Survey,* No. 179. (This is the most valuable single reference for the scholar who wants to trace out in detail the scientific work of Cope and Marsh as it relates to paleontology.)

Merrill, George P. *The First One Hundred Years of American Geology.* New Haven, Yale University Press, 1924.

Osborn, Henry Fairfield. *The Age of Mammals.* New York, Scribners, 1910.

—— *Cope: Master Naturalist.* Princeton, Princeton University Press, 1931

273

(copyrighted by Henry Fairfield Osborn). (This excellent book, the major source for published information on Cope, is now out of print. It contains hundreds of letters written by Cope, which are now in the collections of the American Museum of Natural History. The longer extracts of this correspondence reproduced by permission of Princeton University Press.)

Plate, Robert. *The Dinosaur Hunters: Othniel C. Marsh and Edward D. Cope.* New York, McKay, 1964. (A well-written "action" story, primarily for younger readers.)

Reingold, Nathan. *Science in Nineteenth-century America. A Documentary History.* New York, Hill and Wang, 1964. (Contains excellent editorial introductions to fresh collections of documents.)

Romer, Alfred Sherwood. *Vertebrate Paleontology.* 3d ed. Chicago, University of Chicago Press, 1966.

—— *Notes and comments on Vertebrate Paleontology.* Chicago, University of Chicago Press, 1968.

Schuchert, Charles and Clara Mae LeVene. *O. C. Marsh: Pioneer in Paleontology.* New Haven, Yale University Press, 1940. (This primary reference for Marsh, well-written and well-organized, is unfortunately out of print.)

Scott, William Berryman. *Some Memories of a Paleontologist.* Princeton, Princeton Univeristy Press, 1939.

Stegner, Wallace. *Beyond the Hundredth Meridian.* Sentry Edition. Cambridge, Houghton, 1962.

Sternberg, Charles H. *The Life of a Fossil Hunter.* New York, H. Holt, 1906.

Wallace, E. S. *The Great Reconnaissance: Soldiers, Artists, and Scientists on the Frontier 1848-1861.* Boston, Little, Brown, 1955.

1. SCIENTIST IN THE WHITE HOUSE

Bakeless, John. *Lewis and Clark: Partners in Discovery.* New York, Morrow, 1947.

Bryant, William Cullen. *The Embargo.* Facsimile reproductions of the editions of 1808 and 1809, with an introduction and notes by Thomas O. Mabbott. Gainesville, Scholars, 1955. (This is the poem in which Jefferson's paleontological activities are described by the young Bryant.)

Dos Passos, John. *The Head and Heart of Thomas Jefferson.* Garden City, Doubleday, 1954.

Moore, Thomas. [Epistle] To Thomas Hume, Esq., M.D., from the City of Washington. In *Letters of Thos. Moore,* W. S. Dowden, ed. Oxford, Oxford University Press, 1964. (This poem was undoubtedly the model for Bryant's *The Embargo.* Moore's "Epistles" from Washington give a vivid, if biased, view of the capital and of Jefferson in the early 1800s.)

Osborn, Henry Fairfield. "Thomas Jefferson as a Paleontologist," *Science,* Vol. 82 (1935), pp. 533-538.

## 2. ROCKS AND FOSSILS

Gillispie, Charles C. *Genesis and Geology*. Torchbook ed. New York, Harper, 1959.

## 3. JOSEPH LEIDY

Osborn, Henry Fairfield. "Biographical Memoir of Joseph Leidy, 1823–1871," *Biographical Memoirs of the National Academy of Sciences*, Vol. 7 (1898), pp. 335–396.

## 4. THE BIG BADLANDS

Hauk, Joy Keve. "Badlands. Its Life and Landscape," *Bulletin 2, Badlands Natural History Association*. Interior, South Dakota, 1969. (In cooperation with the National Park Service, U.S. Department of the Interior.)

Osborn, Henry Fairfield. *The Age of Mammals*, pp. 204–227. New York, Scribners, 1910.

## 5. THE BONE HUNTERS COME TO THE SIOUX COUNTRY

Camp, Charles L., ed. *James Clyman: American Frontiersman 1792–1881*. Cleveland, 1928.

Owen, David Dale. *Report of a Geological Survey of Wisconsin, Iowa, and Minnesota; and incidentally a portion of Nebraska Territory*. Philadelphia, 1852.

Strucker, Gilbert F. "Hayden in the Badlands," *The American West*, Vol. 4, No. 1 (1967).

Taylor, Emerson G. *Gouverneur Kemble Warren*. Boston, Houghton, 1932.

Warren, G. K. *Preliminary Report of Explorations in Nebraska and Dakota, in the Years 1855–'56–'57*. Washington, 1875.

White, Charles A. "Biographical Memoir of Ferdinand Vandiveer Hayden, 1829–1887," *Biographical Memoirs of the National Academy of Sciences*, Vol. 3 (1894) pp. 395–413.

## 6. OTHNIEL CHARLES MARSH

Schuchert, Charles. "Biographical Memoir of Othniel Charles Marsh, 1831–1899," *Biographical Memoirs of the National Academy of Sciences*, Vol. 20 (1937), pp. 1–78. (Contains little not also in Schuchert and Le-Vene, cited under "General.")

## 7. EDWARD DRINKER COPE

Frazer, Persifor. "Life and Letters of Edward Drinker Cope," *American Geologist*, Vol. 26 (1900), pp. 67–128.

Osborn, Henry Fairfield. "Biographical Memoir of Edward Drinker Cope,

1840–1897," *Biographical Memoirs of the National Academy of Sciences,* Vol. 13 (1930), pp. 127–317. (Mainly valuable for its bibliography of Cope's writings; that in *Cope: Master Naturalist,* cited under "General," is a shambles.)

## 8. THE SMOKY HILL

Reeside, John B., Jr. "Paleoecology of the Cretaceous Seas of the Western Interior of the United States," *Memoir 67 (1957) of the Geological Society of America,* pp. 505–542.
See also Sternberg, cited under "General."

## 9. BIG BONE CHIEF

Betts, Charles. "The Yale College Expedition of 1870," *Harpers New Monthly Magazine,* October 1871, pp. 663–671.
Grinnell, Joseph. "An Old-time Bone Hunt," *Natural History,* Vol. 23 (1923), pp. 329–336.
Marsh's continuing account, in the form of brief dispatches, of his early western expeditions, from 1868 to 1874, may be found in the *American Journal of Science* for these years, indexed under "Marsh."

## 10. IN SEARCH OF THE GREAT SEA SERPENTS

Cope, E. D. "On the Geology and Paleontology of the Cretaceous Strata of Kansas," *Hayden's Fifth Annual Report (1871) of the U.S. Geological Survey of the Territories,* pp. 318–349.
Huxley, Thomas H. "Review of *Cretaceous Reptiles,*" *Geological Magazine,* Vol. 5 (1868), pp. 432–435.

## 11. BRIDGER BASIN

Leidy, Joseph. *The Extinct Mammalian Fauna of Dakota and Nebraska, Including an Account of Some Allied Forms from Other Localities, Together With a Synopsis of the Mammalian Remains of North America.* Philadelphia, 1869. (Gives an account of pre-Marsh activity in the basin.)
—— "Contributions to the Extinct Vertebrate Fauna of the Western Territories," *Report of the U.S. Geological Survey of the Territories,* Vol. 1 (1873). (Includes Leidy's work in the basin.)
Marsh, O. C. "On the Geology of the Eastern Uinta Mountains," *American Journal of Science,* Vol. 101 (1871), pp. 191–198.
—— "Dinocerata: a Monograph of an Extinct Order of Gigantic Mammals," *Monograph of the United States Geological Survey,* Vol. 10 (1896).
Wheeler, Walter H. "The Uintatheres and the Cope-Marsh War," *Science,* Vol. 131 (1960), pp. 1171–1176.

## 12. WEST OF THE JEMEZ

Cope, E. D. "Report Upon the Extinct Vertebrata Obtained in New Mexico by Parties of the Expedition of 1873," *Geographic Survey West of the 100th Meridian*, Vol. 4 (1877).

—— "Synopsis of the Vertebrate Fauna of the Puerco Series," *Transactions of the American Philosophical Society*, Vol. 16 (1888), pp. 208–361.

Lewis, G. Edward. "Fossil Vertebrates and Sedimentary Rocks of the Front Range Foothills," in *Guide to the Geology of Colorado*, Robert J. Weimer and John D. Haun, eds. Denver, Geological Society of America, etc. 1960.

Simpson, G. G. "The Beginning of the Age of Mammals," *Biological Reviews*, Vol. 12 (1937), pp. 1–47.

—— "The Eocene of the San Juan Basin, New Mexico," *American Journal of Science*, Vol. 246 (1948), pp. 363–385.

—— "Hayden, Cope, and the Eocene of New Mexico," *Proceedings of the Academy of Natural Sciences of Philadelphia*, Vol. 103 (1951), pp. 1–21.

## 13. MARSH AS PARTISAN

This account is based mainly on chapter 6 of Schuchert and LeVene's book on Marsh, cited under "General." Sources not used by them are cited in the text.

## 14. THE BEAUTIFUL JUDITH

Cope, E. D. "The Vertebrata of the Cretaceous Formations of the West," *Report of the U.S. Geological Survey of the Territories*, Vol. 2 (1875). (Gives an account of early explorations of the Judith River Badlands. Cope described his Judith River finds in the *Proceedings of the Academy of Natural Sciences of Philadelphia*, in articles in Vol. 28 (1876), pp. 248–261 and 340–359.)

Hayden, F. V. "Geological Sketch of the Estuary and Fresh Water Deposit of the Bad Lands of the Judith, With Some Remarks upon the Surrounding Formations," *Transactions of the American Philosophical Society*, Vol. 11 (1859), pp. 123–138.

## 15. SUPER-DINOSAURS

Colbert, E. H. *Men and Dinosaurs: The Search in the Field and Laboratory.* New York, Dutton, 1968.

Hatcher, J. B. "Osteology of *Haplocanthus*, with description of a new species, and remarks on the probable habits of the Sauropoda and the age and origin of the *Atlantosaurus* beds," *Memoirs of the Carnegie Museum*, Vol. 2 (1903), pp. 1–72. (Gives an account of the Canon City dinosaur beds.)

Marsh, O. C. "The Dinosaurs of North America," *16th Annual Report of the U.S. Geological Survey*, Part I (1896), pp. 133–244.

Ostrum, John H. and John S. McIntosh. *Marsh's Dinosaurs: The Collections From Como Bluff.* New Haven, Yale University Press, 1966.

Shor, Elizabeth Nobel. *Fossils and Flies.* Norman, University of Oklahoma Press, 1971. (A biography of Williston.)

Williston, Samuel W. "American Jurassic Dinosaurs," *Transactions of the Kansas Academy of Science*, Vol. 6 (1878), pp. 42–46.

## 16. "DAWN HORSES" AND BIRDS WITH TEETH

Cope, E. D. "The Systematic Arrangement of the Order Perissodactyla," *Proceedings of the American Philosophical Society*, Vol. 19 (1881), pp. 377–401.

Marsh, O. C. *Introduction and Succession of Vertebrate Life in America.* New Haven, 1877. (Text of an address to the AAAS, August 30, 1877.)

—— "Odontornithes: a Monograph on the Extinct Toothed Birds of North America," *U.S. Geological Exploration of the 40th Parallel*, Vol. 7 (1880).

Simpson, G. G. *Horses.* New York, Oxford University Press, 1951.

Stirton, R. A. "Phylogeny of North American Equidae," *University of California Publications, Bulletin of the Department of Geological Science*, Vol. 25 (1940), pp. 165–198.

## 17. PRINCE OF COLLECTORS: JOHN BELL HATCHER

Hatcher, J. B. "The Ceratops Beds of Converse County," *American Journal of Science*, Vol. 145 (1893), pp. 135–144.

—— "The Ceratopsia. Based on preliminary studies by Othneil Charles Marsh. Edited and completed by Richard S. Lull," *Monograph of the U.S. Geological Survey*, Vol. 49 (1907).

—— "Narrative and Geography," *Princeton University Expeditions to Patagonia 1896–1899.* Vol. 1 (1903).

Schuchert, Charles. "John Bell Hatcher," *American Geologist*, Vol. 35, pp. 131–141.

## 18. THE TRIUMVIRATE: HAYDEN, POWELL, AND KING

Darrah, W. C. *Powell of the Colorado.* Princeton, Princeton University Press, 1951.

King, Clarence. "Systematic Geology," *Report of the U.S. Geological Exploration of the 40th Parallel*, Vol. 1 (1878).

Powell, John Wesley. *Report on the Lands of the Arid Region of the United States. With a More Detailed Account of the Lands of Utah. House Executive Document 73.* Wallace Stegner, ed. Cambridge, Harvard University Press (Belknap), 1962. (Based on the text of the 2d edition, 1879.)

Stegner, Wallace. *Beyond the Hundredth Meridian.* Sentry ed. Cambridge, Houghton, 1962.

White, Charles A. "Biographical Memoir of Ferdinand Vandiveer Hayden, 1829–1887," *Biographical Memoirs of the National Academy of Sciences,* Vol 3 (1894), pp. 395–413.

Wilkins, Thurman. *Clarence King: A Biography.* New York, Macmillan, 1958.

### 19. COPE AS FINANCIER

Based mostly on Osborn's *Cope: Master Naturalist,* cited under "General."

Cope, E. D. "The Silver Lake of Oregon and its Region," *American Naturalist,* Vol. 23 (1889), pp. 970–982. (Not a technical paper, but evidently a popular article written for pay, and illustrated by Cope's own sketches.)

### 20. REVENGE

Baur, G. "A Review of the Charges Against the Paleontological Department of the U.S. Geological Survey, and of the Defence made by Prof. O. C. Marsh," *American Naturalist,* Vol. 24 (1890), pp. 298–304.

Scott, W. B. *Some Memories of a Paleontologist.* Princeton, Princeton University Press, 1939.

See also the Williston biography by Shor, cited with the references for chapter 15. The newspaper publicity appeared in 1890 in the New York *Herald* for January 12, 17, and some subsequent issues. Separate anti-Marsh articles by various associates of Marsh appeared in the professional journal, *American Naturalist,* during the first few months of 1890.

### 21. AFTER THE BATTLE

This account is based on Schuchert's *O. C. Marsh* and Osborn's *Cope,* as cited under "General."

# INDEX

Adams, Henry, 222
Agassiz, Alexander, 260-61
Ameghino, Carlos and Florentino, 210-11
*American Journal of Science,* 112, 234
*American Naturalist,* 234
Antelope Springs (Nebraska), 79-80, 83
*Archaeopteryx,* 193

Badlands National Monument, 27-29
Baldwin, David, 133-37, 172-73, 238
Ballou, William Hosea, 250
Baur, Georg, 247-48, 253-55
Betts, Charles, 81-83, 105, 106
Big Badlands (of the White River), 20-22, 24-34, 38-39, 41, 45, 147
Big Bone Lick (Kentucky), 3, 5

Big Foot (Sioux chief), 45
Birds, origin of, 168, 193
Birds with teeth, 192-96, 261
Bone Cabin Quarry, 184
*Brachiosaurus,* 173
Bridger, Jim, 101
Bridger basin, 101-24
*Brontosaurus,* 173
Brontotheres, 30, 148, 201
Bryant, William Cullen, 6
Buffalo Bill, 81

Canon City dinosaur locality, 172-73
Carlin, W. E., 174, 175, 177, 178-79
Ceratopsians, 204-7, 211
Clark, William, 4-5
Como Bluff dinosaur locality, 80, 174-83

Cope, Edward Drinker, pre-professional life, 60-70; in Smoky Hill Cretaceous badlands, 94-100; in Bridger basin, 110-15, 121-24; with Wheeler Survey, 125-36; anti-Catholicism, 130; in San Juan basin, 131-36; in Judith River Badlands, 156-64; number of species of fossils described, 162; at Haddonfield, 164-65; at Como Bluff, 181; and Patagonian fossils, 210-11; mining venture, 234-38; in Oregon desert, 239; in Little Missouri Badlands, 240; in Mexico, 241; as herpetologist and ichthyologist, 241-42; job hunting, 243-44; Cope-Marsh war, 247-60; professorship at University of Pennsylvania, 249, 267; final field work in Texas and Dakotas, 267-68; disposal of collections, 268; death, 269; portraits, 25, 69

Cope-Marsh newspaper war, 249-53, 256-60

"Cope's Bible," 219, 240

Cuba (New Mexico), 133

Culbertson, T. A., 34

Custer, George A., 148, 156

Cuvier, Georges, 11-13

Cycads, 263

Dakota formation, 166

Darwin, Charles, 186-87, 210

Delano, Columbus, 150, 151-52

Dinocerata (a group composed mainly of the uintatheres), 114-16, 122

Dinosaur National Monument, 176, 180, 184

Dinosaurs, 167-73, 175-84

Duce, James Terry, 212-13

Earth history, chronology, 9-10, 14-16

Endlich, F. M., 245

*Eohippus,* 189

*Equus,* 191

Evans, John, 33-34

Evolution, organic, 186-93

Fauquier, Francis, 2

Formations, geologic, 15-17

Fort Benton, 158-59

Fort Bridger, 102

Fossils, formation of, 29-31

Franklin, Benjamin, 1

Frazer, Persifor, 245

Geographic Survey West of the One Hundredth Meridian (Wheeler Survey), 126, 217-18

Geological and Geographical Survey of the Rocky Mountain Region (Powell Survey), 215-16

Geological Exploration of the Fortieth Parallel (King Survey), 215, 224-25

Geologic and Geographic Survey of the Territories (Hayden Survey), 103-4, 215, 216-17

Geologic surveys, 102-3, 126, 214-15, 217-18

Geologic time table, 15

Geology, science of, 8-17

Grant, Ulysses S., 150, 151

Grinnell, George, 81, 148

Ground sloths, 3, 210, 211

Hall, James, 34

Harger, Oscar, 107, 246

Harney, William S., 35-57

Hatcher, John Bell, 183-84, 197-213

Hayden, Ferdinand Vandiveer, 34-42, 44-46, 216-20, 226-29

Hayden Survey, 103-4, 215, 216-17
Herbert, Hilary, A., 260-61
*Hesperornis*, 193-96
Horses (evolutionary history), 188-92
Huxley, Thomas Henry, on Leidy
    and Cope, 95; on Marsh, 187-89

*Ichthyornis*, 193, 195-96
*Ichthyosaurus*, 93

Jackson, William Henry, 217
Jefferson, Thomas, 1-7
Jemez Mountains, 125-26, 131
John Day Badlands, 85, 165
Judith River Badlands, 154-64;
    Hatcher in area, 203-4

King, Clarence, 222-25, 227-30
King Survey, 215, 224-25
Kovalevsky, Vladimer, 188, 258

Lakes, Arthur, 170-72, 180-81
Lake Valley (New Mexico), 235-36
Lamarck, Jean Baptiste, 11
Lamy (Juan Baptiste?), 130
Lance Creek formation, 205, 207-8
Leidy, Joseph, 13, 18-22, 34, 35, 95;
    in Bridger basin, 110, 114, 115-16
Lesquereux, Leo, 77
Lewis, Meriwether, 4
Lewis and Clark expedition, 4-5
Little Missouri Badlands, 240
Loup Fork River, 81
Lucas, O. W., 172
Lyell, Charles, 8-11

Mammals, primitive, 136-38; early
    evolution, 139-40; ascendency over
    reptiles, 144-45; Jurassic, 175;
    Cretaceous, 207-10

Marsh, Othniel Charles, pre-profes-
    sional life, 47-59; at Antelope
    Springs, 79-80; at Lake Como, 80;
    and tiger salamander, 79; leader of
    student exploring parties to West
    (1870-73), 81-91; mansion at New
    Haven, 86, 262; discovery of giant
    pterodactyl, 84-85; in the Smoky
    Hill, 84-85, 87-88, 90-91; in Bridger
    basin, 104-24; in Big Badlands
    area, 147; and National Academy
    of Sciences, 149-50, 219-20, 225;
    number of species of fossils de-
    scribed, 162; criticism by Hatcher,
    183-84; and Hayden, 219-20; as
    vertebrate paleontologist of U.S.
    Geological Survey, 233-34, 261,
    262; laboratory professional staff,
    245-48; Cope-Marsh war, 247-60;
    disposal of collections, 264-66;
    death, 266; portraits, 54, 270
Mauvaises Terres, *see* Big Badlands
Meek, Fielding Bradford, 45
*Megalonyx*, 3
Mesozoic-Cenozoic boundary, 141-42
Moran, Thomas, 217
Morgan, J. Pierpont, 212
Morgan, Lewis, 245
Morrison dinosaur locality, 170-71
Morrison formation, 166-67
Mosasaurs, 94, 98-99
Mudge, Benjamin, 72, 195

Nacimiento (or Puerco) formation,
    126, 133-37, 138
National Academy of Sciences, 149-
    50, 219-20, 225
Natural selection, 191-92
New Jersey fossil beds, 95
Niobrara formation, 93-100

Nomenclature, science of biological, 113
North, Frank, 81

Odontornithes, 1, 93-95
Ord, E. O. C., 80, 111
Oreodon, 20-21, 31
Osborn, Henry Fairfield, 187, 197-98, 207, 269
Owen, David Dale, 32-33

Pacific Railroad Reports, 215
Paine, Thomas 6
Paleontology, 10, 11-13
Patagonia, 210-13
Periptychus, 128, 139
Phenacodus, 232, 235
Pine Ridge Indian Reservation, 23
Plesiosaurs, 94, 98
Portheus, 100
Powell, John Wesley, 220-22, 225-28, 229, 244-45, 258-59
Powell Survey, 215-16
Prout, Hiram A., 19-20
Pterodactyls, 84-85, 98, 168
Puerco formation (older name for Nacimiento formation), 126, 133-37, 138

"Quarry No. 9," 175, 181, 183

Raynolds, William, 44-45
Red Beds of Texas, 165, 267
Red Cloud (Sioux chief), 149, 150, 152-53
Reed, W. H., 174, 175, 177-79, 181
Reptiles, decline at end of Mesozoic, 93-94, 142

Salamander, tiger, 79
San Ildefonso, 126-27

San Juan Basin, 125-26
San José formation, 126, 132
Saurischians, 169-70
Sauropods, 170, 173
Schurz, Carl, 225
Scott, William Berryman, 197, 210, 259-60
Sea turtles, fossil, 98
Sheridan, Philip, 80
Sherman, William, 80, 221
Silver Lake (Oregon), 239
Sioux Indians, 32-37, 42-44, 45, 148-49, 156
Sioux Territory, 32-46
Small, William, 2-3
Smoky Hill River, 71-77; fossils of Niobrara shales, 93-100; Cope in Smoky Hill Badlands, 94-100; Marsh in Smoky Hill Badlands, 84-85, 87-88, 90-91
Sternberg, Charles H., 72-78; in Judith River Badlands, 156-58, 160-61, 164; visit to Cope, 164-65; in John Day Badlands, 165; in Texas Redbeds, 165; and Hatcher, 198-200; at Silver Lake, 239
Sternberg Quarry, 198-99
"Super-dinosaurs" (sauropods), 170, 173

Table Mountain Badlands (of Denver basin), 141-42
Teleoceras, 198
Titanotheres (brontotheres), 20, 30, 148, 201
Type specimens, 116
Tyrannosaurus, 170

Uinta basin, 105-6
Uinta Mountains, 102, 104, 105
Uintatheres, 114-16, 122

United States Geological Survey, 226, 232-33

Warren, Gouverneur Kemble, 35-37, 39-44
Wasatch formation, 131-32
Washakie basin, 105
Wheeler, George, 126-28, 132, 217-18

Wheeler Survey, 126, 217-18
Williston, Samuel, 90-91, 238, 246, 248; at Como Bluff, 175, 177-78
Wortman, Jacob, 207, 238
Wounded Knee, 45

Yarrow, H. C., 127
Yellowstone Park, 217

A CATALOG OF SELECTED
# DOVER BOOKS
IN ALL FIELDS OF INTEREST

# A CATALOG OF SELECTED DOVER
# BOOKS IN ALL FIELDS OF INTEREST

DRAWINGS OF REMBRANDT, edited by Seymour Slive. Updated Lippmann, Hofstede de Groot edition, with definitive scholarly apparatus. All portraits, biblical sketches, landscapes, nudes. Oriental figures, classical studies, together with selection of work by followers. 550 illustrations. Total of 630pp. 9⅛ × 12¼.
21485-0, 21486-9 Pa., Two-vol. set $29.90

GHOST AND HORROR STORIES OF AMBROSE BIERCE, Ambrose Bierce. 24 tales vividly imagined, strangely prophetic, and decades ahead of their time in technical skill: "The Damned Thing," "An Inhabitant of Carcosa," "The Eyes of the Panther," "Moxon's Master," and 20 more. 199pp. 5⅜ × 8½.  20767-6 Pa. $3.95

ETHICAL WRITINGS OF MAIMONIDES, Maimonides. Most significant ethical works of great medieval sage, newly translated for utmost precision, readability. Laws Concerning Character Traits, Eight Chapters, more. 192pp. 5⅜ × 8½.
24522-5 Pa. $4.50

THE EXPLORATION OF THE COLORADO RIVER AND ITS CANYONS, J. W. Powell. Full text of Powell's 1,000-mile expedition down the fabled Colorado in 1869. Superb account of terrain, geology, vegetation, Indians, famine, mutiny, treacherous rapids, mighty canyons, during exploration of last unknown part of continental U.S. 400pp. 5⅜ × 8½.  20094-9 Pa. $7.95

HISTORY OF PHILOSOPHY, Julián Marías. Clearest one-volume history on the market. Every major philosopher and dozens of others, to Existentialism and later. 505pp. 5⅜ × 8½.  21739-6 Pa. $9.95

ALL ABOUT LIGHTNING, Martin A. Uman. Highly readable non-technical survey of nature and causes of lightning, thunderstorms, ball lightning, St. Elmo's Fire, much more. Illustrated. 192pp. 5⅜ × 8½.  25237-X Pa. $5.95

SAILING ALONE AROUND THE WORLD, Captain Joshua Slocum. First man to sail around the world, alone, in small boat. One of great feats of seamanship told in delightful manner. 67 illustrations. 294pp. 5⅜ × 8½.  20326-3 Pa. $4.95

LETTERS AND NOTES ON THE MANNERS, CUSTOMS AND CONDITIONS OF THE NORTH AMERICAN INDIANS, George Catlin. Classic account of life among Plains Indians: ceremonies, hunt, warfare, etc. 312 plates. 572pp. of text. 6⅛ × 9¼.  22118-0, 22119-9, Pa. Two-vol. set $17.90

ALASKA: The Harriman Expedition, 1899, John Burroughs, John Muir, et al. Informative, engrossing accounts of two-month, 9,000-mile expedition. Native peoples, wildlife, forests, geography, salmon industry, glaciers, more. Profusely illustrated. 240 black-and-white line drawings. 124 black-and-white photographs. 3 maps. Index. 576pp. 5⅜ × 8½.  25109-8 Pa. $11.95

THE BOOK OF BEASTS: Being a Translation from a Latin Bestiary of the Twelfth Century, T. H. White. Wonderful catalog real and fanciful beasts: manticore, griffin, phoenix, amphivius, jaculus, many more. White's witty erudite commentary on scientific, historical aspects. Fascinating glimpse of medieval mind. Illustrated. 296pp. 5⅜ × 8¼. (Available in U.S. only)      24609-4 Pa. $6.95

FRANK LLOYD WRIGHT: ARCHITECTURE AND NATURE With 160 Illustrations, Donald Hoffmann. Profusely illustrated study of influence of nature—especially prairie—on Wright's designs for Fallingwater, Robie House, Guggenheim Museum, other masterpieces. 96pp. 9¼ × 10¾.      25098-9 Pa. $7.95

FRANK LLOYD WRIGHT'S FALLINGWATER, Donald Hoffmann. Wright's famous waterfall house: planning and construction of organic idea. History of site, owners, Wright's personal involvement. Photographs of various stages of building. Preface by Edgar Kaufmann, Jr. 100 illustrations. 112pp. 9¼ × 10.
23671-4 Pa. $8.95

YEARS WITH FRANK LLOYD WRIGHT: Apprentice to Genius, Edgar Tafel. Insightful memoir by a former apprentice presents a revealing portrait of Wright the man, the inspired teacher, the greatest American architect. 372 black-and-white illustrations. Preface. Index. vi + 228pp. 8¼ × 11.      24801-1 Pa. $10.95

THE STORY OF KING ARTHUR AND HIS KNIGHTS, Howard Pyle. Enchanting version of King Arthur fable has delighted generations with imaginative narratives of exciting adventures and unforgettable illustrations by the author. 41 illustrations. xviii + 313pp. 6⅛ × 9¼.      21445-1 Pa. $6.95

THE GODS OF THE EGYPTIANS, E. A. Wallis Budge. Thorough coverage of numerous gods of ancient Egypt by foremost Egyptologist. Information on evolution of cults, rites and gods; the cult of Osiris; the Book of the Dead and its rites; the sacred animals and birds; Heaven and Hell; and more. 956pp. 6⅛ × 9¼.
22055-9, 22056-7 Pa., Two-vol. set $21.90

A THEOLOGICO-POLITICAL TREATISE, Benedict Spinoza. Also contains unfinished *Political Treatise*. Great classic on religious liberty, theory of government on common consent. R. Elwes translation. Total of 421pp. 5⅜ × 8½.
20249-6 Pa. $6.95

INCIDENTS OF TRAVEL IN CENTRAL AMERICA, CHIAPAS, AND YU-CATAN, John L. Stephens. Almost single-handed discovery of Maya culture; exploration of ruined cities, monuments, temples; customs of Indians. 115 drawings. 892pp. 5⅜ × 8½.      22404-X, 22405-8 Pa., Two-vol. set $15.90

LOS CAPRICHOS, Francisco Goya. 80 plates of wild, grotesque monsters and caricatures. Prado manuscript included. 183pp. 6⅜ × 9⅜.      22384-1 Pa. $5.95

AUTOBIOGRAPHY: The Story of My Experiments with Truth, Mohandas K. Gandhi. Not hagiography, but Gandhi in his own words. Boyhood, legal studies, purification, the growth of the Satyagraha (nonviolent protest) movement. Critical, inspiring work of the man who freed India. 480pp. 5⅜ × 8½. (Available in U.S. only)
24593-4 Pa. $6.95

ILLUSTRATED DICTIONARY OF HISTORIC ARCHITECTURE, edited by Cyril M. Harris. Extraordinary compendium of clear, concise definitions for over 5,000 important architectural terms complemented by over 2,000 line drawings. Covers full spectrum of architecture from ancient ruins to 20th-century Modernism. Preface. 592pp. 7½ × 9⅝. 24444-X Pa. $15.95

THE NIGHT BEFORE CHRISTMAS, Clement Moore. Full text, and woodcuts from original 1848 book. Also critical, historical material. 19 illustrations. 40pp. 4⅝ × 6. 22797-9 Pa. $2.50

THE LESSON OF JAPANESE ARCHITECTURE: 165 Photographs, Jiro Harada. Memorable gallery of 165 photographs taken in the 1930's of exquisite Japanese homes of the well-to-do and historic buildings. 13 line diagrams. 192pp. 8⅜ × 11¼. 24778-3 Pa. $10.95

THE AUTOBIOGRAPHY OF CHARLES DARWIN AND SELECTED LETTERS, edited by Francis Darwin. The fascinating life of eccentric genius composed of an intimate memoir by Darwin (intended for his children); commentary by his son, Francis; hundreds of fragments from notebooks, journals, papers; and letters to and from Lyell, Hooker, Huxley, Wallace and Henslow. xi + 365pp. 5⅜ × 8. 20479-0 Pa. $6.95

WONDERS OF THE SKY: Observing Rainbows, Comets, Eclipses, the Stars and Other Phenomena, Fred Schaaf. Charming, easy-to-read poetic guide to all manner of celestial events visible to the naked eye. Mock suns, glories, Belt of Venus, more. Illustrated. 299pp. 5¼ × 8¼. 24402-4 Pa. $7.95

BURNHAM'S CELESTIAL HANDBOOK, Robert Burnham, Jr. Thorough guide to the stars beyond our solar system. Exhaustive treatment. Alphabetical by constellation: Andromeda to Cetus in Vol. 1; Chamaeleon to Orion in Vol. 2; and Pavo to Vulpecula in Vol. 3. Hundreds of illustrations. Index in Vol. 3. 2,000pp. 6⅛ × 9¼. 23567-X, 23568-8, 23673-0 Pa., Three-vol. set $41.85

STAR NAMES: Their Lore and Meaning, Richard Hinckley Allen. Fascinating history of names various cultures have given to constellations and literary and folkloristic uses that have been made of stars. Indexes to subjects. Arabic and Greek names. Biblical references. Bibliography. 563pp. 5⅜ × 8½. 21079-0 Pa. $8.95

THIRTY YEARS THAT SHOOK PHYSICS: The Story of Quantum Theory, George Gamow. Lucid, accessible introduction to influential theory of energy and matter. Careful explanations of Dirac's anti-particles, Bohr's model of the atom, much more. 12 plates. Numerous drawings. 240pp. 5⅜ × 8½. 24895-X Pa. $5.95

CHINESE DOMESTIC FURNITURE IN PHOTOGRAPHS AND MEASURED DRAWINGS, Gustav Ecke. A rare volume, now affordably priced for antique collectors, furniture buffs and art historians. Detailed review of styles ranging from early Shang to late Ming. Unabridged republication. 161 black-and-white drawings, photos. Total of 224pp. 8⅜ × 11¼. (Available in U.S. only) 25171-3 Pa. $13.95

VINCENT VAN GOGH: A Biography, Julius Meier-Graefe. Dynamic, penetrating study of artist's life, relationship with brother, Theo, painting techniques, travels, more. Readable, engrossing. 160pp. 5⅜ × 8½. (Available in U.S. only) 25253-1 Pa. $4.95

HOW TO WRITE, Gertrude Stein. Gertrude Stein claimed anyone could understand her unconventional writing—here are clues to help. Fascinating improvisations, language experiments, explanations illuminate Stein's craft and the art of writing. Total of 414pp. 4⅝ × 6⅜.                    23144-5 Pa. $6.95

ADVENTURES AT SEA IN THE GREAT AGE OF SAIL: Five Firsthand Narratives, edited by Elliot Snow. Rare true accounts of exploration, whaling, shipwreck, fierce natives, trade, shipboard life, more. 33 illustrations. Introduction. 353pp. 5⅜ × 8½.                    25177-2 Pa. $8.95

THE HERBAL OR GENERAL HISTORY OF PLANTS, John Gerard. Classic descriptions of about 2,850 plants—with over 2,700 illustrations—includes Latin and English names, physical descriptions, varieties, time and place of growth, more. 2,706 illustrations. xlv + 1,678pp. 8½ × 12¼.         23147-X Cloth. $75.00

DOROTHY AND THE WIZARD IN OZ, L. Frank Baum. Dorothy and the Wizard visit the center of the Earth, where people are vegetables, glass houses grow and Oz characters reappear. Classic sequel to *Wizard of Oz*. 256pp. 5⅜ × 8.
24714-7 Pa. $5.95

SONGS OF EXPERIENCE: Facsimile Reproduction with 26 Plates in Full Color, William Blake. This facsimile of Blake's original "Illuminated Book" reproduces 26 full-color plates from a rare 1826 edition. Includes "The Tyger," "London," "Holy Thursday," and other immortal poems. 26 color plates. Printed text of poems. 48pp. 5¼ × 7.                    24636-1 Pa. $3.50

SONGS OF INNOCENCE, William Blake. The first and most popular of Blake's famous "Illuminated Books," in a facsimile edition reproducing all 31 brightly colored plates. Additional printed text of each poem. 64pp. 5¼ × 7.
22764-2 Pa. $3.50

PRECIOUS STONES, Max Bauer. Classic, thorough study of diamonds, rubies, emeralds, garnets, etc.: physical character, occurrence, properties, use, similar topics. 20 plates, 8 in color. 94 figures. 659pp. 6⅛ × 9¼.
21910-0, 21911-9 Pa., Two-vol. set $15.90

ENCYCLOPEDIA OF VICTORIAN NEEDLEWORK, S. F. A. Caulfeild and Blanche Saward. Full, precise descriptions of stitches, techniques for dozens of needlecrafts—most exhaustive reference of its kind. Over 800 figures. Total of 679pp. 8⅛ × 11. Two volumes.         Vol. 1 22800-2 Pa. $11.95
Vol. 2 22801-0 Pa. $11.95

THE MARVELOUS LAND OF OZ, L. Frank Baum. Second Oz book, the Scarecrow and Tin Woodman are back with hero named Tip, Oz magic. 136 illustrations. 287pp. 5⅜ × 8½.                    20692-0 Pa. $5.95

WILD FOWL DECOYS, Joel Barber. Basic book on the subject, by foremost authority and collector. Reveals history of decoy making and rigging, place in American culture, different kinds of decoys, how to make them, and how to use them. 140 plates. 156pp. 7⅞ × 10¾.                    20011-6 Pa. $8.95

HISTORY OF LACE, Mrs. Bury Palliser. Definitive, profusely illustrated chronicle of lace from earliest times to late 19th century. Laces of Italy, Greece, England, France, Belgium, etc. Landmark of needlework scholarship. 266 illustrations. 672pp. 6⅛ × 9¼.                    24742-2 Pa. $14.95

ILLUSTRATED GUIDE TO SHAKER FURNITURE, Robert Meader. All furniture and appurtenances, with much on unknown local styles. 235 photos. 146pp. 9 × 12. 22819-3 Pa. $8.95

WHALE SHIPS AND WHALING: A Pictorial Survey, George Francis Dow. Over 200 vintage engravings, drawings, photographs of barks, brigs, cutters, other vessels. Also harpoons, lances, whaling guns, many other artifacts. Comprehensive text by foremost authority. 207 black-and-white illustrations. 288pp. 6 × 9. 24808-9 Pa. $8.95

THE BERTRAMS, Anthony Trollope. Powerful portrayal of blind self-will and thwarted ambition includes one of Trollope's most heartrending love stories. 497pp. 5⅜ × 8½. 25119-5 Pa. $9.95

ADVENTURES WITH A HAND LENS, Richard Headstrom. Clearly written guide to observing and studying flowers and grasses, fish scales, moth and insect wings, egg cases, buds, feathers, seeds, leaf scars, moss, molds, ferns, common crystals, etc.—all with an ordinary, inexpensive magnifying glass. 209 exact line drawings aid in your discoveries. 220pp. 5⅜ × 8½. 23330-8 Pa. $4.95

RODIN ON ART AND ARTISTS, Auguste Rodin. Great sculptor's candid, wide-ranging comments on meaning of art; great artists; relation of sculpture to poetry, painting, music; philosophy of life, more. 76 superb black-and-white illustrations of Rodin's sculpture, drawings and prints. 119pp. 8⅜ × 11¼. 24487-3 Pa. $7.95

FIFTY CLASSIC FRENCH FILMS, 1912-1982: A Pictorial Record, Anthony Slide. Memorable stills from Grand Illusion, Beauty and the Beast, Hiroshima, Mon Amour, many more. Credits, plot synopses, reviews, etc. 160pp. 8¼ × 11. 25256-6 Pa. $11.95

THE PRINCIPLES OF PSYCHOLOGY, William James. Famous long course complete, unabridged. Stream of thought, time perception, memory, experimental methods; great work decades ahead of its time. 94 figures. 1,391pp. 5⅜ × 8½. 20381-6, 20382-4 Pa., Two-vol. set $23.90

BODIES IN A BOOKSHOP, R. T. Campbell. Challenging mystery of blackmail and murder with ingenious plot and superbly drawn characters. In the best tradition of British suspense fiction. 192pp. 5⅜ × 8½. 24720-1 Pa. $3.95

CALLAS: PORTRAIT OF A PRIMA DONNA, George Jellinek. Renowned commentator on the musical scene chronicles incredible career and life of the most controversial, fascinating, influential operatic personality of our time. 64 black-and-white photographs. 416pp. 5⅜ × 8¼. 25047-4 Pa. $8.95

GEOMETRY, RELATIVITY AND THE FOURTH DIMENSION, Rudolph Rucker. Exposition of fourth dimension, concepts of relativity as Flatland characters continue adventures. Popular, easily followed yet accurate, profound. 141 illustrations. 133pp. 5⅜ × 8½. 23400-2 Pa. $4.95

HOUSEHOLD STORIES BY THE BROTHERS GRIMM, with pictures by Walter Crane. 53 classic stories—Rumpelstiltskin, Rapunzel, Hansel and Gretel, the Fisherman and his Wife, Snow White, Tom Thumb, Sleeping Beauty, Cinderella, and so much more—lavishly illustrated with original 19th century drawings. 114 illustrations. x + 269pp. 5⅜ × 8½. 21080-4 Pa. $4.95

SUNDIALS, Albert Waugh. Far and away the best, most thorough coverage of ideas, mathematics concerned, types, construction, adjusting anywhere. Over 100 illustrations. 230pp. 5⅜ × 8½. 22947-5 Pa. $4.95

PICTURE HISTORY OF THE NORMANDIE: With 190 Illustrations, Frank O. Braynard. Full story of legendary French ocean liner: Art Deco interiors, design innovations, furnishings, celebrities, maiden voyage, tragic fire, much more. Extensive text. 144pp. 8⅜ × 11¾. 25257-4 Pa. $10.95

THE FIRST AMERICAN COOKBOOK: A Facsimile of "American Cookery," 1796, Amelia Simmons. Facsimile of the first American-written cookbook published in the United States contains authentic recipes for colonial favorites—pumpkin pudding, winter squash pudding, spruce beer, Indian slapjacks, and more. Introductory Essay and Glossary of colonial cooking terms. 80pp. 5⅜ × 8½. 24710-4 Pa. $3.50

101 PUZZLES IN THOUGHT AND LOGIC, C. R. Wylie, Jr. Solve murders and robberies, find out which fishermen are liars, how a blind man could possibly identify a color—purely by your own reasoning! 107pp. 5⅜ × 8½. 20367-0 Pa. $2.50

THE BOOK OF WORLD-FAMOUS MUSIC—CLASSICAL, POPULAR AND FOLK, James J. Fuld. Revised and enlarged republication of landmark work in musico-bibliography. Full information about nearly 1,000 songs and compositions including first lines of music and lyrics. New supplement. Index. 800pp. 5⅜ × 8¼. 24857-7 Pa. $15.95

ANTHROPOLOGY AND MODERN LIFE, Franz Boas. Great anthropologist's classic treatise on race and culture. Introduction by Ruth Bunzel. Only inexpensive paperback edition. 255pp. 5⅜ × 8½. 25245-0 Pa. $6.95

THE TALE OF PETER RABBIT, Beatrix Potter. The inimitable Peter's terrifying adventure in Mr. McGregor's garden, with all 27 wonderful, full-color Potter illustrations. 55pp. 4¼ × 5½. (Available in U.S. only) 22827-4 Pa. $1.75

THREE PROPHETIC SCIENCE FICTION NOVELS, H. G. Wells. *When the Sleeper Wakes, A Story of the Days to Come* and *The Time Machine* (full version). 335pp. 5⅜ × 8½. (Available in U.S. only) 20605-X Pa. $6.95

APICIUS COOKERY AND DINING IN IMPERIAL ROME, edited and translated by Joseph Dommers Vehling. Oldest known cookbook in existence offers readers a clear picture of what foods Romans ate, how they prepared them, etc. 49 illustrations. 301pp. 6⅛ × 9¼. 23563-7 Pa. $7.95

SHAKESPEARE LEXICON AND QUOTATION DICTIONARY, Alexander Schmidt. Full definitions, locations, shades of meaning of every word in plays and poems. More than 50,000 exact quotations. 1,485pp. 6½ × 9¼. 22726-X, 22727-8 Pa., Two-vol. set $29.90

THE WORLD'S GREAT SPEECHES, edited by Lewis Copeland and Lawrence W. Lamm. Vast collection of 278 speeches from Greeks to 1970. Powerful and effective models; unique look at history. 842pp. 5⅜ × 8½. 20468-5 Pa. $11.95

THE BLUE FAIRY BOOK, Andrew Lang. The first, most famous collection, with many familiar tales: Little Red Riding Hood, Aladdin and the Wonderful Lamp, Puss in Boots, Sleeping Beauty, Hansel and Gretel, Rumpelstiltskin; 37 in all. 138 illustrations. 390pp. 5⅜ × 8½. 21437-0 Pa. $6.95

THE STORY OF THE CHAMPIONS OF THE ROUND TABLE, Howard Pyle. Sir Launcelot, Sir Tristram and Sir Percival in spirited adventures of love and triumph retold in Pyle's inimitable style. 50 drawings, 31 full-page. xviii + 329pp. 6½ × 9¼. 21883-X Pa. $7.95

AUDUBON AND HIS JOURNALS, Maria Audubon. Unmatched two-volume portrait of the great artist, naturalist and author contains his journals, an excellent biography by his granddaughter, expert annotations by the noted ornithologist, Dr. Elliott Coues, and 37 superb illustrations. Total of 1,200pp. 5⅜ × 8.
Vol. I 25143-8 Pa. $8.95
Vol. II 25144-6 Pa. $8.95

GREAT DINOSAUR HUNTERS AND THEIR DISCOVERIES, Edwin H. Colbert. Fascinating, lavishly illustrated chronicle of dinosaur research, 1820's to 1960. Achievements of Cope, Marsh, Brown, Buckland, Mantell, Huxley, many others. 384pp. 5¼ × 8¼. 24701-5 Pa. $7.95

THE TASTEMAKERS, Russell Lynes. Informal, illustrated social history of American taste 1850's–1950's. First popularized categories Highbrow, Lowbrow, Middlebrow. 129 illustrations. New (1979) afterword. 384pp. 6 × 9.
23993-4 Pa. $8.95

DOUBLE CROSS PURPOSES, Ronald A. Knox. A treasure hunt in the Scottish Highlands, an old map, unidentified corpse, surprise discoveries keep reader guessing in this cleverly intricate tale of financial skullduggery. 2 black-and-white maps. 320pp. 5⅜ × 8½. (Available in U.S. only) 25032-6 Pa. $6.95

AUTHENTIC VICTORIAN DECORATION AND ORNAMENTATION IN FULL COLOR: 46 Plates from "Studies in Design," Christopher Dresser. Superb full-color lithographs reproduced from rare original portfolio of a major Victorian designer. 48pp. 9¼ × 12¼. 25083-0 Pa. $7.95

PRIMITIVE ART, Franz Boas. Remains the best text ever prepared on subject, thoroughly discussing Indian, African, Asian, Australian, and, especially, Northern American primitive art. Over 950 illustrations show ceramics, masks, totem poles, weapons, textiles, paintings, much more. 376pp. 5⅜ × 8. 20025-6 Pa. $7.95

SIDELIGHTS ON RELATIVITY, Albert Einstein. Unabridged republication of two lectures delivered by the great physicist in 1920–21. *Ether and Relativity* and *Geometry and Experience.* Elegant ideas in non-mathematical form, accessible to intelligent layman. vi + 56pp. 5⅜ × 8½. 24511-X Pa. $2.95

THE WIT AND HUMOR OF OSCAR WILDE, edited by Alvin Redman. More than 1,000 ripostes, paradoxes, wisecracks: Work is the curse of the drinking classes, I can resist everything except temptation, etc. 258pp. 5⅜ × 8½. 20602-5 Pa. $4.95

ADVENTURES WITH A MICROSCOPE, Richard Headstrom. 59 adventures with clothing fibers, protozoa, ferns and lichens, roots and leaves, much more. 142 illustrations. 232pp. 5⅜ × 8½. 23471-1 Pa. $3.95

PLANTS OF THE BIBLE, Harold N. Moldenke and Alma L. Moldenke. Standard reference to all 230 plants mentioned in Scriptures. Latin name, biblical reference, uses, modern identity, much more. Unsurpassed encyclopedic resource for scholars, botanists, nature lovers, students of Bible. Bibliography. Indexes. 123 black-and-white illustrations. 384pp. 6 × 9. 25069-5 Pa. $8.95

FAMOUS AMERICAN WOMEN: A Biographical Dictionary from Colonial Times to the Present, Robert McHenry, ed. From Pocahontas to Rosa Parks, 1,035 distinguished American women documented in separate biographical entries. Accurate, up-to-date data, numerous categories, spans 400 years. Indices. 493pp. 6½ × 9¼. 24523-3 Pa. $10.95

THE FABULOUS INTERIORS OF THE GREAT OCEAN LINERS IN HISTORIC PHOTOGRAPHS, William H. Miller, Jr. Some 200 superb photographs capture exquisite interiors of world's great "floating palaces"—1890's to 1980's: *Titanic, Ile de France, Queen Elizabeth, United States, Europa,* more. Approx. 200 black-and-white photographs. Captions. Text. Introduction. 160pp. 8⅜ × 11¼. 24756-2 Pa. $9.95

THE GREAT LUXURY LINERS, 1927–1954: A Photographic Record, William H. Miller, Jr. Nostalgic tribute to heyday of ocean liners. 186 photos of Ile de France, Normandie, Leviathan, Queen Elizabeth, United States, many others. Interior and exterior views. Introduction. Captions. 160pp. 9 × 12. 24056-8 Pa. $10.95

A NATURAL HISTORY OF THE DUCKS, John Charles Phillips. Great landmark of ornithology offers complete detailed coverage of nearly 200 species and subspecies of ducks: gadwall, sheldrake, merganser, pintail, many more. 74 full-color plates, 102 black-and-white. Bibliography. Total of 1,920pp. 8⅜ × 11¼. 25141-1, 25142-X Cloth. Two-vol. set $100.00

THE SEAWEED HANDBOOK: An Illustrated Guide to Seaweeds from North Carolina to Canada, Thomas F. Lee. Concise reference covers 78 species. Scientific and common names, habitat, distribution, more. Finding keys for easy identification. 224pp. 5⅜ × 8½. 25215-9 Pa. $6.95

THE TEN BOOKS OF ARCHITECTURE: The 1755 Leoni Edition, Leon Battista Alberti. Rare classic helped introduce the glories of ancient architecture to the Renaissance. 68 black-and-white plates. 336pp. 8⅜ × 11¼. 25239-6 Pa. $14.95

MISS MACKENZIE, Anthony Trollope. Minor masterpieces by Victorian master unmasks many truths about life in 19th-century England. First inexpensive edition in years. 392pp. 5⅜ × 8½. 25201-9 Pa. $8.95

THE RIME OF THE ANCIENT MARINER, Gustave Doré, Samuel Taylor Coleridge. Dramatic engravings considered by many to be his greatest work. The terrifying space of the open sea, the storms and whirlpools of an unknown ocean, the ice of Antarctica, more—all rendered in a powerful, chilling manner. Full text. 38 plates. 77pp. 9¼ × 12. 22305-1 Pa. $4.95

THE EXPEDITIONS OF ZEBULON MONTGOMERY PIKE, Zebulon Montgomery Pike. Fascinating first-hand accounts (1805–6) of exploration of Mississippi River, Indian wars, capture by Spanish dragoons, much more. 1,088pp. 5⅜ × 8½. 25254-X, 25255-8 Pa. Two-vol. set $25.90

A CONCISE HISTORY OF PHOTOGRAPHY: Third Revised Edition, Helmut Gernsheim. Best one-volume history—camera obscura, photochemistry, daguerreotypes, evolution of cameras, film, more. Also artistic aspects—landscape, portraits, fine art, etc. 281 black-and-white photographs. 26 in color. 176pp. 8⅜ × 11¼. 25128-4 Pa. $13.95

THE DORÉ BIBLE ILLUSTRATIONS, Gustave Doré. 241 detailed plates from the Bible: the Creation scenes, Adam and Eve, Flood, Babylon, battle sequences, life of Jesus, etc. Each plate is accompanied by the verses from the King James version of the Bible. 241pp. 9 × 12. 23004-X Pa. $9.95

HUGGER-MUGGER IN THE LOUVRE, Elliot Paul. Second Homer Evans mystery-comedy. Theft at the Louvre involves sleuth in hilarious, madcap caper. "A knockout."—Books. 336pp. 5⅜ × 8½. 25185-3 Pa. $5.95

FLATLAND, E. A. Abbott. Intriguing and enormously popular science-fiction classic explores the complexities of trying to survive as a two-dimensional being in a three-dimensional world. Amusingly illustrated by the author. 16 illustrations. 103pp. 5⅜ × 8½. 20001-9 Pa. $2.50

THE HISTORY OF THE LEWIS AND CLARK EXPEDITION, Meriwether Lewis and William Clark, edited by Elliott Coues. Classic edition of Lewis and Clark's day-by-day journals that later became the basis for U.S. claims to Oregon and the West. Accurate and invaluable geographical, botanical, biological, meteorological and anthropological material. Total of 1,508pp. 5⅜ × 8½.
21268-8, 21269-6, 21270-X Pa. Three-vol. set $26.85

LANGUAGE, TRUTH AND LOGIC, Alfred J. Ayer. Famous, clear introduction to Vienna, Cambridge schools of Logical Positivism. Role of philosophy, elimination of metaphysics, nature of analysis, etc. 160pp. 5⅜ × 8½. (Available in U.S. and Canada only) 20010-8 Pa. $3.95

MATHEMATICS FOR THE NONMATHEMATICIAN, Morris Kline. Detailed, college-level treatment of mathematics in cultural and historical context, with numerous exercises. For liberal arts students. Preface. Recommended Reading Lists. Tables. Index. Numerous black-and-white figures. xvi + 641pp. 5⅜ × 8½.
24823-2 Pa. $11.95

HANDBOOK OF PICTORIAL SYMBOLS, Rudolph Modley. 3,250 signs and symbols, many systems in full; official or heavy commercial use. Arranged by subject. Most in Pictorial Archive series. 143pp. 8⅛ × 11. 23357-X Pa. $6.95

INCIDENTS OF TRAVEL IN YUCATAN, John L. Stephens. Classic (1843) exploration of jungles of Yucatan, looking for evidences of Maya civilization. Travel adventures, Mexican and Indian culture, etc. Total of 669pp. 5⅜ × 8½.
20926-1, 20927-X Pa., Two-vol. set $11.90

DEGAS: An Intimate Portrait, Ambroise Vollard. Charming, anecdotal memoir by famous art dealer of one of the greatest 19th-century French painters. 14 black-and-white illustrations. Introduction by Harold L. Van Doren. 96pp. 5⅜ × 8½.
25131-4 Pa. **$4.95**

PERSONAL NARRATIVE OF A PILGRIMAGE TO ALMANDINAH AND MECCAH, Richard Burton. Great travel classic by remarkably colorful personality. Burton, disguised as a Moroccan, visited sacred shrines of Islam, narrowly escaping death. 47 illustrations. 959pp. 5⅜ × 8½.     21217-3, 21218-1 Pa., Two-vol. set **$19.90**

PHRASE AND WORD ORIGINS, A. H. Holt. Entertaining, reliable, modern study of more than 1,200 colorful words, phrases, origins and histories. Much unexpected information. 254pp. 5⅜ × 8½.     20758-7 Pa. **$5.95**

THE RED THUMB MARK, R. Austin Freeman. In this first Dr. Thorndyke case, the great scientific detective draws fascinating conclusions from the nature of a single fingerprint. Exciting story, authentic science. 320pp. 5⅜ × 8½. (Available in U.S. only)     25210-8 Pa. **$6.95**

AN EGYPTIAN HIEROGLYPHIC DICTIONARY, E. A. Wallis Budge. Monumental work containing about 25,000 words or terms that occur in texts ranging from 3000 B.C. to 600 A.D. Each entry consists of a transliteration of the word, the word in hieroglyphs, and the meaning in English. 1,314pp. 6⅜ × 10.
23615-3, 23616-1 Pa., Two-vol. set **$31.90**

THE COMPLEAT STRATEGYST: Being a Primer on the Theory of Games of Strategy, J. D. Williams. Highly entertaining classic describes, with many illustrated examples, how to select best strategies in conflict situations. Prefaces. Appendices. xvi + 268pp. 5⅜ × 8½.     25101-2 Pa. **$5.95**

THE ROAD TO OZ, L. Frank Baum. Dorothy meets the Shaggy Man, little Button-Bright and the Rainbow's beautiful daughter in this delightful trip to the magical Land of Oz. 272pp. 5⅜ × 8.     25208-6 Pa. **$5.95**

POINT AND LINE TO PLANE, Wassily Kandinsky. Seminal exposition of role of point, line, other elements in non-objective painting. Essential to understanding 20th-century art. 127 illustrations. 192pp. 6½ × 9¼.     23808-3 Pa. **$5.95**

LADY ANNA, Anthony Trollope. Moving chronicle of Countess Lovel's bitter struggle to win for herself and daughter Anna their rightful rank and fortune—perhaps at cost of sanity itself. 384pp. 5⅜ × 8½.     24669-8 Pa. **$8.95**

EGYPTIAN MAGIC, E. A. Wallis Budge. Sums up all that is known about magic in Ancient Egypt: the role of magic in controlling the gods, powerful amulets that warded off evil spirits, scarabs of immortality, use of wax images, formulas and spells, the secret name, much more. 253pp. 5⅜ × 8½.     22681-6 Pa. **$4.50**

THE DANCE OF SIVA, Ananda Coomaraswamy. Preeminent authority unfolds the vast metaphysic of India: the revelation of her art, conception of the universe, social organization, etc. 27 reproductions of art masterpieces. 192pp. 5⅜ × 8½.
24817-8 Pa. **$5.95**

CHRISTMAS CUSTOMS AND TRADITIONS, Clement A. Miles. Origin, evolution, significance of religious, secular practices. Caroling, gifts, yule logs, much more. Full, scholarly yet fascinating; non-sectarian. 400pp. 5⅜ × 8½.
23354-5 Pa. $6.95

THE HUMAN FIGURE IN MOTION, Eadweard Muybridge. More than 4,500 stopped-action photos, in action series, showing undraped men, women, children jumping, lying down, throwing, sitting, wrestling, carrying, etc. 390pp. 7⅞ × 10⅝.
20204-6 Cloth. $21.95

THE MAN WHO WAS THURSDAY, Gilbert Keith Chesterton. Witty, fast-paced novel about a club of anarchists in turn-of-the-century London. Brilliant social, religious, philosophical speculations. 128pp. 5⅜ × 8½.
25121-7 Pa. $3.95

A CEZANNE SKETCHBOOK: Figures, Portraits, Landscapes and Still Lifes, Paul Cezanne. Great artist experiments with tonal effects, light, mass, other qualities in over 100 drawings. A revealing view of developing master painter, precursor of Cubism. 102 black-and-white illustrations. 144pp. 8¾ × 6⅝.
24790-2 Pa. $5.95

AN ENCYCLOPEDIA OF BATTLES: Accounts of Over 1,560 Battles from 1479 B.C. to the Present, David Eggenberger. Presents essential details of every major battle in recorded history, from the first battle of Megiddo in 1479 B.C. to Grenada in 1984. List of Battle Maps. New Appendix covering the years 1967–1984. Index. 99 illustrations. 544pp. 6½ × 9¼.
24913-1 Pa. $14.95

AN ETYMOLOGICAL DICTIONARY OF MODERN ENGLISH, Ernest Weekley. Richest, fullest work, by foremost British lexicographer. Detailed word histories. Inexhaustible. Total of 856pp. 6½ × 9¼.
21873-2, 21874-0 Pa., Two-vol. set $17.00

WEBSTER'S AMERICAN MILITARY BIOGRAPHIES, edited by Robert McHenry. Over 1,000 figures who shaped 3 centuries of American military history. Detailed biographies of Nathan Hale, Douglas MacArthur, Mary Hallaren, others. Chronologies of engagements, more. Introduction. Addenda. 1,033 entries in alphabetical order. xi + 548pp. 6½ × 9¼. (Available in U.S. only)
24758-9 Pa. $13.95

LIFE IN ANCIENT EGYPT, Adolf Erman. Detailed older account, with much not in more recent books: domestic life, religion, magic, medicine, commerce, and whatever else needed for complete picture. Many illustrations. 597pp. 5⅜ × 8½.
22632-8 Pa. $8.95

HISTORIC COSTUME IN PICTURES, Braun & Schneider. Over 1,450 costumed figures shown, covering a wide variety of peoples: kings, emperors, nobles, priests, servants, soldiers, scholars, townsfolk, peasants, merchants, courtiers, cavaliers, and more. 256pp. 8⅜ × 11¼.
23150-X Pa. $9.95

THE NOTEBOOKS OF LEONARDO DA VINCI, edited by J. P. Richter. Extracts from manuscripts reveal great genius; on painting, sculpture, anatomy, sciences, geography, etc. Both Italian and English. 186 ms. pages reproduced, plus 500 additional drawings, including studies for *Last Supper, Sforza* monument, etc. 860pp. 7⅞ × 10¾. (Available in U.S. only) 22572-0, 22573-9 Pa., Two-vol. set $31.90

THE ART NOUVEAU STYLE BOOK OF ALPHONSE MUCHA: All 72 Plates from "Documents Decoratifs" in Original Color, Alphonse Mucha. Rare copyright-free design portfolio by high priest of Art Nouveau. Jewelry, wallpaper, stained glass, furniture, figure studies, plant and animal motifs, etc. Only complete one-volume edition. 80pp. 9⅜ × 12¼. 24044-4 Pa. $9.95

ANIMALS: 1,419 COPYRIGHT-FREE ILLUSTRATIONS OF MAMMALS, BIRDS, FISH, INSECTS, ETC., edited by Jim Harter. Clear wood engravings present, in extremely lifelike poses, over 1,000 species of animals. One of the most extensive pictorial sourcebooks of its kind. Captions. Index. 284pp. 9 × 12.
23766-4 Pa. $9.95

OBELISTS FLY HIGH, C. Daly King. Masterpiece of American detective fiction, long out of print, involves murder on a 1935 transcontinental flight—"a very thrilling story"—NY Times. Unabridged and unaltered republication of the edition published by William Collins Sons & Co. Ltd., London, 1935. 288pp. 5⅜ × 8½. (Available in U.S. only) 25036-9 Pa. $5.95

VICTORIAN AND EDWARDIAN FASHION: A Photographic Survey, Alison Gernsheim. First fashion history completely illustrated by contemporary photographs. Full text plus 235 photos, 1840-1914, in which many celebrities appear. 240pp. 6½ × 9¼. 24205-6 Pa. $6.95

THE ART OF THE FRENCH ILLUSTRATED BOOK, 1700-1914, Gordon N. Ray. Over 630 superb book illustrations by Fragonard, Delacroix, Daumier, Doré, Grandville, Manet, Mucha, Steinlen, Toulouse-Lautrec and many others. Preface. Introduction. 633 halftones. Indices of artists, authors & titles, binders and provenances. Appendices. Bibliography. 608pp. 8⅜ × 11¼. 25086-5 Pa. $24.95

THE WONDERFUL WIZARD OF OZ, L. Frank Baum. Facsimile in full color of America's finest children's classic. 143 illustrations by W. W. Denslow. 267pp. 5⅜ × 8½. 20691-2 Pa. $7.95

FRONTIERS OF MODERN PHYSICS: New Perspectives on Cosmology, Relativity, Black Holes and Extraterrestrial Intelligence, Tony Rothman, et al. For the intelligent layman. Subjects include: cosmological models of the universe; black holes; the neutrino; the search for extraterrestrial intelligence. Introduction. 46 black-and-white illustrations. 192pp. 5⅜ × 8½. 24587-X Pa. $7.95

THE FRIENDLY STARS, Martha Evans Martin & Donald Howard Menzel. Classic text marshalls the stars together in an engaging, non-technical survey, presenting them as sources of beauty in night sky. 23 illustrations. Foreword. 2 star charts. Index. 147pp. 5⅜ × 8½. 21099-5 Pa. $3.95

FADS AND FALLACIES IN THE NAME OF SCIENCE, Martin Gardner. Fair, witty appraisal of cranks, quacks, and quackeries of science and pseudoscience: hollow earth, Velikovsky, orgone energy, Dianetics, flying saucers, Bridey Murphy, food and medical fads, etc. Revised, expanded In the Name of Science. "A very able and even-tempered presentation."—The New Yorker. 363pp. 5⅜ × 8.
20394-8 Pa. $6.95

ANCIENT EGYPT: ITS CULTURE AND HISTORY, J. E Manchip White. From pre-dynastics through Ptolemies: society, history, political structure, religion, daily life, literature, cultural heritage. 48 plates. 217pp. 5⅜ × 8½. 22548-8 Pa. $5.95

# CATALOG OF DOVER BOOKS

SIR HARRY HOTSPUR OF HUMBLETHWAITE, Anthony Trollope. Incisive, unconventional psychological study of a conflict between a wealthy baronet, his idealistic daughter, and their scapegrace cousin. The 1870 novel in its first inexpensive edition in years. 250pp. 5⅜ × 8½. 24953-0 Pa. $5.95

LASERS AND HOLOGRAPHY, Winston E. Kock. Sound introduction to burgeoning field, expanded (1981) for second edition. Wave patterns, coherence, lasers, diffraction, zone plates, properties of holograms, recent advances. 84 illustrations. 160pp. 5⅜ × 8¼. (Except in United Kingdom) 24041-X Pa. $3.95

INTRODUCTION TO ARTIFICIAL INTELLIGENCE: SECOND, EN-LARGED EDITION, Philip C. Jackson, Jr. Comprehensive survey of artificial intelligence—the study of how machines (computers) can be made to act intelligently. Includes introductory and advanced material. Extensive notes updating the main text. 132 black-and-white illustrations. 512pp. 5⅜ × 8½. 24864-X Pa. $8.95

HISTORY OF INDIAN AND INDONESIAN ART, Ananda K. Coomaraswamy. Over 400 illustrations illuminate classic study of Indian art from earliest Harappa finds to early 20th century. Provides philosophical, religious and social insights. 304pp. 6⅜ × 9⅜. 25005-9 Pa. $9.95

THE GOLEM, Gustav Meyrink. Most famous supernatural novel in modern European literature, set in Ghetto of Old Prague around 1890. Compelling story of mystical experiences, strange transformations, profound terror. 13 black-and-white illustrations. 224pp. 5⅜ × 8½. (Available in U.S. only) 25025-3 Pa. $6.95

PICTORIAL ENCYCLOPEDIA OF HISTORIC ARCHITECTURAL PLANS, DETAILS AND ELEMENTS: With 1,880 Line Drawings of Arches, Domes, Doorways, Facades, Gables, Windows, etc., John Theodore Haneman. Sourcebook of inspiration for architects, designers, others. Bibliography. Captions. 141pp. 9 × 12. 24605-1 Pa. $7.95

BENCHLEY LOST AND FOUND, Robert Benchley. Finest humor from early 30's, about pet peeves, child psychologists, post office and others. Mostly unavailable elsewhere. 73 illustrations by Peter Arno and others. 183pp. 5⅜ × 8½. 22410-4 Pa. $4.95

ERTÉ GRAPHICS, Erté. Collection of striking color graphics: *Seasons, Alphabet, Numerals, Aces* and *Precious Stones*. 50 plates, including 4 on covers. 48pp. 9⅜ × 12¼. 23580-7 Pa. $7.95

THE JOURNAL OF HENRY D. THOREAU, edited by Bradford Torrey, F. H. Allen. Complete reprinting of 14 volumes, 1837–61, over two million words; the sourcebooks for *Walden*, etc. Definitive. All original sketches, plus 75 photographs. 1,804pp. 8½ × 12¼. 20312-3, 20313-1 Cloth., Two-vol. set $120.00

CASTLES: THEIR CONSTRUCTION AND HISTORY, Sidney Toy. Traces castle development from ancient roots. Nearly 200 photographs and drawings illustrate moats, keeps, baileys, many other features. Caernarvon, Dover Castles, Hadrian's Wall, Tower of London, dozens more. 256pp. 5⅜ × 8¼. 24898-4 Pa. $6.95

AMERICAN CLIPPER SHIPS: 1833–1858, Octavius T. Howe & Frederick C. Matthews. Fully-illustrated, encyclopedic review of 352 clipper ships from the period of America's greatest maritime supremacy. Introduction. 109 halftones. 5 black-and-white line illustrations. Index. Total of 928pp. 5⅜ × 8½.
25115-2, 25116-0 Pa., Two-vol. set $17.90

TOWARDS A NEW ARCHITECTURE, Le Corbusier. Pioneering manifesto by great architect, near legendary founder of "International School." Technical and aesthetic theories, views on industry, economics, relation of form to function, "mass-production spirit," much more. Profusely illustrated. Unabridged translation of 13th French edition. Introduction by Frederick Etchells. 320pp. 6⅛ × 9¼. (Available in U.S. only)
25023-7 Pa. $8.95

THE BOOK OF KELLS, edited by Blanche Cirker. Inexpensive collection of 32 full-color, full-page plates from the greatest illuminated manuscript of the Middle Ages, painstakingly reproduced from rare facsimile edition. Publisher's Note. Captions. 32pp. 9⅜ × 12¼.
24345-1 Pa. $4.95

BEST SCIENCE FICTION STORIES OF H. G. WELLS, H. G. Wells. Full novel *The Invisible Man*, plus 17 short stories: "The Crystal Egg," "Aepyornis Island," "The Strange Orchid," etc. 303pp. 5⅜ × 8½. (Available in U.S. only)
21531-8 Pa. $6.95

AMERICAN SAILING SHIPS: Their Plans and History, Charles G. Davis. Photos, construction details of schooners, frigates, clippers, other sailcraft of 18th to early 20th centuries—plus entertaining discourse on design, rigging, nautical lore, much more. 137 black-and-white illustrations. 240pp. 6⅛ × 9¼.
24658-2 Pa. $6.95

ENTERTAINING MATHEMATICAL PUZZLES, Martin Gardner. Selection of author's favorite conundrums involving arithmetic, money, speed, etc., with lively commentary. Complete solutions. 112pp. 5⅜ × 8½. 25211-6 Pa. $2.95

THE WILL TO BELIEVE, HUMAN IMMORTALITY, William James. Two books bound together. Effect of irrational on logical, and arguments for human immortality. 402pp. 5⅜ × 8½. 20291-7 Pa. $7.95

THE HAUNTED MONASTERY and THE CHINESE MAZE MURDERS, Robert Van Gulik. 2 full novels by Van Gulik continue adventures of Judge Dee and his companions. An evil Taoist monastery, seemingly supernatural events; overgrown topiary maze that hides strange crimes. Set in 7th-century China. 27 illustrations. 328pp. 5⅜ × 8½. 23502-5 Pa. $6.95

CELEBRATED CASES OF JUDGE DEE (DEE GOONG AN), translated by Robert Van Gulik. Authentic 18th-century Chinese detective novel; Dee and associates solve three interlocked cases. Led to Van Gulik's own stories with same characters. Extensive introduction. 9 illustrations. 237pp. 5⅜ × 8½.
23337-5 Pa. $4.95

*Prices subject to change without notice.*
Available at your book dealer or write for free catalog to Dept. GI, Dover Publications, Inc., 31 East 2nd St., Mineola, N.Y. 11501. Dover publishes more than 175 books each year on science, elementary and advanced mathematics, biology, music, art, literary history, social sciences and other areas.